Encyclopaedia of Modern

BRITISH ARMY REGIMENTS

Encyclopaedia of Modern

BRITISH ARMY REGIMENTS

David Griffin

Patrick Stephens, Wellingborough

First published in 1985

British Library Cataloguing in Publication Data

Griffin, David
Encyclopaedia of modern British army regiments.
1. Great Britain, *Army*—Dictionaries
355.3'1'0941 UA649

ISBN 0-85059-708-0

Patrick Stephens Limited is part of the Thorsons Publishing Group, Denington Estate, Wellingborough, Northamptonshire, NN8 2RQ, England.

Printed in Great Britain by Butler & Tanner Limited, Frome, Somerset.

10 9 8 7 6 5 4 3 2

Contents

Introduction

'One way or another the roots of tradition strike down deep. The soldier feels the regiment solid about him'— General Sir Ian Hamilton, 1921.

In the pages of this book I have attempted to make a register of the many distinctions and customs which have been handed down within the regiments of the British Army in order to sustain the *esprit de corps* which is considered vital to their high standard of pride and discipline. The reason why traditions are regarded so highly is not always appreciated, and fanciful rituals and uniforms are all too readily dismissed as being irrelevant to modern soldiering; it is an undisputable fact, however, that tradition maintains the regiment's continuity, and it is this that gives substance and credibility to the pageantry.

The Army's 'teeth' owe their present uneven shape to a system of regional brigades which was established in 1948 to create a greater working flexibility for the much-reduced regiments of post-war Britain. These brigades had the unhappy effect of suppressing the individuality of their component regiments, however, and their true purpose became evident in the late 1950s, when large scale amalgamations were ordered for the regiments by brigade, six of which paid the ultimate price and merged all of their battalions to become 'large regiments' themselves. In consequence, a new system was needed to accommodate the medley of regiments large, small and in between, and, in 1968, the division came in to embrace brigade and regiment alike (see appendices). The division offers no securer future for the one-battalion regiments, whose lineage has altered little in 300 years, but the newer 'large regiments' have developed a fine sense of confidence from their multifarious traditions, and stand out amongst the best in the Army today.

In order to understand fully the make-up of a regiment's traditions it is necessary first to look at its pedigree, as illustrated by 'family trees' in this book. These tables help us to picture the formation of the regiments, and the origins of their strange titles, many of which might require explanation: the *Guards* concept came in with Charles II, who classed all of his early regiments as 'personal bodyguards' in order to appease a Parliament suspicious of standing armies. The reign of James II saw the first *fuzileers* and *Horse*, the former a type of foot soldier whose title derived from his firearm, and whose elite standing in the infantry was imitated by the regiments of *light infantry* over a century later. Similarly, the *Horse* was regarded as a superior breed of cavalry, quite distinct from the more numerous *dragoons* who started out as mounted infantry; in 1746, however, a budget was made of the mounted arm, and the prestigious *Horse*, by then little more than an expensive relic of 1685, had its three senior regiments relegated to *dragoons* for reasons of economy. The term *dragoon guards* was given to these regiments to preserve their dignity, and the remaining regiments of *Horse* duly came out as *dragoon guards* in 1788, at a time when many of the old *dragoon* regiments were being converted to a light role. Together with the *light Horse* raised in 1759 these *light dragoons* were equipped with swift chargers and uniforms to reflect their new panache, and went on to become *hussars* and *lancers*, following Continental trends. Of the infantry (the *foot*) it need only be mentioned that their territorial titles first came in 1782, when regiments not already endowed with a royal designation were required to adopt a county name, and 'to cultivate a connection with that county which might at all times be useful towards recruiting'.

Each section of the book deals with one of the modern Army's 57 regiments, in order of seniority, and begins with a list of its honorary distinctions and battle honours as they appear on their revered 'flags'; these are the very embodiment of regimental tradition, and are variously known as a Standard (Household Cavalry and Dragoon Guards), a Guidon (hussars and lancers), and the Colours (Guards and infantry). The battle honour, defined as being a public commemoration of a victory, is displayed on the drums and Colours to create a sense of pride in the regiment's achievements, and to remind us of those who died in its service. Battle honours of units blessed with a multi-regimental ancestry are labelled, in this book, with the parent regiments whose labours actually secured the honour(s). Before the review of 1881, the science of awarding battle honours proved to be a very haphazard affair and many were the battles whose official recognition did not come until long after their cause and effects had been forgotten. In cases such as this the regiment which claimed the honour is indicated in order to give an idea of its service record. Space does not permit all of the modern regiment's inherited honours to be displayed on its appointments, but almost all pre-1914 ones are (except for the very largest regiments), and, ideally, ten from each of the World Wars (more in the larger regiments). Battle honours of World Wars 1 and 2 are captioned with abbreviations of the former regiments from whose Colours they came, though these need not have been the only founder regiments to have been granted the honour, as only principal honours are emblazoned on the drums and Colours.

Regimental customs and privileges are mentioned where known, save those which are too common, or too private to be unearthed. In order to appreciate privileges such as officers of regiments in alliance being able to frequent each others' mess, it is necessary to understand that, under normal circumstances, it is unthinkable for any officer, or NCO, to visit any mess other than his own. One privilege that is common to many units, and which may require explanation, is that of belonging to the Wolfe Society, a brotherhood whose member regiments still send representatives to the annual dinner at Westerham in Kent, the birthplace of James Wolfe. The Society was formed some years after the death of General Wolfe for the sons of Westerham and the regiments that had been associated with him during his lifetime.

The British regiment has a talent for gathering nicknames and marches, two aspects of tradition which I have included in the text to give a colourful, and often amusing, insight into regimental 'character'.

Dress uniform is, perhaps, the best area of regimental expression and every section of the book has a list of regimental differences in dress and insignia. Many nuances are not immediately obvious, and their origins even less so, but their effect on regimental pride is inestimable. The newer 'amalgams' benefit by having a wealth of inherited traditions to draw upon, and many interesting uniforms have been developed as a result. The Royal Scots Dragoon Guards, Queen's Own Highlanders and Royal Anglian Regiment have been particularly inventive in their choice of dress.

The point that all this helps to underline is that the modern British regiment, unlike its counterpart in other armies, operates best out of a sense of its own esteem and disdainfully rejects any move towards featureless units in faceless legions. Any special distinction that sets a regiment apart from its contemporaries is greatly cherished and passed on for future generations to flaunt with a sense of historic pride.

David Griffin
Leicester 1984

The Regiments

The Life Guards

Insignia

The Royal Arms.

The Royal Crest above an entwined, reversed *LG*.

Honours

Dettingen, Peninsula, Waterloo, Tel-el-kebir, Egypt 1882, Relief of Kimberley, Paardeberg, South Africa 1899–1900.

Mons, Le Cateau, Marne 1914, Aisne 1914, Messines 1914, Ypres 1914, 1915, 1917, Somme 1916, 1918, Arras 1917, 1918, Hindenburg Line, France & Flanders 1914–18.

Soleuvre, Brussels, Nederrijn, North-West Europe 1944–45, Iraq 1941, Palmyra, Syria 1941, El Alamein, North Africa 1942–45, Italy 1944.

Anniversaries

Waterloo Day (June 18).

Customs

The Loyal Toast is dispensed with on informal occasions.

The Household Cavalry is the only cavalry regiment still to carry Squadron Standards.

Colonels of the Household Cavalry traditionally supply the ancient appointments of bodyguard to the Sovereign (Gold Stick and Silver Stick).

Lieutenant Colonels are addressed by rank and Warrant Officers by 'mister' in the Household Cavalry.

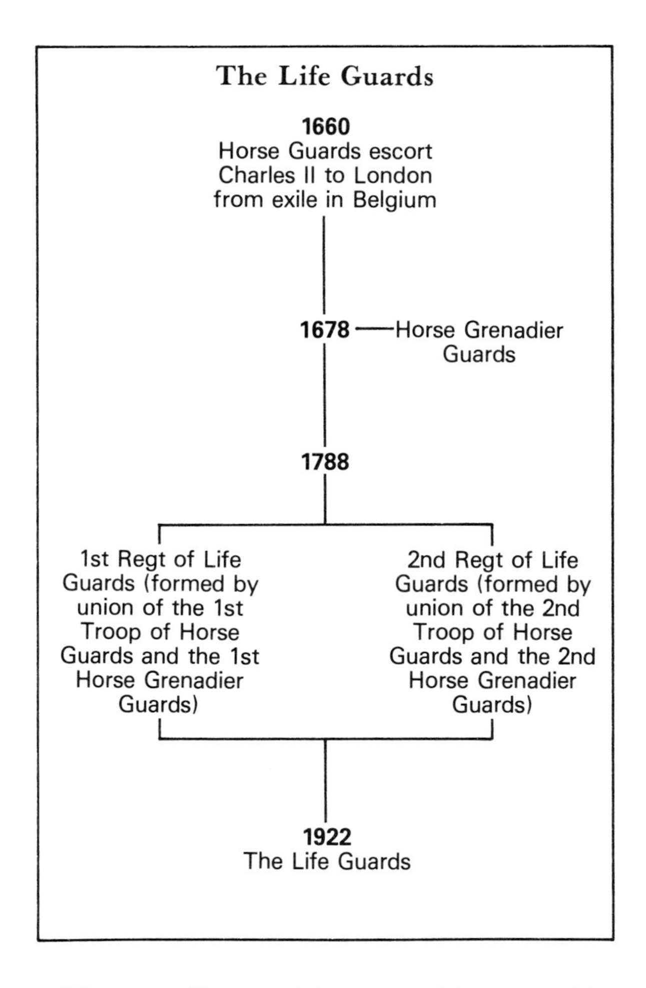

The term 'Sergeant' is not used because of its derivation from the word 'servant', a legacy of the 18th century, when such a word would be considered unsuitable for a regiment of noble breeding.

NCOs observe the traditional ritual of 'hanging the brick' at Christmas time. This old ceremony consists of hanging an ebony 'brick' over the mess

Above left *Life Guards' French hornist.*

Above right *A Farrier-Corporal at work. The ancient skills of the Household Cavalry farriers now serve all of London's military horses, including those of the Metropolitan Police.*

Below *The Life Guards band at rehearsal.*

Life Guards display troop with lances fronted by trumpeters and drummer in State coats.

bar as a sign of unlimited drinking throughout the period.

Mascot

None.

Dress distinctions

A blue dress cap with scarlet band and piping, mounted with the Regimental cap badge, the Royal Cipher within a crowned circle. The cap peak is edged in gold braid according to rank: one row, Trooper; two rows, Lance Corporal; three rows, Corporal of Horse; four rows, Squadron Quartermaster Corporal; and five rows, Corporal Major and Trumpet Major. A blue side hat with scarlet top, piped in yellow. Buttons are stamped with the lion and crown above an entwined, reversed *LG*. The blue dress overalls are stylised with two scarlet stripes and centre welt down the outer seams (introduced for the 2nd Life Guards in 1832). Officers may wear buff breeches with brown riding boots.

Mounted Review Order: a white-metal helmet (1842 pattern), on which is fixed an enamel Garter and cross upon a star, surrounded by laurel and oak leaves and surmounted by a Crown, all in brass (gilt for officers). A white horsehair plume (red for Trumpeters) tied from a dome. The brass curb chain is worn beneath the lower lip in this Regiment. A scarlet tunic faced and piped in blue; officers have gold laurels and oak leaf embroidered on the skirts, collars, and cuffs. Gold aiguilettes (1821) are worn from officers' right and NCOs' left shoulder. A nickel-silver cuirass (1821) with brass shoulder scales, overlaid with a white cartouche belt on which is laid a red flask-cord: a relic of the time when the cavalry carried firearms. White breeches, black jackboots, and spurs (1812). White gauntlets (1812). An 1883 pattern State Sword with white slings and knot. Farriers wear a black helmet plume, blue tunic, and white leather axe-belt. A ceremonial axe is carried. Red cloaks with blue collars are worn in foul weather.

Musicians have differences in uniform on State Occasions: a blue velvet cap, a long crimson coat heavily embellished in gold lace (the State Coat), and gold sword belt and slings.

Officers' horse saddlery is covered by a blue cloth shabraque with a wide scarlet border, its corners embroidered with the Garter Star encompassed by battle honour scrolls. Soldiers' saddlery is covered by a white sheepskin. Horse manes are dressed to the right (offside).

Marches

Milanollo, the Quick March (1st Life Guards). *Men of Harlech*, the Quick March (2nd Life Guards). *The Life Guards' Slow March*.

Nicknames

'The Bangers': Guards' terminology for the Household Cavalry and the noise it creates at the trot. Also 'Lumpers' from their weight.

'The Cheesemongers': a slanderous expression of the 1790s. The French Revolutionary War had soaked up Britain's most eligible recruits and the Life Guards were forced to lower their standard of intake. Many old hands quit in disgust and likened the Corps to nothing better than a band of cheesemongers. The slur lost its bite in later years, however, as at Waterloo the Regiment charged to the war cry 'Come on the Cheeses!'

'The Fly-slicers': an 18th century observation of Guardsmen sitting on horseback beneath London's arches idly swatting at flies with their swords.

'The Piccadilly Butchers': a rather unjustified comment on the Regiment's handling of the Burdett Riots in 1810.

'The Roast and Boiled': a satirical reference to the Life Guards' privileged lifestyle in the 18th century, which seems to have been based on a daily diet of roast beef and boiled potatoes.

'The Ticky Tins': the Blues' impression of the Life Guards; implying dirty equipment.

Recruiting

Nationwide. RHQ: Combermere Barracks, Windsor.

The Blues and Royals

Insignia

The Royal Arms: the traditional emblem of the Royal Horse Guards.

An eagle on a plinth inscribed '105' within the Garter: the Imperial Eagle was formerly carried on the dress and appointments of the Royal Dragoons to commemorate the capture of a French Eagle standard at Waterloo.

Honours

Tangier 1662–80 (Royals); Dettingen, Warburg (Blues/Royals); Beaumont, Willems, Fuentes d'Onor (Royals); Peninsula, Waterloo (Blues/Royals); Balaklava, Sevastopol (Royals); Tel-el-kebir, Egypt 1882, Relief of Kimberley, Paardeberg (Blues); Relief of Ladysmith (Royals); South Africa 1899–1902 (Blues/Royals).

Le Cateau, Marne 1914, Messines 1914 (Blues); Ypres 1914, 1915, 1917 (Blues/Royals); Gheluvelt (Blues); Frezenburg, Loos, Arras 1917 (Blues/Royals); Somme 1918, Amiens, Hindenburg Line, Cambrai 1918 (Royals); Sambre (Blues); Pursuit to Mons (Royals); France & Flanders 1914–18 (Blues/Royals).

Soleuvre, Brussels (Blues); Nederrijn, North-West Europe 1944–45 (Blues/Royals); Iraq 1941, Palmyra (Blues); Syria 1941 (Blues/Royals); Knightsbridge (Royals); El Alamein (Blues/Royals); Advance on Tripoli (Royals); North Africa 1941–43 (Blues/Royals); Sicily 1943 (Royals); Italy 1943–44 (Blues/Royals).

Anniversaries

Waterloo Day (June 18): the Waterloo tradition was important for both founder Regiments; the Blues in the fiery charge of Somerset's Cavalry Brigade, which forced Napoleon's *cuirassiers* to abandon their attack on the British squares, and the Royals for the charge of the Union Brigade, in which Captain Clark and Corporal Styles captured the Regimental Eagle of the French 105th. It was in recognition of the Blues' glorious part in the battle that the Regiment was accepted as being part of the Household Cavalry, in 1821.

Before 1914 it was the practice of Kaiser Wilhelm, the Royals' Colonel-in-Chief, to send a wreath every year to be carried on the Regiment's Guidon at the Waterloo Parade.

Customs

The Loyal Toast is not drunk in the Regiment.

The Freedom of London (confirmed to the Royals in 1963).

A Guidon (Royals) is carried in addition to a Standard (Blues).

Officer's inspection. The Warrant Officer at right, a Life Guardsman, wears the patrol jacket preserved from the Victorian age.

Royal Dragoons' Freedom of the City of London, 1963.

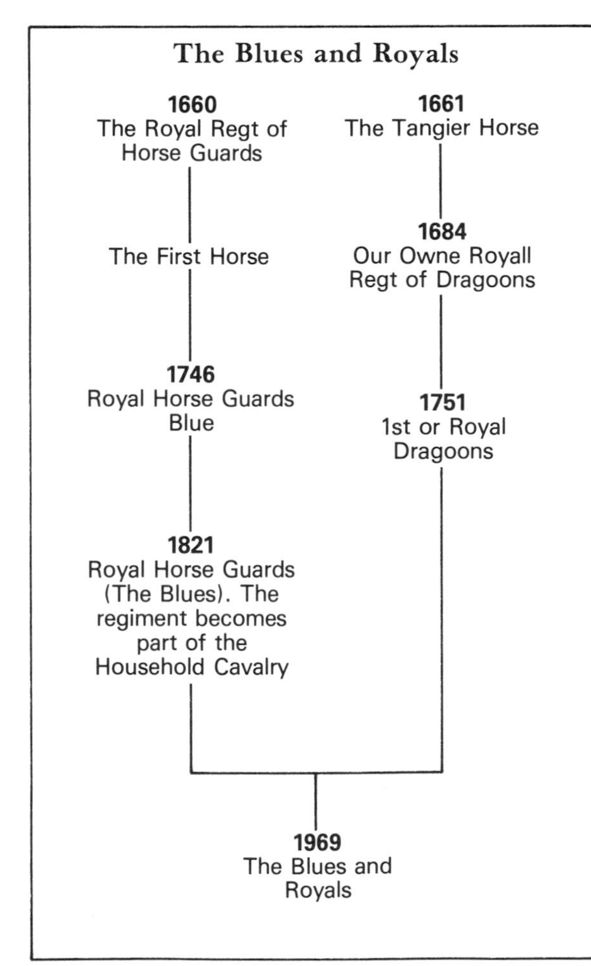

The junior commissioned rank is referred to by the cavalry term for a Standard-bearer, 'Cornet', a former practice of the Blues.

Soldiers may salute with the hand even when bare-headed, an old custom of the Blues said to have originated with Granby's cavalry charge at the Battle of Warburg in 1760. The Marquis of Granby was Colonel of the Royal Horse Guards Blue at the time, and rumour had it that his wig made little effort to withstand the rigours of the charge, hence the expression 'going at it bald-headed'.

Mascot

The Royal Dragoons kept a goose mascot which they rescued in Ireland. It was presented to the King and Queen in 1925, and died in Egypt while the Regiment was serving there.

Dress distinctions

A blue dress cap with scarlet band and piping, mounted with Regimental badge, the Royal Cipher within a crowned circle, bronzed. Buttons are embossed with a crowned *RHG* over *1st D*. Red lanyards are worn by officers in service dress, and white by other ranks. The Napoleonic Eagle badge is worn on blue cloth backing on the upper left sleeve. The stable-belt is striped blue/scarlet/blue. Dress overalls are fashioned with a broad scarlet stripe down the seams.

Mounted Review Order: a white-metal helmet as for the Life Guards, except that a scarlet plume, treated to resemble yak's hair, is worn by all ranks. The curb chain is longer, to be worn beneath the chin. A blue tunic, faced and piped in scarlet, with a brass Napoleonic Eagle on the left sleeve. The Eagle

Dismounted troopers 'going on' at Horse Guards.

was the collar badge of the Royal Dragoons until 1948, when it became the cap badge also. A cuirass, cartouche belt, breeches, jackboots and spurs as for the Life Guards. Blue cloaks with red collars are worn in foul weather. Musicians' State Dress as for the Life Guards. Officers' horse saddlery is covered by a scarlet cloth shabraque edged in gold oak-leaf lace. Soldiers' saddlery is covered by a black sheepskin. Horse manes are dressed to the left (nearside).

Marches

The Grand March from Verdi's *Aida* (Blues) is played today with *The Royals. Spectamur Agendo*, a former march of the Royal Dragoons, named after their motto. *Keel Row/Moneymusk*, the traditional March Past of the Household Cavalry.

Nicknames

'The Aldershot Guards': the Royal Dragoons, from

The mounted band in foul weather cloaks, 1950s.

the time when only tall men were enlisted, to meet the demands of the heavy cavalry. The cavalry under Queen Victoria was classed by the weight and size of horse and rider: the Household Cavalry, 1st (Royal) Dragoons, and the Scots Greys comprised the 'heavies', the Dragoon Guards, 6th (Inniskilling) Dragoons, and the lancers were considered 'medium', and the hussars made up the light cavalry.

'The Bird-catchers': a term common to the Royal Dragoons and the Scots Greys in respect of their capture of French regimental Eagles at Waterloo. The Royals' prize was taken in the Charge of the Union Brigade (Royals, Greys, and Inniskillings).

'The Blues': the Royal Horse Guards' famous nickname prior to amalgamation in 1969, when the name officially became part of the title. The soubriquet stemmed from the Regiment's use of blue coats during the time of its first Colonel, Aubrey de Vere, Earl of Oxford. The name varied to 'Oxford Blues' in 1690 to distinguish the Regiment from William III's Dutch 'Blew' Guards.

'The Royals': the 1st (Royal) Dragoons prior to amalgamation.

'The Spectamurs': the Royal Dragoons, from their motto *Spectamur Agendo* (By our deeds we are known).

'The Tangier Cuirassiers': the Tangier Horse, from the body armour worn by the regiments of Horse in the 17th century.

'The Tasty Blues': Life Guards' terminology, implies slovenly turn-out.

Recruiting

Nationwide. RHQ: Combermere Barracks, Windsor.

The Tangier Horse capture a Moor standard during a sortie out of Tangier. The regiment made many useful attacks on the enemy during 22 years in Africa.

The Royal Horse Artillery

Insignia

The Royal Cipher within a crowned oval Garter.

A gun between two scrolls, that above inscribed *Ubique*, that below inscribed *Quo fas et gloria ducunt*, the whole ensigned with the Crown.

Honour titles

In 1925 all batteries of the Royal Artillery were authorised to assume titles which had a bearing on their fighting past: 'A' (The Chestnut Troop); 'F' (Sphinx) Battery; 'G' Battery (Mercer's Troop, at Waterloo); 'H' Battery (Ramsey's Troop, at Waterloo); 'I' Battery (Bull's Troop); 'J' Battery (Sidi Rezegh); 'L' (Nery) Battery; 'N' Battery (The Eagle Troop); 'O' Battery (The Rocket Troop); AND 'Q' (Sanna's Post) Battery.

Anniversaries

Founders Day: November 11 is kept to celebrate the day in 1793 when two troops of horsed artillery were raised to join two experimental troops born in the January. The union officially marked the birth of the Regiment.

Battery days: each Battery celebrates the anniversary of its own battle honour namesake. 'I' Battery keep May 5 as Drivers' Day in honour of Captain Bull's Troop in the Peninsula and at Waterloo, but particularly 2nd Captain Norman Ramsey's section

The Royal Horse Artillery

1793
RHA formed as the first branch of the Artillery in which all ranks were mounted

1816
The Rocket Troop and others formed during the Napoleonic Wars disbanded

1855
Regiment reorganised as a Horse Brigade

1947
The ceremonial troop renamed King's Troop. Other batteries organised in regiments of the RHA

The Lines horses of the King's Troop are Light Irish Draught cobs of bay, brown and black. The blacks are kept for royal and military funerals.

and its famous gallop to save the guns at Fuentes d'Onor in 1811.

Customs
The King's Troop has duties to fire salutes on royal birthdays and anniversaries, and occasions of State. It has to find the Queen's Life Guard when the Household Cavalry is at summer camp.

Mascot
None.

Dress distinctions
As for the Royal Regiment of Artillery, except: the soldiers' collar badge is the same as the Regimental Crest (the Royal Cipher within a crowned oval Garter) and a stable-belt of light blue with a narrow centre stripe.

Full dress: a black fur busby with red bag, yellow cords, and white plume (red for musicians); a blue shell jacket with scarlet collar and yellow braid; blue riding breeches with a broad red stripe down the outer seams.

Marches
The Keel Row and *Bonnie Dundee* are played as canters, otherwise as for the Royal Regiment of Artillery.

Nicknames
'The Galloping Gunners': from the Regiment's ability to go into action in support of the cavalry.

'The Four-wheeled Hussars': a reference to the gunners' hussar-style dress and their custom of riding on the guns and limbers.

'The Right of the Line': the Regiment's seniority in the Army, and its right to lead and take the right flank on parade, originated in 1857. In that year the Duke of Cambridge submitted to Queen Victoria that as the Foot Artillery had been accorded precedence over the infantry (in 1756), then the Horse Artillery should have priority of the cavalry (and thus the Army). The Household Cavalry objected, however, and RHA precedence was commuted, in 1873, to be second to the Life Guards and the Royal Horse Guards; the right to take the right flank and march at the head of all other regiments on parade was made subject to the guns being present.

Recruiting
Nationwide. RHQ: London

1st The Queen's Dragoon Guards

Insignia
The Austrian Eagle: Adopted by the 1st (King's) Dragoon Guards from the Arms of Emperor Franz

Above *Queen Elizabeth The Queen Mother inspecting the Regiment, 1983.*

Below *'The Welsh Tankies'. Ferret scout cars of the Regiment on patrol in Martyr's Square, Beirut, 1983.*

Joseph I of Austria, who was Colonel-in-Chief of the Regiment from 1896 to 1914.

The cipher of Queen Caroline within the Garter: this device was taken up by the Queen's Bays on becoming The Queen's Own Royal Regiment of Horse in 1727, on the accession of George II. His Queen was Caroline of Anspach.

Pro Rege et Patria: the Regimental motto of the Queen's Bays (For King and Country) is borne on the Standard, and marks the Regiment's Royal connections; the Bays' dispensation from the Loyal Toast is maintained in 1QDG today.

Honours

Blenheim, Ramillies, Oudenarde, Malplaquet, Dettingen (KDG); Warburg (KDG/Bays); Beaumont (KDG); Willems (Bays); Waterloo, Sevastopol (KDG); Lucknow (Bays); Taku Forts, Pekin 1860, South Africa 1879 (KDG); South Africa 1901–02 (KDG/Bays).

Mons, Le Cateau, Marne 1914, Messines 1914, Ypres 1914–15 (Bays); Somme 1916, 1918 (KDG/Bays); Morval (KDG); Scarpe 1917, Cambrai 1917, 1918, Amiens, Pursuit to Mons (Bays); France & Flanders 1914–18 (KDG).

Afghanistan 1919 (KDG).

Somme 1940 (Bays); Beda Fomm, Defence of Tobruk (KDG); Gazala (Bays); Defence of Alamein Line (KDG); El Alamein, El Agheila (Bays); Advance on Tripoli, Tebaga Gap (KDG); El Hamma (Bays); Tunis, North Africa 1941–43 (KDG/Bays); Monte Camino, Gothic Line (KDG); Coriano, Lamone Crossing, Rimini Line, Argenta Gap (Bays); Italy 1943–44 (KDG).

Anniversaries

Waterloo/Gazala Day: the Regiment's day of celebration is a fusion of the founder Regiments' principal battle anniversaries: Waterloo Day of the KDG and Gazala Day of the Queen's Bays. It is customary, on this day, for officers and Sergeants to dine together in the tradition of the KDG, whose officers sat and shared their rations with other ranks of the Regiment on the field of Waterloo. Gazala Day honours the Bays who were equipped with second-hand tanks and moved up to the Gazala Line, where they were in action for 19 days continuously. At the end of the Battle of Knightsbridge the Bays were the only British armoured unit left operationally effective.

Customs

Information not available.

Mascot

None.

The King's Dragoon Guards charge Tartar infantry in China, 1860.

The Mounted Band of the Queen's Bays, 1890. The white helmet plumes of the band contrast with black plumes worn by the sabre squadrons following. The whitish buff drum banners are emblazoned with a gold gothic Bays *and laurel wreath, and the battle honour 'Lucknow' below.*

Dress distinctions

A blue dress cap mounted with the Austrian Eagle badge. Collar badges: a Gothic-style *Bays* within a crowned bay-leaf wreath on blue backing, the former badge of the Queen's Bays. Buttons are embossed with a Gothic *Q* over *DG* within the Garter, superimposed upon a crowned star. A stable-belt of Royal blue.

Full dress: a brass helmet with white plume; scarlet tunic faced blue, and trimmed in yellow cord; blue overalls with a broad white stripe down the outer seam (Bays).

Marches

Radetsky/Rusty Buckles, the Regimental March is a combination of those formerly played in the founder Regiments. *The Radetsky March* was composed in 1848 by Johann Strauss, and introduced to the KDG by Bandmaster Herr Schramm. *Rusty Buckles* relates to the old nickname of the Queen's Bays, and was adapted from the Regimental Slow March of the same name. The Slow March of the King's Dragoon Guards was based on themes from an opera by the Italian composer Mercadente.

Nicknames

'The Welsh Tankies': 1QDG is the armoured regiment for Wales and the border counties.

'The Bays': the 2nd Dragoon Guards acquired their nickname from their practice of riding nothing but bay mounts, a custom begun in 1767, and confirmed in 1799. Similarly, the KDG were known for their black mounts, once the distinguishing mark of the Regiments of Horse.

'The KDGs': from the initial letters of King's Dragoon Guards, sometimes read as 'The King's Dancing Girls'.

'The Rusty Buckles': a name given to the 2nd Dragoon Guards after their return from Ireland in the 18th century, where constant rain had rusted all the horse irons. Other regiments had in the meantime been issued with brass bits and buckles.

'The Traders Union': the King's Dragoon Guards, from their experience with industrial riots in the 19th century.

Recruiting

Wales, Shropshire and old Herefordshire. RHQ: Maindy Barracks, Cardiff.

1st The Queen's Dragoon Guards

1685 Queen's Regt of Horse	**1685** Earl of Peterborough's Horse
1714 The King's Horse	**1714** Princess of Wales's Own Regt of Horse
	1727 Queen's Own Horse
1746 1st or King's Dragoon Guards	**1746** 2nd or Queen's Dragoon Guards
	1872 2nd Dragoon Guards (Queen's Bays)
	1921 The Queen's Bays (2nd Dragoon Guards)

1959
1st The Queen's Dragoon Guards

The Royal Scots Dragoon Guards (Carabiniers and Greys)

Insignia

The Badge of the Order of the Thistle with motto *Nemo me impune lacessit*: the ancient Guidon device of the Scots Greys now forms the centre design on the RSDG Standard.

An eagle superimposed upon crossed carbines: the Imperial Eagle badge of the Scots Greys was worn to commemorate the capture of a Regimental Eagle of the French 45th at Waterloo. Crossed

3rd Dragoon Guards at the start of Napier's Expedition to the heart of Abbysinia in 1868.

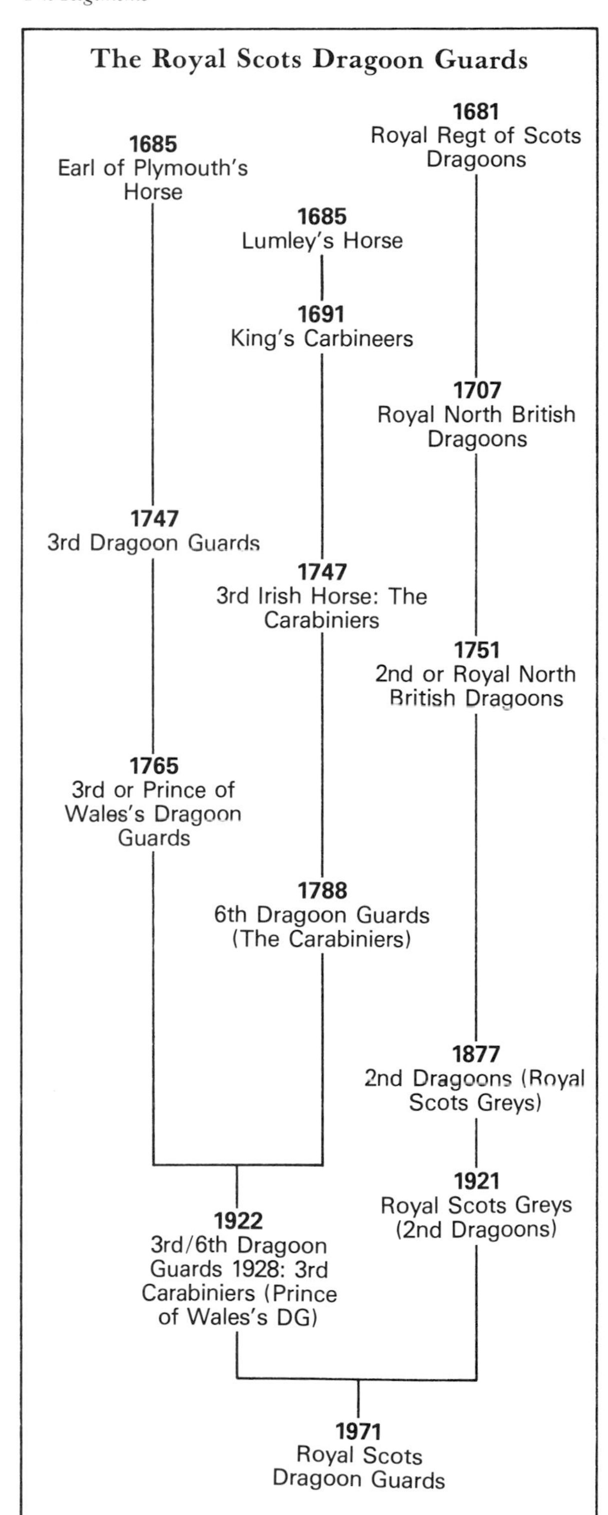

Sgt Ewart capturing the Eagle in the Charge of the Union Brigade at Waterloo.

carbines are known to have graced Regimental appointments of the Carabiniers from as early as 1770.

The Prince of Wales' plume: the 3rd Dragoon Guards assumed the 'Prince of Wales' title in 1765, on the occasion of the third birthday of Prince George Augustus Frederick. His emblem is emblazoned on the Standard together with the Red Dragon of Wales in the tradition of the Regiment.

Honours

Blenheim, Ramillies, Oudenarde, Malplaquet (3DG/Carbs/Greys); Dettingen (3DG/Carbs); Warburg (3DG/Carbs/Greys); Beaumont (3DG); Willems (3DG/Greys); Talavera, Albuhera, Vittoria, Peninsula (3DG); Waterloo, Balaklava, Sevastopol (Greys); Delhi 1857 (Carbs); Abyssinia (3DG); Afghanistan 1879–80 (Carbs); Relief of Kimberley, Paardeberg (Greys); South Africa 1899–1902 (3DG/ Carbs/ Greys).

Retreat from Mons, Marne 1914 (Carbs/Greys); Aisne 1914, Messines 1914, Ypres 1914, 1915, Arras 1917, Cambrai 1917, 1918, Amiens, Somme 1918 (3DG/Carbs/Greys); Hindenburg Line (3DG/Greys); Pursuit to Mons (Carbs/Greys).

Merjayun, Alam el Halfa, El Alamein, Nofilia, Salerno, Hill 112, Falaise Gap, Hochwald, Aller (Greys); Imphal, Nunshigum, Kanglatombi, Bishenpur, Kennedy Peak, Irrawaddy, Sagaing, Ava, Mandalay (3rd Carbs).

Anniversaries

Waterloo Day (June 18): the Scots Greys' charge with the Union Brigade at Waterloo, and the subsequent capture of a French Eagle by Segeant Ewart, is celebrated in the RSDG with the same fervour as the Greys applied to their Waterloo Day. On

Trooper in No 2 dress.

Drummer in No 2 dress with the Atholl bonnet.

Waterloo Day 1956 the Eagle trophy was taken from the Royal Hospital at Chelsea, where it had been lodged since the battle, to Edinburgh, where it was ceremonially borne to the Greys' headquarters in the Castle.

Nunshigum Day (April 13): the Regimental Day of the 3rd Carabiniers is observed in the old way, with 'B' Squadron led on parade by its Sergeant Major. The absence of officers symbolises a critical moment in the 1944 battle for the control of the Nunshigum Ridge, when all the officer tank commanders had been picked off by Japanese snipers. This was not the first counter-attack on the jungle-clad ridge, eight miles from Imphal, and with the situation rendered desperate yet again, Sergeant Major Craddock organised the 3rd Carabiniers with the Indian dogras and drove the enemy from their entrenched positions along the crest of the ridge.

The Regimental birthday (July 2): the principal day of celebration commemorates the union of the Royal Scots Greys and the 3rd Carabiniers at Holyrood House in 1971.

Customs

The Loyal Toast: officers of the Regiment are allowed to drink the Loyal Toast seated, a privilege of both the Greys and the 3rd Dragoon Guards from the reign of George III. The old King dined regularly with the Greys and the practice is thought to have developed from a time when he began to find it inconvenient to rise for the Toast.

The Royal Standard: the RSDG has the unique honour, as did the Greys before them, of having permission to fly the Scottish Royal Standard over headquarters.

The Queen's banner: in the presence of Queen Elizabeth II, and on her birthday, the Pipe Major carries Her Majesty's personal pipe banner presented to the Royal Scots Greys in 1968.

Mascot

None.

Dress distinctions

A blue dress cap with a band of yellow vandyke and

Drummer in full dress reminiscent of that of the Scots Greys.

Piper in full dress; the sporran tassels are marked in the plume colours of the 3rd Dragoon Guards — red and black.

yellow piping, mounted with the Regimental badge on black backing, a Napoleonic Eagle with 'Waterloo' superimposed upon crossed carbines. The yellow vandyke was adopted around 1800 for the stable caps of the Scots Greys. It was changed to white in the 1840s, but a return was made to yellow with the formation of the RSDG in consideration of the yellow facings worn by the 3rd Carabiniers. Officers' caps are distinguished by thistle buttons and gold braid on the peak. The stable-belt is blue with adjacent stripes of grey/yellow/red. The side hat is blue with a yellow vandyke. Collar badges and buttons as the cap badge. The Prince of Wales' plume and motto is worn by all ranks on the left sleeve; white worsted for No 2 dress, and embroidered in silver for officers and No 1 dress.

Dress overalls are fashioned with a twin yellow stripe down the outer seams, a legacy of the 3rd Carabiniers, whose custom it was to wear light cavalry pattern overalls in the tradition of the 6th Dragoon Guards (The Carabiniers).

The curious mixture of heavy and light dragoon uniform can be traced to an order of 1851, which required the Carabiniers to be converted to a Regiment of light cavalry. When heavy status was restored in 1863 an application was made for the Regiment to continue with its unique style of dress: a blue heavy pattern tunic and helmet, with light pattern overalls and equipment.

Bandsmen are allowed to wear a grenade badge above the Regimental badge. This follows a custom of the Greys, whose musicians were recognised by the grenade badge. The tradition goes back to the early 18th century, when the 'musick' would march in the van of the Regiment with the grenadiers. Drummers may wear Royal Stewart trews, or Dalyell tartan for Regimental use.

Full dress: a bearskin with a white plume secured by a brass grenade socket on the left. The grenade is embossed with the Royal Arms, St Andrew's Cross and the honour 'Waterloo', and is worn by right of the grenadier cap sanctioned to the Greys to mark

the victory at Ramillies in 1706, where the Greys charged the French *Regiment du Roi* and secured a prize of fur caps. The grenadier caps worn by the Regiment evolved through several period styles to the bearskin worn in the RSDG today. On the back of soldiers' bearskins is the Horse of Hanover in silver, a distinction discarded by officers of the Greys during the Napoleonic Wars. Bandsmen wear a long scarlet plume over the crest of the bearskin in the manner adopted by the Greys in 1830. The scarlet tunic is faced in yellow after the 3rd Carabiniers. Pipers wear a Highland feather bonnet fashioned with the yellow vandyke and Regimental badge, a blue Lowland doublet piped in yellow with gold thistle-pattern lace on the wings, black waist and cross belts, and a Royal Stewart plaid and kilt.

Marches

3rd Dragoon Guards, the Regimental Quick March. *Garb of Old Gaul,* the Regimental Slow March (Greys). *Men of Harlech,* the Mounted Walk (3DG). *The Keel Row,* the Mounted Trot (Greys). *Bonnie Dundee*, the Canter (Greys). *My Home*, the Pipes Slow March. *Highland Laddie*, the Pipes Quick March. *Scotland the Brave*, combined band Quick March.

When the band is performing in the Officers' Mess it is customary for them to play *God Bless The Prince of Wales*, a time-honoured practice of the 3rd Dragoon Guards' mess, and the *Imperial Russian Anthem* in memory of Czar Nicholas II, one time Colonel-in-Chief of the Scots Greys.

It was a custom in the Carabiniers for the Viennese folk tune *Ach du Lieber Augustin* to be played instead of the normal cavalry reveille. This was introduced by Colonel Porter in 1898.

Nicknames

'The Bird-catchers': a reputation shared by the Greys and the Royal Dragoons following their success in capturing French regimental Eagles at Waterloo.

'The Bubbly Jocks': an old name for the Scots Greys, probably inspired by their eagle badge, because *Bubbly Jock* was an old Scottish term for a turkey cock.

'The Carbs': the Carabiniers (6th Dragoon Guards). The term *Carabinier* dates from the year 1690, when William III bestowed the title 'King's Carabineers' on the Regiment in recognition of their expert use of the carbine firearm at the Battle of the Boyne.

'Ces terribles chevaux gris': Napoleon's supposed description of the Greys at Waterloo.

'The Greys': a shortened form of 'Scots Greys', the nickname of the 2nd Dragoons from about 1700 to 1877, when it became part of the Regiment's title. The name is thought to have come from the Regiment's exclusive use of grey mounts, but this theory is refuted by some modern authorities, who ascribe the name to iron-grey coats worn by the Scotch dragoons in the 17th century. The 2nd

Dragoons were famous for their greys nonetheless, and horses of that colour are still procured for RSDG ceremonials whenever possible.

'The Old Canaries': the 3rd Dragoon Guards, from their yellow facings.

'Tichborne's Own': Sir Roger Tichborne attracted a great deal of publicity for himself, and this appellation for his Regiment, the Carabiniers, at the so-called Trial of the Tichborne Claimant in 1873.

Recruiting

Scotland. RHQ: Edinburgh Castle.

The 4th/7th Royal Dragoon Guards

Insignia

The Star of the Order of St Patrick with motto *Quis separabit*: from the Standard of the 4th (Royal Irish) Dragoon Guards.

The Harp and Crown.

The Coronet of Her late Majesty the Empress and Queen Frederick of Germany as Princess Royal of Great Britain and Ireland: from the Standard of the 7th Dragoon Guards.

Honours

Blenheim, Ramillies, Oudenarde, Malplaquet, Dettingen, Warburg (7th); Peninsula (4th); South Africa 1846–47 (7th); Balaklava, Sevastopol (4th); Tel-el-kebir, Egypt 1882 (4th/7th); South Africa 1900–02 (7th).

Mons, Marne 1914, Aisne 1914, (4th); La Bassée 1914, (7th); Ypres 1914, 1915 (4th); Somme 1916, 1918 (4th/7th); Cambrai 1917, 1918 (4th); Amiens, Hindenburg Line (7th); Pursuit to Mons (4th/7th).

Dyle, Dunkirk 1940, Normandy Landing, Odon, Mont Pincon, Nederrijn, Geilenkirchen, Rhineland, Cleve, Rhine.

Top left *The Royal Scots Dragoon Guards drummer follows Greys' tradition with his white bearskin and black horse. The offside banner is yellow and embroidered with the Prince of Wales' plume upon crossed carbines, and the nearside banner is red after the Greys, and shows their Eagle and motto, 'Second to none'.*

Above left *A Simkin watercolour of an officer of Carabiniers, 1888. Note the light cavalry pattern shoulder-belt and breeches.*

Above right *The 4th/7th Royal Dragoon Guards' Regimental Standard.*

Right *Cuneo's painting of the Presentation of the New Standard to the 4th/7th Royal Dragoon Guards by Field Marshal Sir Gerald Templer, at Fallingbostel on May 23 1958.*

The surrender of the keys of the Citadel of Cairo to the 4th Dragoon Guards on September 14 1882.

'The Black Horse', circa 1904. The troopers' helmet plumes are black and white, and facings black.

Anniversaries

Dettingen Day (June 12): Cornet Richardson suffered 30 sabre cuts in defence of the Regimental Standard, which afterwards was presented to him.

Normandy Day (June 6): the 4th/7th won a reputation for being 'the first and last' in and out of the engagements following the Normandy beach landings.

Customs

The Regiment has the only Military Travelling (Freemasons) Lodge, warranted to 4DG in 1758.

Mascot

None.

Dress distinctions

A blue dress cap mounted with the Regimental cap badge, the Star of the Order of St Patrick, with the Princess Royal's Coronet on the cross of St George in the centre. The side hat is red with blue flaps piped yellow. Buttons are embossed with the Coronet of the Princess Royal. The stable-belt has dark red over narrow yellow over blue stripes. A Regimental arm badge is worn below the left shoulder: a black diamond bearing one gold over two maroon chevrons.

Marches

Inseparable (Slow) and *St Patrick's Day* (Quick).

Nicknames

'Arran's Cuirassiers': a byname for the Earl of Arran's Horse, predecessors of the 4th Dragoon Guards. The name alluded to the cuirass, or body armour, worn by the regiments of Horse at this period.

'The Black Horse': a mid-18th century nickname of the 7th Dragoon Guards, from the Regimental facing colour. The Regimental Journal, begun in 1893, was entitled *The Black Horse Gazette*.

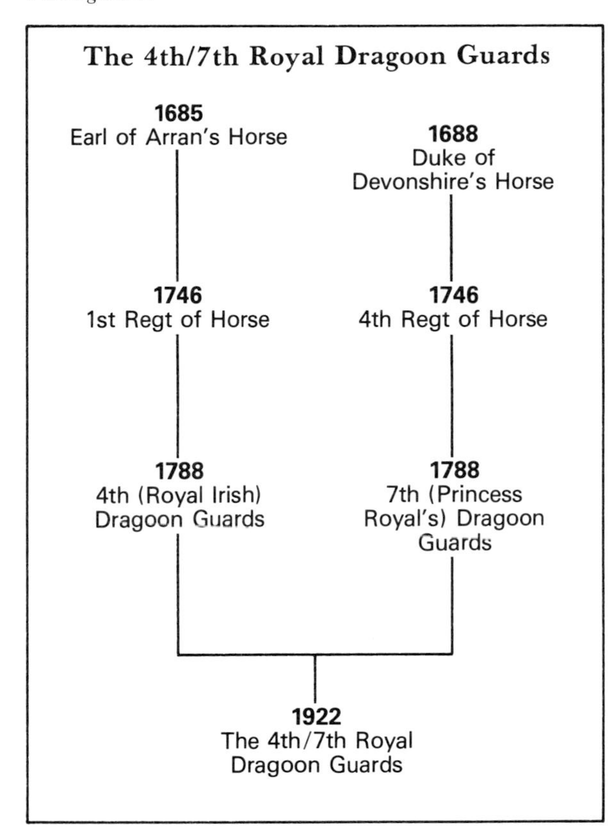

'The Virgin Mary's Bodyguard': a ribbing given to the 'Black Horse' during the reign of George II, when they were sent to assist the army of Archduchess Maria Theresa of Austria.

'The Blue Horse': an 18th century term for the 4th Dragoon Guards, from the Regimental facings.

'The Buttermilks': the 4th Dragoon Guards spent long periods in Ireland during the 18th century, much of it in farming the local stations.

'The Ligoniers': Earl Ligonier was Colonel of the Black Horse from 1720 to 1749, during which time he raised the Regiment to be a model of discipline and efficiency. In 1898 the 7th DG, in absence of a Regimental badge, adopted the Earl's crest, a demi-lion issuing from a coronet with the motto *Quo fata vocant* (Where fate calls).

'The Mounted Micks': the 4th (Royal Irish) Dragoon Guards. Although the 4th/7th is not essentially an Irish regiment the traditions of the 4th Dragoon Guards connected with St Patrick's Day are maintained on March 17.

Recruiting

North and West Yorkshire. RHQ: Catterick Garrison.

The 5th Royal Inniskilling Dragoon Guards

Insignia

The Castle of Inniskilling with St George's colours above the monogram *VDG:* the badges of the founder Regiments combined.

V.PCW.DG on a blue ground: the initials of the 5th Princess Charlotte of Wales's Dragoon Guards

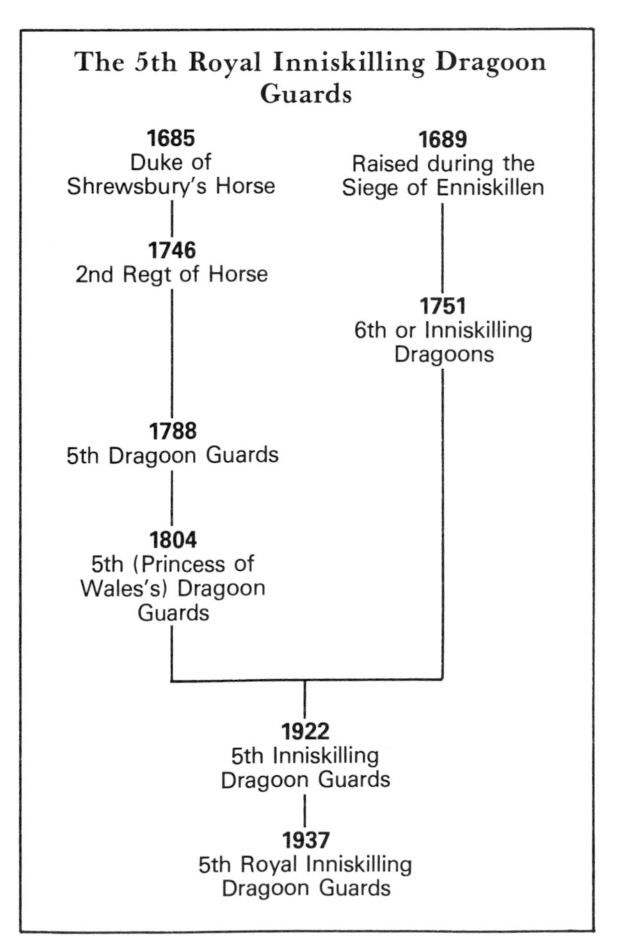

6th (Inniskilling)
Dragoons
Trooper
1751

Above far left *Regimental trumpeters of the 2nd Division Colour Party at a Freedom ceremony for the British Army of the Rhine. Their helmet plumes are red, and their collars blue and mounted with the Castle badge.*

Above left *A painting of a private in the 6th Dragoons, circa 1751. The saddlecloth, housings, and facings are yellow.*

Left *The Inniskillings charge into the stationary Russian cavalry 'with a wild cheer'. Balaklava, 1854.*

Above *Sir James Yorke Scarlett before the Heavy Brigade at Balaklava. Scarlett was sorely missed as Commander of the 5th Dragoon Guards when he was promoted to Brigadier shortly before they sailed to the Crimea.*

are emblazoned on the Standard.

The Castle of Inniskilling on a blue ground: the 6th (Inniskilling) Dragoons were formed of Protestant fighters in the town of Enniskillen during the siege of 1689. The symbol for the fortified town was added to the appointments of the Regiment in the early 18th century.

The White Horse of Hanover: the Horse emblem is carried on the Standards and Guidons of all British cavalry Regiments of the line as a matter of course, but was granted to the 5th Dragoon Guards as a Regimental badge in 1804, when they became 'The Princess Charlotte of Wales'.

Honours

Blenheim, Ramillies, Oudenarde, Malplaquet (5DG); Warburg (6D); Beaumont (5DG); Willems (6D); Salamanca, Vittoria, Toulouse, Peninsula (5DG); Waterloo (6D); Balaklava, Sevastopol (5DG/6D); Defence of Ladysmith (5DG); South Africa 1899–1902 (5DG/6D).

Mons, Le Cateau, Marne 1914, Messines 1914, Ypres 1914, 1915 (5DG); Somme 1916, 1918, Cambrai 1917, 1918, Amiens (5DG/6D); Hindenburg Line (6D); Pursuit to Mons (5DG/6D).

Withdrawal to Escaut, St Omer–La Bassée, Dunkirk 1940, Mont Pincon, Lower Maas, Roer.

The Hook, Korea 1951–52.

Anniversaries

Salamanca Day (July 22): a French Drum Major's mace, the 'Salamanca Staff', is carried on parade, its inscription reads: 'This trophy was taken in the charge by the 5th Dragoon Guards at the Battle of Salamanca, 22nd July, 1812, in which, amongst others, the 66th French Regiment was annihilated. Major General Ponsonby begs leave to present it to the 5th Dragoon Guards to be carried by the Trumpet Major on all occasions of review as a memory of That Glorious Day'.

Oates Sunday: the former Regimental Day of the Inniskilling Dragoons is observed now on the Sunday nearest to St Patrick's Day. The original celebration for St Patrick has been modified to honour the memory of Captain Oates of the Inniskillings, who, on March 17 1912, walked knowingly to his death in order to give his comrades on the South Pole Expedition a better chance of survival.

Customs

From 1930 the Salamanca Staff has been carried on special occasions. The Belgian National Anthem is played before the Loyal Toast in honour of the Colonel, King Leopold.

Mascot

None.

Dress distinctions

A dark green dress cap (5DG) with a primrose yellow band and piping (6D), mounted with the Regimental cap badge, a crowned *V* superimposed upon *DG*. A primrose yellow side hat with dark green flaps piped yellow. Collar badge, the Castle (of Inniskilling). Buttons are embossed with the Castle beneath *V* and flanked by *D* and *G* within the words *Vestigia nulla retrorsum* (No going backward), the old motto of the 5th Dragoon Guards. The Sergeants' arm badge is the Horse of Hanover in silver. The stable-belt is striped red over yellow, the bands separated by a narrow green strip.

Full dress: a white-metal helmet (6D) fixed with a red and white falling plume (5DG), a scarlet tunic faced in blue, and green overalls (5DG) fashioned with a broad yellow stripe down the outer seams.

Marches

The Soldiers' Chorus (5DG) and *Il Travatore* (slow). *Fare Thee Well Inniskilling* (the Quick).

Nicknames

'The Green Horse': one of a series of similar names from the 18th century used to differentiate between the old regiments of Horse. The 2nd Horse (later the 5th Dragoon Guards) were distinguished by green facings.

'The Old Farmers': like most Horse regiments the 5th Dragoon Guards spent many long years in Ireland during the 18th century and many of its members turned their hands to farming.

'The Skillingers': the 6th (Inniskilling) Dragoons.

Recruiting

Northern Ireland, Cumbria and Cheshire. RHQ: Chester Castle.

The Queen's Own Hussars

Insignia

The *QO* cipher above the White Horse of Hanover, within the Garter: the Regimental Crest is a combination of founder Regiments' badges. The *QO* cipher was inherited from the 7th Hussars and dates from 1727, when the Regiment was honoured as 'The Queen's Own'. The Horse of Hanover has been worn on the appointments of the 3rd since 1714, when it was created 'The King's Own'.

Nec aspera terrent: the motto of the House of Hanover (Nor do difficulties deter) was granted to

An exhibition stand of the Royal Armoured Corps showing, among other things, silver statuettes of a mounted officer of the 7th Hussars and a desert rat.

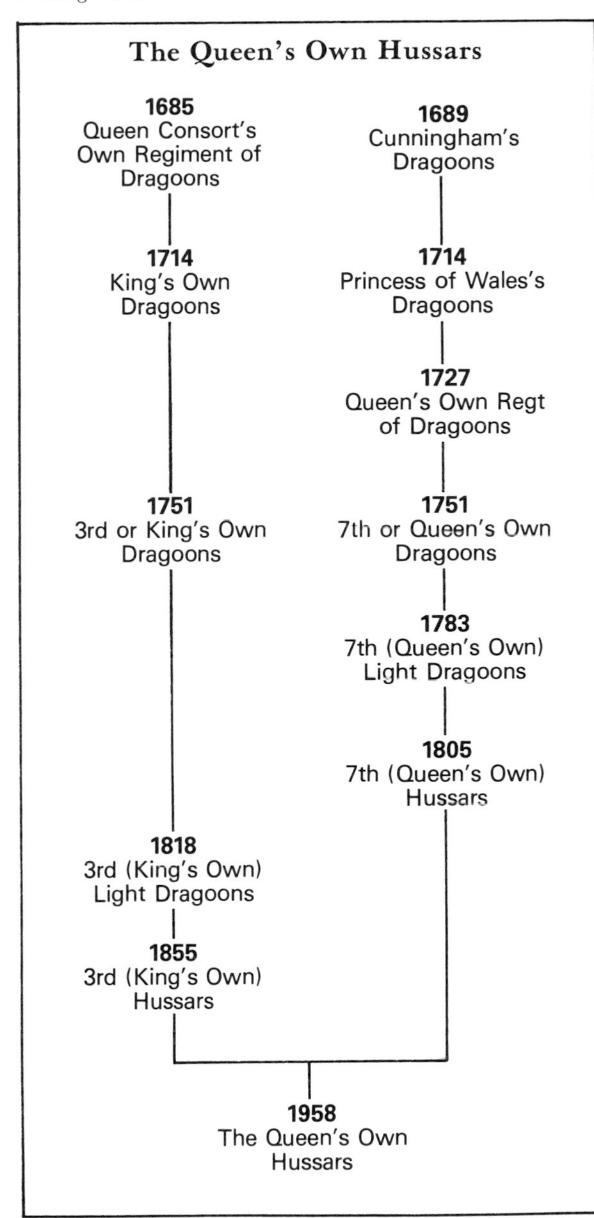

the 3rd in 1714 with the Hanover badge.

Honours

Dettingen (3rd/7th); Warburg, Beaumont, Willems (7th); Salamanca, Vittoria (3rd); Orthes (7th); Toulouse (3rd); Peninsula (3rd/7th); Waterloo (7th); Cabool 1842, Moodkee, Ferozeshah, Sobraon, Chillianwallah, Goojerat, Punjaub (3rd); Lucknow (7th); South Africa 1901–02 (3rd/7th).

Retreat from Mons, Marne 1914, Ypres 1914, 1915, Cambrai 1917, 1918, Somme 1918, Amiens, France & Flanders 1914–18 (3rd); Khan Baghdadi, Sharquat, Mesopotamia 1917–18 (7th).

Egyptian Frontier 1940 (7th); Buq Buq (3rd); Beda Fomm (3rd/7th); Sidi Rezegh 1941 (7th); El Alamein (3rd); North Africa 1940–42 (3rd/7th); Citta della Pieve (3rd); Ancona (7th); Italy 1944–45 (3rd/7th); Crete (3rd); Burma 1942 (7th).

Anniversaries

Dettingen Day: the Dettingen tradition inherited from the 3rd Hussars has many facets, each of which tells of the extraordinary gallantry displayed by their Regimental forerunners in the battle (see 'Customs' entry).

Waterloo Day (June 18): 'Waterloo' was the main battle honour of the 7th Hussars, and the QOH has undertaken to continue the Waterloo Day celebrations in memory of the gallant rearguard action near Quatre Bras, where the 7th was decimated.

El Alamein Day (October 23): the Battle of El Alamein is commemorated in tribute to the 3rd Hussars, who were almost annihilated fighting alongside the 2nd New Zealand Division in the desert battle. The Regiment's armour is still emblazoned with the Fern Leaf emblem of New Zealand.

Customs

The QOH maintain a drum horse to carry replicas of the magnificent kettle-drums captured at Dettingen in 1743; these are paraded without banners in the way of the 3rd Hussars to show off their beauty and engraved battle honours. The 3rd enjoyed a dispensation from the Loyal Toast because of their obvious loyalty in the presence of the King at Dettingen.

Mascot

None.

Dress distinctions

A scarlet dress cap mounted with the Horse of Hanover badge. The officers, RSM, and Bandmaster wear the Regimental Crest in No 1 dress: the Horse of Hanover and *QO* cipher within the Garter. A scarlet side hat piped yellow. An arm badge is worn on the left sleeve by every member of the Regiment: the silver and scarlet *Maid of Warsaw* was awarded to the 7th Hussars by the commander of the 2nd Polish Corps in recognition of their valour in supporting the Poles throughout the Italian Campaign of 1944–5. The stable-belt is striped blue/yellow/blue, with a scarlet line on each stripe.

No 1 dress is personalised by blue ranking and a scarlet collar. These distinctions were granted to the

Above *Amalgamation Parade, 1958, with the 3rd Hussars' famous drum horse. The drummer's silver collar was presented to the Regiment by Lady Southampton in 1772.*

Left *An officer of the 7th Hussars in 1833. The Regiment was easily recognised by the distinctive dog-tooth edging to its saddlecloths.*

3rd Hussars in respect of their traditional uniform colourings. Blue has been evident in the Regiment's dress since its foundation as the Queen Consort's Dragoons in 1685, when the musicians wore hat plumes of that colour to complement the Queen's livery.

Officers' Sam Browne belts are not of the universal pattern, but have a special cross-belt with the Regimental cipher embossed thereon.

Full dress (musicians) follows that of the former 3rd Hussars: blue busby bag and white plume.

Marches

Suppé's *Light Cavalry,* the Quick March was introduced for the 1958 amalgamation and has no history of Regimental use. The former Regimental Marches *Robert The Devil* and *Bannocks o' Barley Meal* are played as an extra. *Colonel Bland,* the Regimental Slow March, now combined with *Garb of Old Gaul,* combines marches of the founder Regiments.

Colonel Bland was Commander of the 3rd Dragoons at the time of Dettingen. *Bonnie Dundee,* one of the old marches of the Scottish-born 7th; played before and after the Regimental March as a canter. *Encore,* authorised to the 7th Hussars about 1898 as a Trot Past.

Nicknames

'Bland's Dragoons': a popular name for the 3rd or King's Own Dragoons following their success at Dettingen (1743).

'The Lilywhites': the 7th Hussars, from the white facings and saddlecloths worn during the time of George III. Officers were allowed the distinction of a white strip collar on the frock coat.

'The Moodkee Wallahs': a reputation carried by the 3rd Light Dragoons after their formidable charge at the Battle of Moodkee in 1845, in which they suffered more killed outright than any other regiment engaged.

'The Saucy Seventh': the 7th Hussars.

'The Strawboots': the 7th Dragoons during the Warburg Campaign of 1760, when inadequate footwear was insulated or replaced with straw.

'The Young Eyes': the 7th Hussars, origin obscure.

'Lord Adam Gordon's Life Guards': a sardonic reference to the length of time spent by the 3rd Dragoons under that officer in Scotland at the height of the Jacobite rebellion.

Recruiting

Warwickshire, West Midlands and old Worcestershire. RHQ: Warwick.

The Queen's Royal Irish Hussars

Insignia

The Irish Harp surmounted by the Royal Crest: this was the badge of the 8th Hussars, whose designation was 'The King's Royal Irish'.

Mente et manu: the Regimental motto of the 4th Hussars (With mind and hand).

The Munster Garrison at the Freedom of the City in 1982. An Irish Guards' Drum Major leads the bands of the QRIH and 17/21 Lancers, two regiments whose close fellowship goes back to the bloody days of the Crimean War.

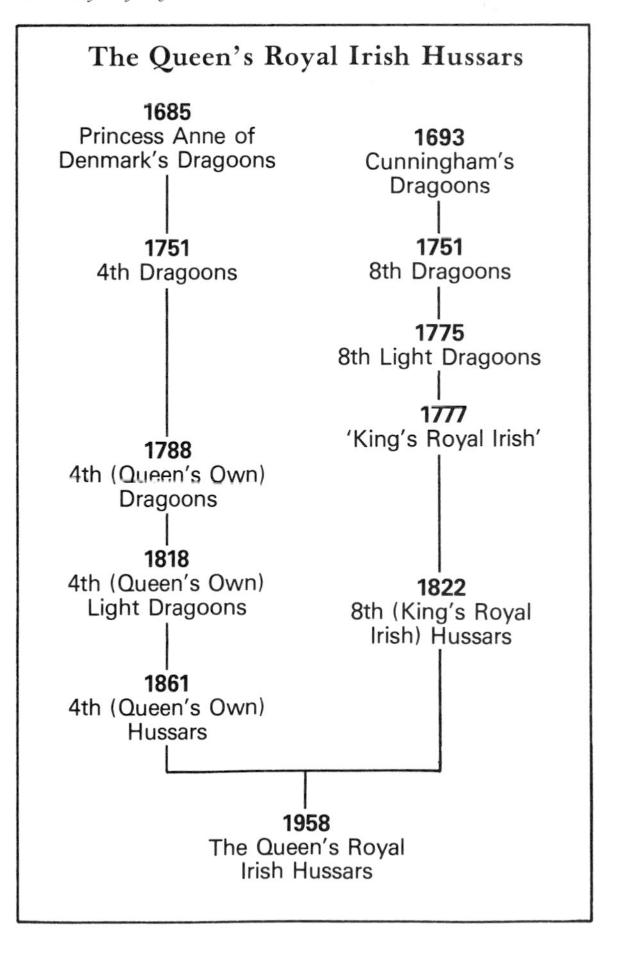

Above *Pepper's (the 8th) Dragoons at Almenara in 1710.*

Left *Officer of the 4th Light Dragoons in the French-style dress worn after the Crimean War.*

Pristinae virtutis memores: the Regimental motto of the 8th Hussars (The memory of former valour) is thought to be connected with the battle honour 'Leswaree'.

Honours

Dettingen (4th); Leswaree, Hindoostan* (8th); Talavera, Albuhera, Salamanca, Vittoria, Toulouse, Peninsula, Ghuznee 1839, Afghanistan 1839 (4th); Alma, Balaklava, Inkerman, Sevastopol (4th/8th); Central India, Afghanistan 1879–80, South Africa 1900–02 (8th).

Mons, Marne 1914, Ypres 1914, 1915 (4th); Givenchy 1914, Somme 1916, 1918 (8th); Cambrai 1917, 1918 (4th/8th); Bapaume 1918 (8th); Amiens (4th/8th); Albert 1918, France & Flanders 1914–18 (18th).

Villers Bocage, Roer, Rhine, Gazala (8th); Alam

* It should be noted that where the modern and original spelling differ, the original is given, even where this leads to inconsistency in the honours list.

el Halfa (4th); El Alamein (4th/8th); North Africa 1941–42 (8th); Coriano, Proasteion, Greece 1941 (4th).

Korea 1950–51, Imjin (8th).

'Leswaree' and 'Hindoostan' are rare battle honours, and were unique to the 8th Hussars in the cavalry. In March 1825 the Regiment was authorised to add the Harp and these honours to its Guidon.

Anniversaries

Balaklava Day (October 25): the Charge of the Light Brigade is commemorated in the Regiment because both the 4th and 8th Hussars were part of the five regiments which comprised the Brigade at Balaklava.

Customs

Information not available.

Mascot

None.

Dress distinctions

A scarlet dress cap mounted with the Harp badge within a circle surmounted by the Royal Crest. On a scroll beneath, the motto *Mente et manu.* The circle comes from the cap badge of the 4th Hussars. Officers wear a badge of entwined *QRIH* beneath the Royal Crest on the beret. A green side hat with yellow piping. Officers' side hats are shaped 'tent like' in the style of a Napoleonic stable cap, with gold braiding. Officers wear a brown bandolier with brass pickers, and a silver pouch embossed with a brass entwined *QRIH* beneath the Royal Crest. Yellow lanyards. NCOs arm badge: the Harp. Lance corporals wear two chevrons. The stable-belt is green with narrow yellow on blue centre stripes.

Marches

Litany Of Loretto (the Slow) based on Italian plainsong and collected in 1890. *Berkeley's Dragoons* (4H) and *St Patrick's Day* (8H) — (Quick).

Nicknames

'The Cross-belts': a nickname gained by the 8th Dragoons after the battle of Almenara in 1710, where they defeated a unit of Spanish Horse, and, 'exulting in victory', stripped the enemy of their sword-belts to wear as a mark of victory. At this time only Horse regiments carried their swords from a shoulder-belt, and moves were made to try and stop the 8th Dragoons' breach of protocol. It was not until 1769 that General Saverne was able to write, 'By the King's order cross-belts were expressly confirmed to the 8th Dragoons, with an addition of carrying their swords like the regiments of Horse, by their cross-belts, which before they carried in their waist-belts'. When the 8th became a regiment of light dragoons in 1775 it was found that cross-belts were common in the light horse, and it is thought that the 8th might have applied for another form of recognition for its part in the Battle of Almenara, hence the title 'King's Royal Irish', sanctioned in 1777.

'Paget's Irregular Horse': a name acquired by the 4th Light Dragoons from a loose form of drill they adopted in Afghanistan in 1839.

'The Twenty-fives': from the combined numbers of the 8th Hussars and 17th Lancers, who formed a fellowship during the Crimean War.

Recruiting

Northern Ireland, Surrey, Sussex and Greater London. RHQ: London.

The 9th/12th Royal Lancers (Prince of Wales's)

Insignia

The Plume of the Prince of Wales upon crossed lances, within the Garter: the 12th Light Dragoons took on the Prince of Wales' title in 1768, and bore his badge and motto from then on.

The cipher of Queen Elizabeth The Queen Mother: The Colonel-in-Chief's emblem.

The cipher of Queen Adelaide reversed and interlaced: the 9th Lancers were granted the right to bear the cipher in 1830, when the new King inspected the Regiment in Hyde Park and honoured it with the title 'Queen's Royal' Lancers. The emblem seems not to have been displayed at first, but eventually came into use as the Regimental button design.

The Sphinx superscribed 'Egypt': the 12th Light Dragoons were one of the few cavalry units to go on the Egyptian expedition of 1801 and remained to be

Above left *12th Lancers Guidon Presentation, 1956. The 12th was the first regiment to receive a Guidon after their restoration to the light cavalry. Before 1956 battle honours were displayed on the drum banners.*

Above right *The band of the 9th/12th Lancers. The band was issued with traditional Full Dress in the 1980s — scarlet helmet top and plume.*

Right *The charge of the 9th Lancers at Mons in 1914.*

Below right *'The Delhi Spearmen' of the 1920s. Note Queen Adelaide's cypher and the gong suspended within a tripod of lances.*

one of only two which could display the Sphinx on its appointments.

Honours

Salamanca, Peninsula, Waterloo (12th); Punniar, Sobraon, Chillianwallah, Goojerat, Punjaub (9th); South Africa 1851–53, Sevastopol, Central India (12th); Delhi 1857, Lucknow, Charasiah, Kabul 1879, Kandahar 1880, Afghanistan 1878–80 (9th); Modder River, Relief of Kimberley, Paardeberg (12th); South Africa 1899–1902 (9th/12th).

Mons (12th); Retreat from Mons, Marne 1914, Aisne 1914, Messines 1914, Ypres 1914, 1915, Somme 1916, 1918, Arras 1917, Cambrai 1917, 1918 (9th/12th); Rosieres (9th); Sambre (12th); Pursuit to Mons (9th).

Dyle, Dunkirk 1940 (12th); Somme 1940 (9th); North-West Europe 1940 (9th/12th); Chor es Sufan (12th); Gazala (9th/12th); Ruweisat (9th); El Alamein (9th/12th); El Hamma (9th); Tunis (12th); North Africa 1941–43, (9th/12th); Defence of Lamone Bridgehead, Argenta Gap, (9th); Bologna (12th); Italy 1944–45 (9th/12th).

Anniversaries

Mons/Moy Day: the Regimental Day commemorates the last mounted charges made with the lance (August 1914). No specific date is set for the festivities, but usually a convenient weekend in June or July.

Customs

The 12th Lancers maintained the ritual of playing a medley of five hymns every evening: *Sicilian Vespers, Hymn—the Russian National Anthem, Evening Hymn, God Bless The Prince of Wales,* and *God Save the King.* This custom is thought to have originated during the Regiment's Mediterranean tour of 1794, when the officers had an audience with the Pope at Civitavecchia to receive good conduct medals. It is likely that he made a request then for the hymns to be played in the Regiment on a regular basis. Another, spurious, theory has it that the hymns were played as a penance for raiding a monastery during the Peninsula War.

An old campaign friendship born in South Africa in 1851 with the 43rd Regiment was continued by the 12th Lancers with the Oxfordshire Light Infantry.

Mascot

None.

Dress distinctions

A scarlet dress cap with blue piping and quarter welts, mounted with the Regimental badge, the Prince of Wales' Plume, crowned, and superimposed upon crossed lances. A scarlet side hat piped yellow. Officers' side hats are blue piped gold. Buttons are embossed with an entwined and reversed *PW* superimposed upon crossed lances and surmounted by a crown. Lanyards of red and yellow. The stable-belt is yellow edged in red, with a wider red centre stripe.

Marches

God Bless The Prince Of Wales, Coburg and *Men Of Harlech.*

Nicknames

'The Delhi Spearmen': a repuation earned by the

QUEEN'S

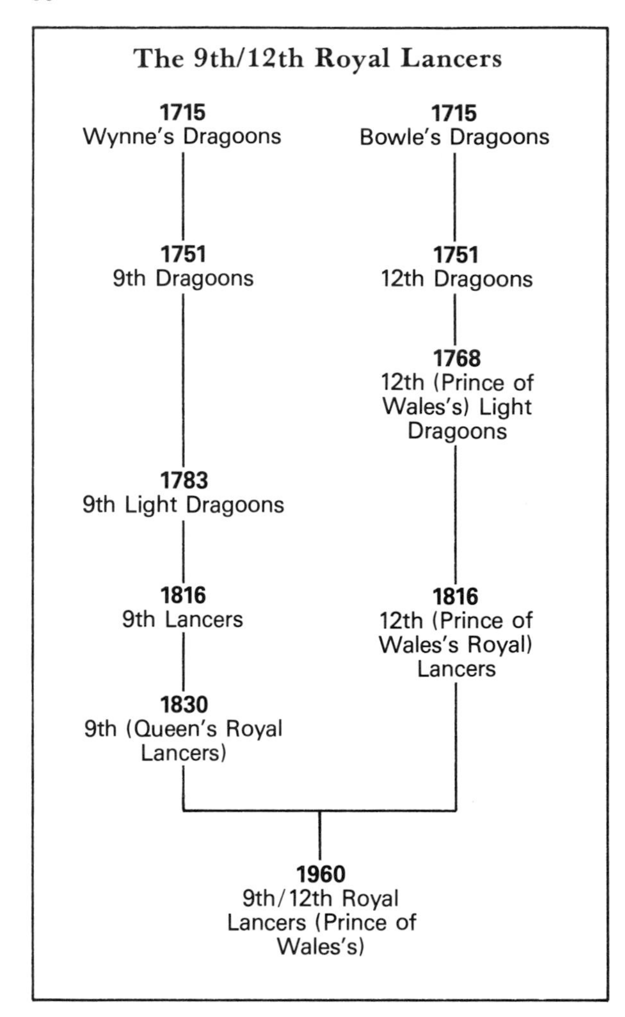

9th Lancers fighting at the Siege of Delhi in 1857. The Regiment gained more VCs, with the exception of the Royal Artillery, than any other unit engaged. The name was later taken by the Regimental Journal.

'The Magpies': the 9th Lancers, from their helmet plume of black and white. The Regiment was unusual in not having the upper part of the helmet in the facing colour (red). Helmets of the 9th Lancers were covered in blue cloth.

'The Supple Twelfth': the 12th Light Dragoons had a reputation for alacrity in action throughout the Peninsula War particularly in their celebrated charge against Foy's Division at Salamanca.

Recruiting

Derbyshire, Leicestershire, Northamptonshire and Greater London. RHQ: Glen Parva Barracks, Leicester.

The Royal Hussars (Prince of Wales's Own)

Insignia

The Prince of Wales' Plume: the 10th Light Dragoons were chosen by the Prince of Wales in 1783 to carry his title and emblem, three plumes issuing from a coronet with the motto *Ich dien.* Although he allowed Prince George to have the Colonelcy of the 10th, the King would not indulge his passion to lead the Regiment on the fields of Spain. The 10th Hussars continued to enjoy a long association with successive Princes of Wales.

The crest of the late Prince Albert with motto *Treu und fest*: worn on the dress and appointments of the 11th Hussars from 1840, when Prince Albert 'adopted' the Regiment, designed a new uniform for it and raised it to the hussars. The Prince was introduced to the Regiment in 1840, when he came to England for his impending marriage to Queen Victoria and met the 11th at Dover for the march to Canterbury.

The Red Dragon and Rising Sun: emblems emblazoned on the Guidon which relate to the Welsh connection in the Regiment's title.

The Sphinx with 'Egypt': awarded to the 11th

The trumpet on which it is believed the 'Advance' was sounded in the Charge of the Light Brigade.

Light Dragoons in 1802 in recognition of the services of 'C' Squadron as escort to General Abercromby during the Egyptian Campaign of the previous year. For this the unit was permitted to assume senior squadron status in the Regiment.

Honours

Warburg (10th/11th); Beaumont, Willems, Salamanca (11th); Peninsula, Waterloo (10th/11th); Bhurtpore, Alma, Balaklava, Inkerman (11th); Sevastopol (10th/11th); Ali Masjid, Afghanistan 1878–79, Egypt 1884, Relief of Kimberley, Paardeberg, South Africa 1899–1902 (10th).

Le Cateau, Retreat from Mons, Messines 1914, (11th); Ypres 1914, 1915 (10th/11th); Loos, (10th); Somme 1916, 1918 (10th/11th); Arras 1917, 1918 (10th); Cambrai 1917, 1918 (11th); Avre (10th); Amiens (10th/11th); Pursuit to Mons (10th).

Somme 1940 (10th); Villers Bocage, Rhine (11th); North-West Europe 1940, 1944–45, Egyptian Frontier 1940, Beda Fomm (11th); Saunnu (10th); El Alamein, Tunis (10th/11th); Argenta Gap (10th); Italy 1943–45 (11th).

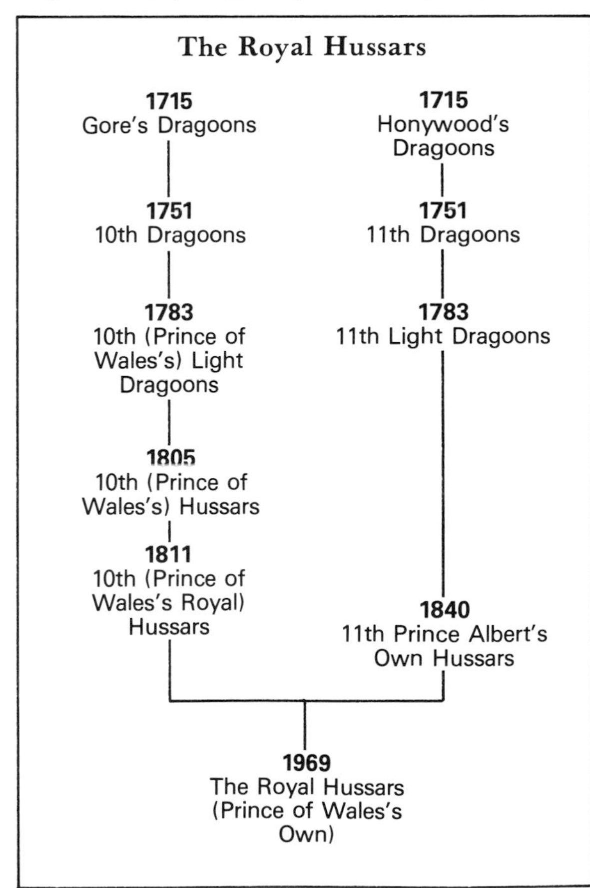

Bandsmen of the 11th Hussars by Harry Payne. Musicians in this regiment were remarkable for their grey fur busbies. The busby bag, breeches and drum banners were of regimental crimson.

Anniversaries

El Alamein Day (October 23): the anniversary of the Battle of El Alamein was selected to be the Regimental Day in view of the glorious victory shared by the armoured units of the 10th and 11th Hussars.

Customs

In the 11th Hussars 'C' Squadron had the unusual privilege of parading on the right flank of the Regiment (see above).

Last Post is sounded at 21.50 hrs — the time of Lord Cardigan's death.

Mascot

None.

Dress distinctions

A crimson dress cap (11th) mounted with the Prince

Orlando Norie's painting of the 10th Hussars at Aldershot Camp in 1868. Their uniform is distinguished by a scarlet busby bag and a black and white busby plume.

of Wales' plume (10th). The distinctive reddish-brown beret was also inherited from the 11th Hussars. A crimson side hat piped in yellow (11th). Buttons are embossed with the Prince of Wales' plume. The stable-belt is striped yellow/red/yellow, and edged in blue. Dress overalls are crimson after the style of the 11th Hussars.

Marches

God Bless The Prince of Wales. The Merry Month of May, the former Regimental March of the 10th Hussars. *Coburg,* the March of the 11th Hussars took its name from Prince Albert's family title.

The 10th Hussars were known for their custom of playing two hymns just before Last Post — *Thy Will Be Done* and *As Pants The Hart for Cooling Streams.*

Nicknames

'The Cherrypickers': the famous nickname of the 11th Hussars, and now the byname for the Royal Hussars, began life as an aspersion on Lieutenant Wood's patrol of the 11th Light Dragoons caught by the French whilst foraging in an orchard at San Martin de Trebejo, on August 15 1811. The name achieved respectability in time and was found to be particularly appropriate in 1840, when the 11th adopted cherry-coloured breeches.

'Baker's Light Bobs': the 10th Hussars in the Sudan 1884, after their field commander, Colonel Valentine Baker.

'Cardigan's Bloodhounds': a sobriquet for the 11th Hussars under the jurisdiction of the Earl of Cardigan. Although Cardigan was universally unpopular throughout his career, his Regiment enjoyed an unprecedented standard of excellence and bearing under his command.

'The Cherubims': a social comment on the 11th Hussars at the height of fashion in the 1840s. The word has no clear definition, but is thought to have been a corruption of 'Cherrypickers', and a subtle allusion to the Regiment's distinctive cerise breeches ('Cherrybums').

'The Don't Dance Tenth': officers of the 10th Hussars were reputed to have had a haughty disdain for the social art of dance, an exercise which might have spoilt the hang of their expensive uniforms.

'The Shiny Tenth': the 10th Hussars were known for their magnificent style of dress, especially during the reign of George IV. Shoulder-belts adorned with ornate chains, scarlet levee overalls and horse leathers decorated with cowrie shells were all relics of the Regency hussar carried into the Victorian age by the 10th. (Also 'Chainy Tenth'.)

Recruiting

Oxfordshire, Buckinghamshire, Berkshire, Hampshire, Wiltshire and Gloucestershire. RHQ: Lower Barracks, Winchester.

The 13th/18th Royal Hussars (Queen Mary's Own)

Insignia

The cipher *QMO* interlaced: the 18th Hussars were created 'Queen Mary's Own' in 1910.

Viret in aeturnam: the motto of the 13th Hussars (It flourishes for ever) relates to the Regiment's nickname 'Evergreens'.

Pro Rege, pro lege, pro Patria conamur: the motto of the 18th Hussars (We strive for King, laws, and country).

Honours

Albuhera, Vittoria, Orthes, Toulouse (13th); Peninsula, Waterloo (13th/18th); Alma, Balaklava, Inkerman, Sevastopol (13th); Defence of Ladysmith (18th); Relief of Ladysmith (13th); South Africa 1899–1902 (13th/18th).

Above *The 18th Hussars, brigaded with their old Peninsula comrades the 10th Hussars, routing French 'heavies' at Waterloo.*

Above right *Cavalry regiments, 1965. 'The Lilywhites' may be recognised by their white caps at right.*

Mons, Marne 1914, Aisne 1914, Messines 1914, Ypres 1914, 1915, Somme 1916, 1918, Cambrai 1917, 1918, Amiens, Hindenburg Line (18th); France & Flanders 1914–18 (13th/18th); Kut al Amara 1917, Baghdad, Sharquat, Mesopotamia 1916–18 (13th).

Ypres–Comines Canal, Normandy Landing, Caen, Mont Pincon, Geilenkirchen, Roer, Rhineland, Goch, North-West Europe 1940, 1944–45.

Anniversaries

Balaklava Day (October 25): the former Regimental Day of the 13th Hussars is perpetuated to commemorate their lead in the Charge of the Light Brigade.

Normandy Day (June 6): 13th/18th was one of the first units to go ashore on the Normandy beaches in their specially equipped DD tanks.

Lajj Day (March 5): the former celebration of the 13th Hussars' last mounted charge, in Mesopotamia, is observed today as a Regimental holiday.

Customs

Information not available.

Mascot

None.

Dress distinctions

A white dress cap with a blue band, mounted with the Regimental badge, the *QMO* cipher interlaced and crowned (18th), and superimposed by the title scroll (13th). A white side hat piped in yellow, with

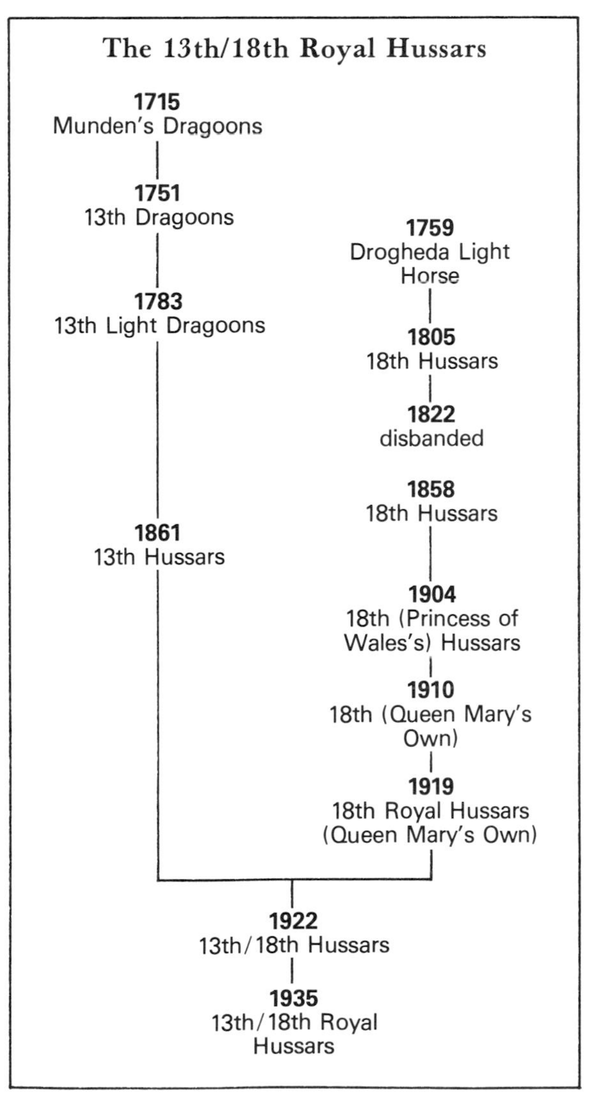

Simkin's Officer of 13th Hussars. This Victorian uniform is almost identical to 13/18 full dress today.

blue flaps and peak. White lanyards. The stable-belt is striped blue and white. A white/blue diamond patch is worn on the upper left sleeve; NCOs wear an entwined *QMO* over their chevrons.

Regimental full dress is based upon that of the 13th Hussars: a white busby bag and plume, white tunic collar and twin white overall stripes.

An application was made in 1981 for the officers to wear cummerbunds in mess dress based on the pattern of those worn by Skinner's Horse, with which the Regiment has an association.

Marches

Balaklava. Right Of The Line (the 13th Light Dragoons rode on the right flank of the Light Brigade at Balaklava). *The Regimental March Of The 13th Hussars* (1903). *The Regimental March Of The 18th Hussars,* introduced in 1903 and based on the old Irish air *The Rose Tree. A Life On The Ocean Wave,* played on occasion to commemorate the Normandy landings of 1944.

Nicknames

'The Lilywhites': from the 13th Hussars, who were known as 'The Lilywhite Hussars' after their white facings and distinctions.

'Yorkshire's Cavalry': a modern self-styled name. The Regiment is of South Yorkshire extraction.

'Baker's Dozen': an old name for the 13th Hussars.

'The Droghedas': from the Marquis of Drogheda, who raised the 18th in 1759 and commanded the Regiment until 1822, when it was sent to Dublin and disbanded.

'The Evergreens': an old reference to the 13th, probably from its facing colour. When the Regiment was in red coats, from 1715 to 1783, and 1836 to 1840, green was the facing colour, but when light cavalry blue was taken on green was considered unsuitable, and buff substituted. This was pipeclayed and eventually changed to white.

'The Ragged Brigade': a description of the effects of campaign on the 13th and 14th Light Dragoons in the later stages of the Peninsula War. The 13th made a remarkable transition after the war and became known as 'The Geraniums' from its colourful dress.

Recruiting

South Yorkshire. RHQ: York.

The 14th/20th King's Hussars

Insignia

A Prussian Eagle: the black Prussian Eagle is borne on the Guidon by privilege of the 14th Hussars, who were granted the right to wear the emblem in 1799 in honour of the marriage of the Princess Royal of Prussia to His Royal Highness the Duke of York in 1791. The association between Princess and Regiment began in 1798, when the 14th Light Dragoons

The band of the 14th/20th King's Hussars in traditional guise pass by the regiment's ultra-modern armour. Note the Gurkha bandsmen near the rear of the column.

had occasion to escort the Princess to London. After this Princess Frederika became known as 'The Royal Patroness' of the Regiment.

Crossed kukris: the 14th/20th was invited by the 6th Gurkha Rifles to display the Gurkha badge on its appointments in 1947 to cement the close wartime relationship that existed between the Hussars and 43rd Gurkha Lorried Brigade. The badge was approved in 1950, and a strong association is maintained with 6GR today.

The Red Rose of Lancaster: the Rose is carried on the Guidon to mark the Regiment's recruiting area in Manchester and Lancashire.

Honours

Vimiera, (20th); Douro, Talavera, Fuentes d'Onor, Salamanca, Vittoria, Pyrenees, Orthes (14th); Peninsula (14th/20th); Chillianwallah, Goojerat, Punjaub, Persia, Central India (14th); Suakin 1885 (20th); Relief of Ladysmith (14th); South Africa 1900-02 (14th/20th).

Mons, Retreat from Mons, Marne 1914, Aisne 1914, Messines 1914, Ypres 1914, 1915, Cambrai 1917, 1918, Somme 1918, Amiens, Sambre (20th); Tigris 1916, Kut al Amara 1917, Baghdad, Mesopotamia 1915–18, Persia 1918 (14th).

Bologna, Medicina, Italy 1945.

'Vimiera' was inherited from the 20th Light Dragoons, disbanded in 1819. This Regiment was the only cavalry unit available to Wellington in the battle, and earned the battle honour in a dashing charge against the French at a time when the infantry were hard pressed.

'Douro' is borne by no other cavalry regiment and only three regiments altogether.

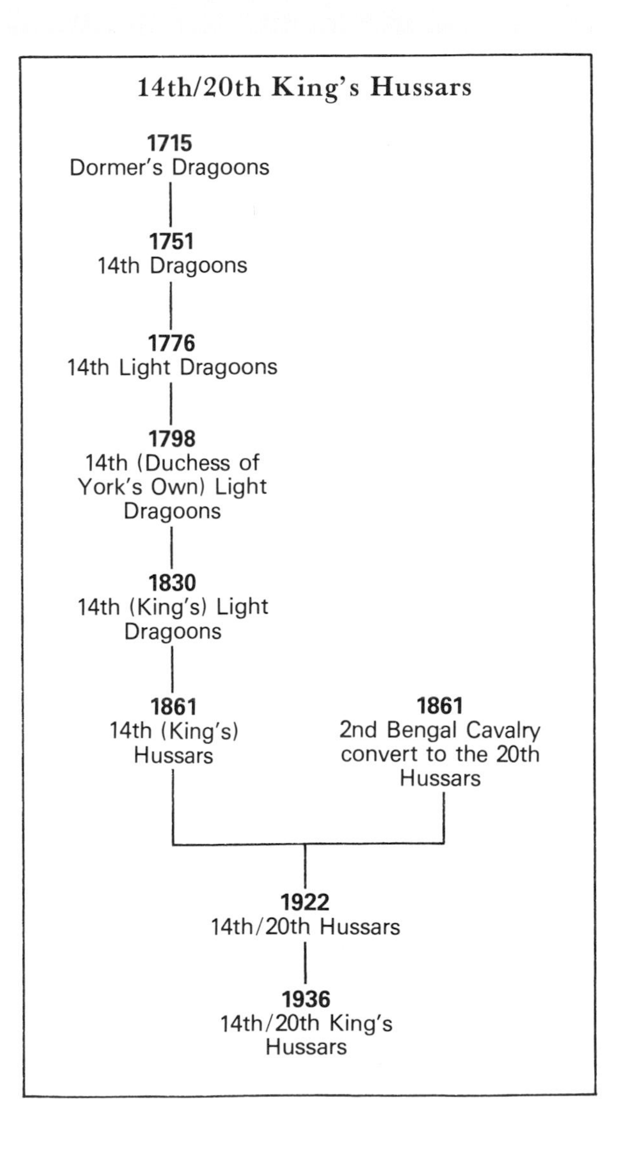

Above left *The 14th/20th King's Hussars' Regimental Guidon.*

Above right *B Squadron march past, Colonel's Parade, 1981. The Corporal's full dress is distinguished by a yellow busby bag, tunic braiding, and overalls stripes.*

Below *Light dragoons looting King Joseph's carriages in the aftermath of Vittoria, 1813.*

'Medicina' is probably the Regiment's proudest battle honour. It records the dramatic assault made on the German Paratroop stronghold in Medicina in 1945. 'C' Squadron 14th/20th, in league with the 6th Gurkha Rifles, broke into the Italian town at dusk on April 16 and overwhelmed the garrison by the sheer violence and surprise of their attack.

Anniversaries

Ramnuggur Day (November 22): this day is held to honour the men of the 14th Light Dragoons who charged a force of Sikh cavalry which had crossed the River Chenab near Ramnuggur in 1848. Lieutenant Colonel Havelock pressed his Regiment's initial successes and was brought down with 43 of his men. The victory is commemorated in the Sergeants' Mess, with all officers and SNCOs present and the Ramnuggur Cup is passed round for the ritual toast to 'The Heroes of Ramnuggur'.

Ramadi Day (September 28): the 14th Hussars' Mesopotamian campaign against the Turks is commemorated in the Corporals' Mess with a celebration of the action of Ramadi in 1916.

Customs

A wartime association with the 6th Gurkha Rifles is actively maintained. The Gurkhas often participate in Regimental activities, and an ornate kukri has pride of place amongst the mess silver.

A silver chamber pot (The Emperor), secured by the 14th at the Battle of Vittoria, occupies a prominent position in the Regimental silver and is used in mess rituals.

Mascot

None.

Dress distinctions

A scarlet dress cap mounted with the black Prussian Eagle badge. Officers wear the Eagle in gold on the beret, and tank crew wear the badge on a diagonal blue over yellow patch. A scarlet side hat piped in yellow. Collar badges: a lion and crown within the Garter. The crossed kukris arm badge is worn by all ranks. The stable-belt is striped blue/yellow/blue.

Full dress follows that of the 14th Hussars: a yellow busby bag and white plume.

Yellow was the facing colour of the 14th Light Dragoons before their change to (Prussian) orange in 1798. After an inspection by King William IV in 1830 the facings were altered to Royal blue.

The 14th Hussars had certain interesting deviations in their dress characteristics. Officers sported no gold button gimp below the busby plume, as was normal in the hussars, and the Sergeants' arm badge was worn by all non-commissioned ranks.

Marches

Royal Sussex, the Regimental march was authorised to the 14th/20th in 1961, but had been in use by the 14th since 1801, when the Regimental band was found to be unfit to perform, and the band of the 35th (Sussex) Regiment was enlisted to play for the Light Dragoons with their own march. *The Eagle,* the Regimental Slow March. *Rory O'More,* the Regimental Gallop. *Up Light Loo,* the Regimental Trot.

Nicknames

'The Emperor's Chambermaids': a name which relates to the 14th Light Dragoons and their siezure of a magnificent silver chamber pot from Joseph Bonaparte's coach in the rout of Vittoria.

'Charles O'Malley's Own': a reference to Lever's novel, in which the hero served with the 14th Hussars.

'The Hawks': a name for the 14th Hussars (kept alive by the title of the Regimental Journal) from the Prussian Eagle badge.

'Nobody's Own': a comment on the 20th Hussars' lack of Royal title.

'The Ramnuggur Boys': a reputation won by the 14th with their superb charge at Ramnuggur in 1848.

Recruiting

Lancashire, Greater Manchester and the Isle of Man. RHQ: Manchester.

15th/19th The King's Royal Hussars

Insignia

The Crest of England within the Garter: the former badge of the 15th Hussars.

The Elephant superscribed 'Assaye': awarded to the 19th Light Dragoons on an Honorary Guidon by the Honorable East India Company in 1803 for their part in the victory at Assaye. The Guidon was lost not long after presentation, but Squadron Guidons were issued to the Regiment on its return

Officers Mess staff in the reign of George V dressed in the Royal livery granted by King George III in 1801, and still worn today.

to England in 1807, each carrying the Elephant emblem. The Regiment was disbanded in 1821, but the 19th Hussars was allowed to adopt its Elephant device along with the honours 'Mysore', 'Seringapatam' and 'Niagara'.

Merebimur: the motto of the 15th Hussars (We shall be worthy of our honours) is worn on the cap badge and Guidon.

Honours

Emsdorff (15th); Mysore (19th); Villers-en-Couches, Willems (15th); Seringapatam (19th); Egmont-op-Zee, Sahagun, Vittoria (15th); Niagara (19th); Peninsula, Waterloo, Afghanistan 1879–80 (15th); Tel-al-kebir, Egypt 1882–84, Nile 1884, Abu klea, Defence of Ladysmith, South Africa 1899–1902 (19th).

Le Cateau (19th); Retreat from Mons, Marne 1914, Aisne 1914 (15th/19th); Armentieres (19th); Ypres 1914, 1915 (15th/19th); Bellewaarde (15th); Somme 1916, 1918, Cambrai 1916, 1918 (15th/19th); Rosiere (15th); Amiens (19th); Pursuit to Mons (15th/19th); France & Flanders 1914–18 (15th).

Withdrawal to Escaut, Seine 1944, Nederrijn, Rhineland, Hochwald, Rhine, Ibeenburen, Aller, North-West Europe 1940, 1944–45.

The honours 'Emsdorff', 'Villers-en-Couches', and 'Sahagun' are borne by no other regiment. The 15th experienced unprecedented glory after the battle for Emsdorff to which they went when only a few months in service. Amongst the accolades heaped upon the corps in the aftermath of the battle was the inscription, 'five battalion of foot defeated and taken by this Regiment, with their Colours and nine pieces of cannon, at Emsdorff, 16th July, 1760.' In addition the badge of crossed Bourbon flags, points down, was carried on officers' horse furniture until mechanisation.

Anniversaries

Sahagun Day (December 21): the operation to surprise the garrison at Sahagun was made by Paget's Hussar Brigade (10th and 15th) in the snow-covered mountains of Spain in 1808. Paget wrote of their episode, 'You will be pleased to hear that I have had an affair with the French cavalry and have given them a good licking. It was those lucky rogues, the 15th — who always happen to be under my hand, when there is anything to be done'.

Esla Day (May 31): this celebration serves to recall the crossing of the treacherous Esla River in 1813, where men of the 51st (Yorkshire) Light Infantry had to take hold of the stirrups of the 15th Hussars to avoid being swept away. The two Regiments formed a fellowship thereafter and would meet on Esla Day to compete in sport for a picture of the crossing.

Customs

No Loyal Toast.

Mascot

None.

Dress distinctions

A scarlet dress cap mounted with the Regimental badge, the Crest of England within the Garter with the motto *Merebimur*. A scarlet patch is worn behind the badge on the beret to signify the Regiment's Royal distinctions. A scarlet side hat piped yellow (15th). The stable-belt is blue with twin centre stripes, yellow on red. Bandsmen are issued with full dress, distinguished by a busby of 15th Regimental pattern (scarlet bag and plume).

Marches

The Bold King's Hussars/Haste to The Wedding, the Regimental Quick March combines the marches of the 15th and 19th Hussars respectively. *Elliott's Light Horse/Denmark*, the Regimental Slow March is a combination of the founder Regiments' slow

Above left *Sabretache of the 19th Light Dragoons, with its Elephant and 'Assaye' honour (1818).*
Above right *Elliott's Light Horse, 1760.*
Below *The 15th Hussars charge at Sahagun, 1808.*

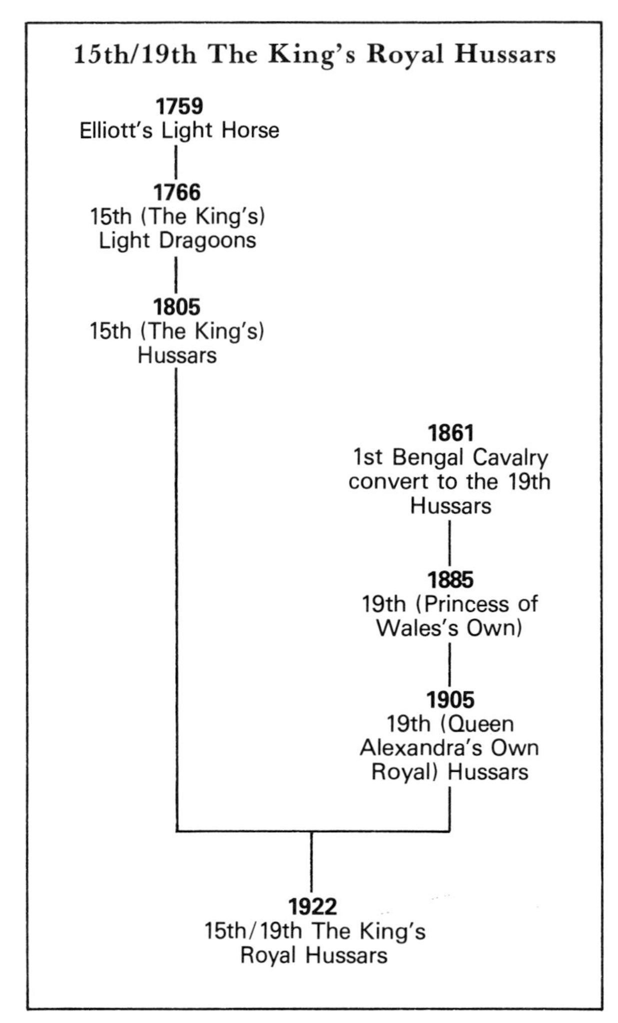

marches. Denmark was the family name and origin of Queen Alexandra, whose title was used by the 19th Hussars.

Nicknames

'The Geordie Hussars': a modern name which alludes to the Regiment's recruiting area.

'The Five and Nines': from the Regimental numerals.

'The Fighting Fifteenth': from its birth in 1759 to the end of Napoleonic Wars the 15th maintained an unsurpassed record in battle.

'The Tabs': an enduring nickname, from the title of Elliott's Horse, whose number was made up of striking journeymen tailors.

Recruiting

Tyne and Wear and the North-East. RHQ: Fenham Barracks, Newcastle-upon-Tyne.

16th/5th The Queen's Royal Lancers

Insignia

The cipher of Queen Charlotte within the Garter, juxtaposed with the Irish Harp within a circle inscribed *Quis separabit*, beneath a Crown, and superimposed upon crossed lances: the right to bear the cipher dates from 1766, when King George III made an inspection of his light horse. Much impressed with their bearing he bade the 15th assume the honourary title 'The King's', and the 16th 'The Queen's'. The Irish Harp and motto (Who shall separate us?) comes from the banners of the 5th Lancers.

Aut cursu, aut cominus armis: the motto of the 16th Lancers (Either in the charge, or hand to hand).

Honours

Blenheim, Ramillies, Oudenarde, Malplaquet (5th); Beaumont, Willems, Talavera, Fuentes d'Onor, Salamanca, Vittoria, Nive, Peninsula, Waterloo, Bhurtpore, Ghuznee, Afghanistan 1839, Maharajpore, Aliwal, Sobraon (16th); Suakin 1885, Defence of Ladysmith (5th); Relief of Kimberley, Paardeberg (16th); South Africa 1899–1902 (5th/16th).

'The Pursuit'. The 16th Lancers at Bhurtpore in 1826.

Above *16th/5th The Queen's Royal Lancers fanfare trumpeters in full dress scarlet tunics at St James' Palace, 1981.*

Left *The charge of the 5th Lancers at Elandslaagte, in the Second Boer War, ranks as one of the most outstanding lance charges in British military history.*

Mons, Le Cateau (5th/16th); Retreat from Mons (5th); Marne 1914, Aisne 1914; Messines 1914; Ypres 1914, 1915 (5th/16th); Bellewaarde, Arras (16th); Cambrai 1917 (5th/16th); Somme 1918 (16th); St Quentin, Pursuit to Mons (5th).

Fondouk, Bordj, Djebel Kournine, Tunis, North Africa 1942–43, Cassino II, Liri Valley, Advance to Florence, Argenta Gap, Italy 1944–45.

Anniversaries

Aliwal Day (January 28): the 16th Lancers' period in India is regarded as a time of great accomplishment and January 28 is kept as a day of celebration to honour the valour and perseverance of the Regiment in turning the Sikh army to flight at the Battle of Aliwal in 1848. The day climaxes in true theatrical fashion with 'The Aliwal Review'. After the battle it was noticed that many of the Regiment's lance-pennons had become corrugated due to the effects of drying blood and soon after began the Regimental practice of flying crimped pennons as a lasting tribute to they who had fallen at Aliwal.

Customs

The Loyal Toast: the reason why the Loyal Toast is not drunk in the Regiment is lost in legend, but

The Regimental Guidon.

Presentation of the New Guidon Parade, 1983. The Guidon flutters proudly above the lance-pennons of the regiment.

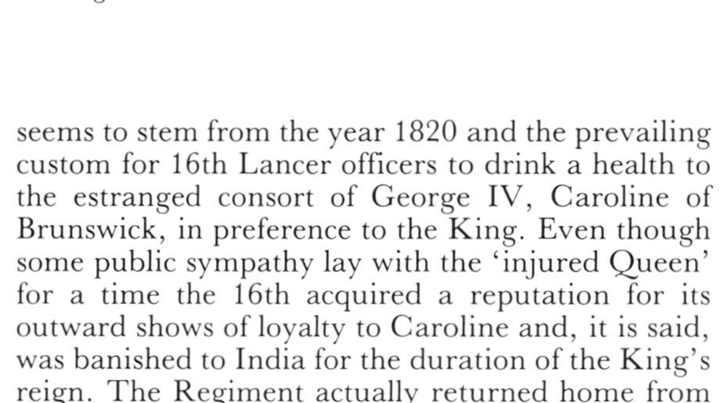

seems to stem from the year 1820 and the prevailing custom for 16th Lancer officers to drink a health to the estranged consort of George IV, Caroline of Brunswick, in preference to the King. Even though some public sympathy lay with the 'injured Queen' for a time the 16th acquired a reputation for its outward shows of loyalty to Caroline and, it is said, was banished to India for the duration of the King's reign. The Regiment actually returned home from India in 1846.

Mascot

None.

Dress distinctions

A scarlet dress cap with blue piping and quarter welts, mounted with the Regimental cap badge, the figure '16' superimposed upon crowned crossed lances. A scarlet side hat with blue flaps and peak. Collar badges: as the Regimental crest (the *C* cipher within the Garter combined with the Irish Harp within a circle, on crossed lances). Buttons are embossed with the Irish Harp on crossed lances (5th). The stable-belt is striped equally red/yellow/blue.

Officers' Sam Browne belts are worn reversed, a custom inherited from the 16th Lancers and inadvertently started by King Alfonso of Spain in his capacity as Colonel-in-Chief of the Regiment from 1905 to 1939. The King arrived on one visit of inspection with his Sam Browne fastened on back to front; the Regimental officers switched theirs to comply and never again wore them in the conventional manner.

Bandsmen are accoutred in the scarlet lancer tunics and blue-topped helmets made famous by the 16th. This order of dress was evident in the 16th/5th prior to World War 2, but was not issued again until 1979.

The 5th Lancers almost ceased to exist after the Irish 'troubles' of 1921, and made little contribution to the amalgamation of 1922, hence the predominance of 16th dress styles.

Marches

Scarlet and Green: the Regimental Quick March, and Journal, take their name from the union of the 16th and 5th Lancers and the scarlet of the 16th (from the scarlet tunic) and the green of the 5th Royal Irish Lancers symbolised in their helmet plume.

The Queen Charlotte: the Regimental Slow March was inspired by the Regiment's titular head, and wife of George III, Charlotte of Mecklenburg.

Nicknames

'The Brummagem Uhlans': the 16th Lancers, from their high intake of Birmingham lads during the First World War. *Uhlan* is German for lancer.

'The Daily Advertisers': the 5th Lancers, origin obscure.

'The Redbreasts': the 5th Lancers, from their scarlet facings.

'The Scarlet Lancers': the universal nickname for the 16th Lancers comes from the scarlet tunic, which was exclusive to the 16th in the light cavalry after 1846. Scarlet coatees were decreed for the light cavalry by King William IV, but most regiments had returned to blue by 1840. When the 16th came home from India in 1846 their scarlet coatees caused some interest due to their rarity and the Colonel

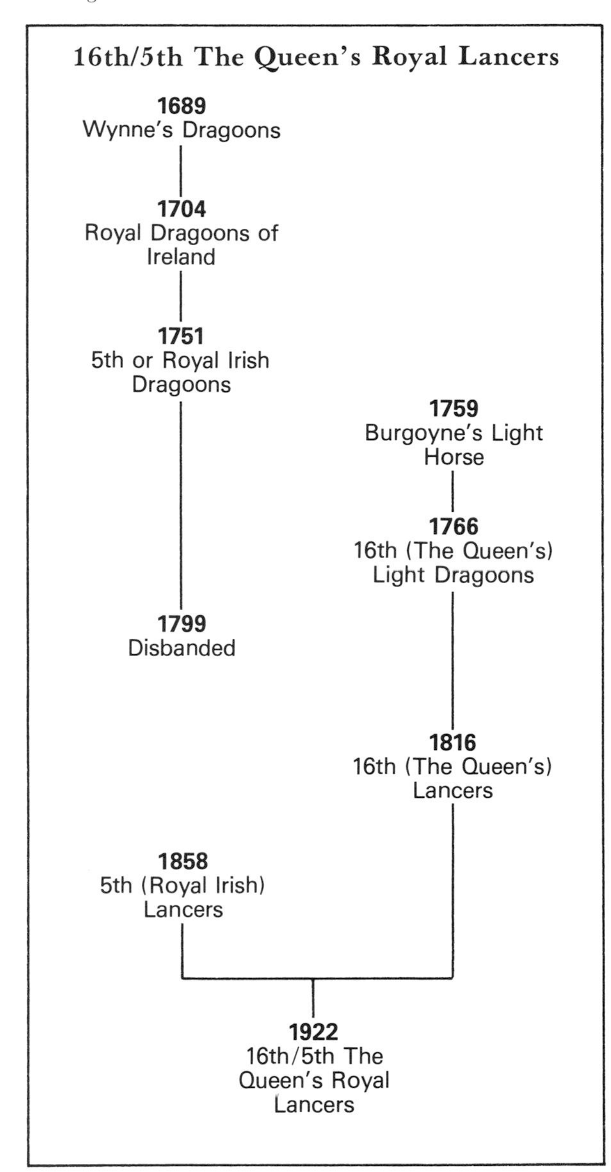

received permission for his Regiment to continue in scarlet.

Recruiting

Staffordshire and the West Midlands. RHQ: Stafford.

Historical note: the rise and fall of the Irish Dragoons

Wynne's Dragoons, raised from the Protestant garrison of Enniskillen in 1689, came to prominence during the campaigns of Marlborough. The pinnacle of their career was reached in 1704, when, at the Battle of Blenheim, three French kettle drums were captured and the Regiment was honoured as The Royal Dragoons of Ireland. Two years later the Regiment charged with the Scots Greys at Ramillies, and succeeded in defeating the French *Regiment du Roi*, for which they were authorised by Queen Anne to share in a prize of fur caps, to be worn thereafter as a mark of victory.

The kettle drums are still at the disposal of the 16th/5th, but the grenadier cap privilege was sadly neglected, and despite much correspondence in the 1760s for their restoration, the grenadier caps which made the Greys famous were disallowed to the 5th Dragoons.

The varying fortunes of the 5th came to a dramatic end in 1799, when the Regiment was disbanded for allowing Irish insurgents to infiltrate its ranks and cause its downfall. The causes of disbandment were read out at the head of every regiment in the Army, and although the 5th rose again from the ashes like the Phoenix, its line of descent had been interrupted and its seniority lost, which is why the 16th took precedence in the title on amalgamation.

The 17th/21st Lancers

Insignia

The Death's Head 'Or Glory': the motto was adopted for the formation of the 17th Light Dragoons in 1759 to immortalise the heroic death of General Wolfe at Quebec. The connection lay with Colonel Hale, late of the 47th Foot, who carried news of the victory to London, and was rewarded with a commission to raise a Regiment of light horse; this duly became the 17th Lancers. Because of this link with General Wolfe the Regiment holds membership in the Wolfe Society.

The Imperial Cipher: awarded to the 21st Lancers, together with the title 'Empress of India's', in recognition of their brave charge at the Battle of Omdurman in 1898.

Honours

Alma, Balaklava, Inkerman, Sevastopol, Central India, South Africa 1879 (17th); Khartoum (21st); South Africa 1900–02 (17th).

Festubert 1914, Somme 1916, 1918, Morval, Cambrai 1917, 1918, St Quentin, Avre, Lys, Hazebrouck, Amiens, Pursuit to Mons, France & Flanders 1914–18 (17th); North-West Frontier India 1915–16 (21st).

Tebourba Gap, Kasserine, Fondouk, El Kourzia, Tunis, North Africa 1942–43, Cassino II, Capture of Perugia, Argenta Gap, Italy 1944–45.

Anniversaries

Balaklava Day (October 25): the 17th Lancers' fine reputation for discipline and efficiency was epitomised in their magnificent lead of the Charge of the Light Brigade.

Khartoum Day (September 2): 'Khartoum' is significant in being the only battle honour gained by the 21st Lancers prior to World War I. The 21st had suffered a certain amount of ridicule for its prior lack of honours, but the celebrated desert charge at Omdurman lifted this stigma and transformed Regimental image at a stroke.

Customs

The 17th has always had a reputation for being a very exclusive regiment and, it is said, has never had to canvass for recruits.

Mascot

The 17th kept a variety of unofficial mascots in Victorian times, including a black bear.

Dress distinctions

A blue dress cap with a white band, piping, and quarter welts, mounted with the Regimental motto, the Death's Head above a scroll inscribed 'Or Glory'. A white side hat with blue flaps, piped in yellow. The stable-belt is blue with twin narrow white stripes. Buttons and collar badges are as the cap badge. Full dress: a lancer helmet with white top and plume, and blue tunic and overalls faced and lined in white (after the 17th Lancers).

Above far left *17th/21st Lancers' Sergeant in full dress.*

Above left *Lord Bingham in the uniform of the 17th Lancers, 1833. He succeeded to the title of Lord Lucan in 1839, and went on to command the Cavalry Division in the Crimean War.*

Left *The 21st spill into the Dervish trap at Omdurman, 1898. The survivors were forced to beat off the enemy with their carbines.*

Marches

Wagner's *Rienzi* (Slow) and *The White Lancer* (Quick).

Nicknames

'The Death Or Glory Boys': the established nickname of the 17th Lancers, and now the 17th/21st, from the Death's head motto. It was fashionable at one time to shorten the name to 'The Deaths'.

'Bingham's Dandies': the 17th was remarkable for the well-fitting uniforms of its officers and men under the command of Lord Bingham (1826–37).

'The Grey Lancers': the 21st, from their unique French grey facings.

'The Hooks and Eyes': the 21st Lancers, from the shape of the Regimental number.

'The Horse Marines': a detachment of the 17th Light Dragoons served abroad *The Hermione* in 1795.

'The Tots': an upper-class name for the Regiment, from the German *Totenkopf* (Deathshead). The *Totenkopf Hussars* were a Prussian regiment in

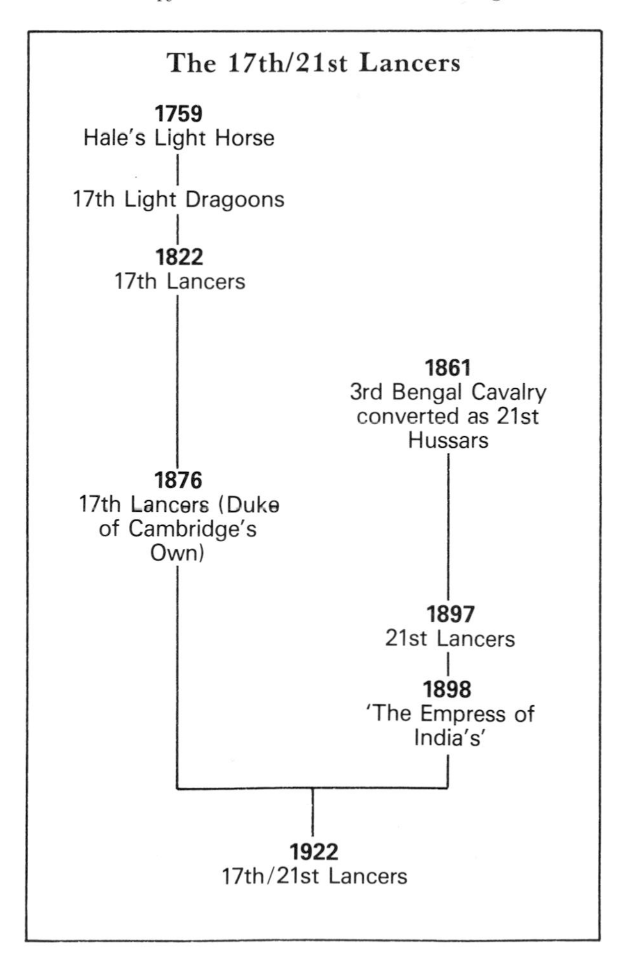

Balaklava Day, 1983. 'The Death or Glory Boys' on exercise with their companions in the Charge of the Light Brigade, the Royal Hussars and the Queen's Royal Irish Hussars.

the army of Frederick the Great, whose fame rested on their black uniforms and Death's head insignia.

'The White Lancers': a nickname of the 17th Lancers which alluded to their distinctive facing colour. The name was extended to the Regimental March and Journal.

Recruiting

Nottinghamshire, Lincolnshire and South Humberside. RHQ: Prince William of Gloucester Barracks, Grantham.

The Royal Tank Regiment

Insignia

An early tank encircled by a wreath of laurel and surmounted by a Crown, with the motto *Fear naught.*

Honours

Somme 1916, 1918, Arras 1917, 1918, Messines 1916, Ypres 1917, Cambrai 1917, Villers Bretonneaux, Amiens, Bapaume 1918, Hindenburg Line, France & Flanders 1916–18.

Rhine, North-West Europe 1940, 1944–45, Abyssinia 1940, Tobruk 1941, El Alamein, North Africa 1940–43, Italy 1943–45, Greece 1941, Burma 1942. Korea 1951–53.

Anniversaries

Cambrai Day (November 20) commemorates the 1917 battle.

Customs

Standards are carried as in the more senior regiments of the Royal Armoured Corps.

Mascot.

None.

Dress distinctions

A black beret mounted with the tank badge. A white tank emblem is worn on the upper right sleeve and

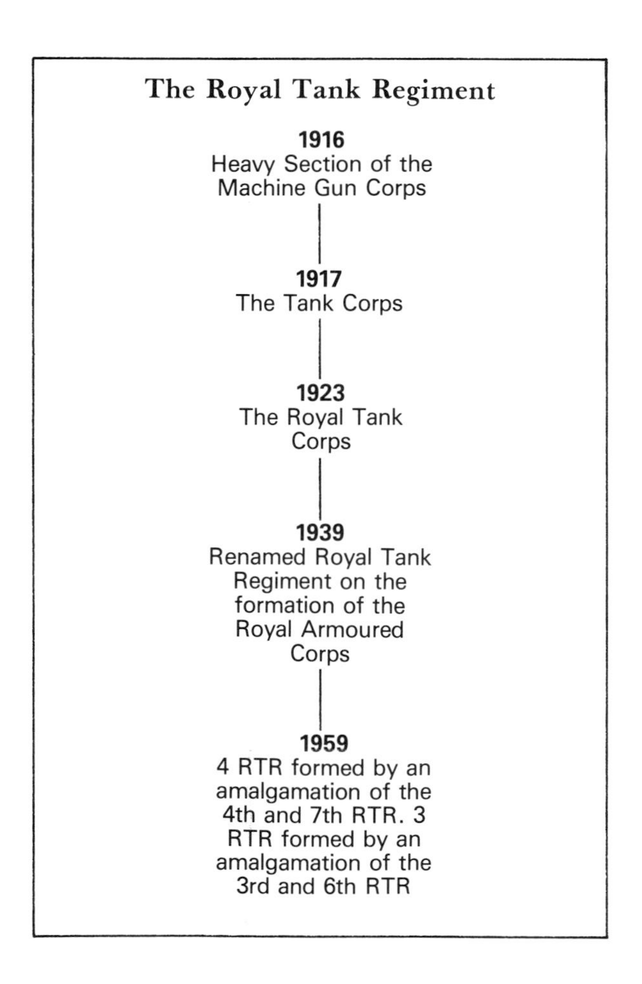

Above *RTR Instructor, in the distinctive black overalls, with a scimitar crew from the 9th/12th Lancers on the ranges.*

Below *Standard-bearer, 5th RTR, at Leeds.*

shoulder flashes: 2RTR yellow with central colours, 3RTR green and 4RTR blue. The stable-belt of Regimental colours—brown/red/green—signifies early struggles: through mud, through blood to the green fields beyond. Bandsmen wear a brown/red/green cut feather hackle in the beret and gold cuff braid with waistbelts of gold/black/gold.

Marches

My Boy Willie, the Regimental Quick March. *The Royal Tank Regiment*, the Regimental Slow March. *Lippe Detmold* (1RTR). *Saffron* (2RTR). *On The Quarterdeck* (3RTR). *Blue Flash* (4RTR).

Nicknames

'The Tankies': 4RTR, a Scottish unit.

Recruiting

1RTR: Merseyside, Blackburn, Burnley, Oldham, Leeds, Halifax and Wakefield. 2RTR: Cambridgeshire, Bedfordshire, Hertfordshire, Norfolk, Suffolk, Essex, Kent and Greater London. 3RTR: Cornwall, Devon, Dorset, Somerset, Avon. 4RTR: Scotland. RHQ: Horseferry Road, London.

The Royal Regiment of Artillery

Insignia

A gun between two scrolls, that above inscribed *Ubique*, that beneath inscribed *Quo fas et gloria ducunt*, the whole ensigned with the Crown: the gun represented is a hybrid RML and 9 pdr, Waterloo type. The mottoes *Ubique* (Everywhere) and *Quo fas et gloria ducunt* (Whither right and glory lead) are shared with the Corps of Royal Engineers, with whom the Regiment has an affinity.

Honour titles

The Royal Artillery is the only regiment not to

Above *Royal Regiment of Artillery on Palace duty.*

Above right *The guns are regarded as the colours, to be put before all, and never abandoned in battle.*

Below *The moustachioed axe-bearer troops the Axe on Battle Axe Day. Battle Axe Company, now suspended, was descended from Eyre's Company at Martinique, where a captured French drum and pioneer's axe were bestowed upon the company for its outstanding services.*

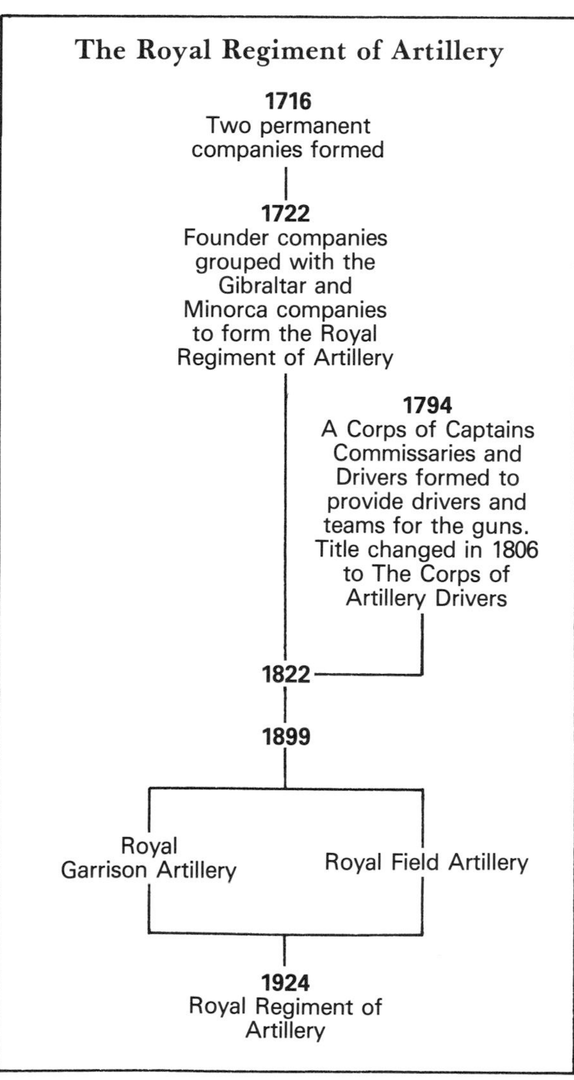

Saving the guns at Le Cateau.

display battle honours, its widespread service in all theatres of war is represented simply in the motto *Ubique*.

In 1925 all batteries of the Regiment were required to assume a 'battle honour title' inspired by a great moment in their history. This gave the batteries a sense of continuity, as their operational titles tend to change as the Regiment develops. The system of enumerating batteries, introduced in 1947, clearly shows those which have been put into 'suspended animation':

5th, Gibraltar 1779–83 Battery; 8th, Alma Battery; 9th, Plassey Battery; 10th, Assaye Battery; 12th, Minden Battery; 13th, Martinique 1809 Battery; 14th, Cole's Kop Battery; 16th, Battery Sandham's Company (at Waterloo); 17th, Corunna Battery; 18th, Quebec 1759 Battery; 19th, Gibraltar 1779–83 Battery; 25th, Asten Battery; 26th, Louisburg Battery; 27th, Battery Strange's Company (Indian Mutiny); 29th, Corunna Battery; 30th, Battery Rodger's Company (at Waterloo); 32nd, Minden Battery; 34th, Seringapatam Battery; 37th, Le Cateau Battery; 43rd, Battery Lloyd's Company (at Waterloo); 46th, Talavera Battery; 49th, Inkerman Battery; 51st, Kabul 1842 Battery; 52nd, Niagara Battery; 53rd, Louisburg Battery; 54th, Maharajpore Battery; 55th, Residency Battery; 57th, Bhurtpore Battery; 58th, Battery Eyre's Company; 66th, Colenso Battery; 74th, Battle Axe Company; 76th, Maude's Battery; 79th, Kirkee Battery; 88th, Aracan Battery; 94th, New Zealand Battery; 97th, Battery Lawson's Company (Peninsula War); 132nd, Battery The Bengal Rocket Troop; 137th, Java Battery; 143rd, Battery, Tomb's Troop (Indian Mutiny); 170th, Imjin Battery; 171st, Broken Wheel Battery (Egypt 1882); and 176th, Abu klea Battery.

The Regiment is a member of the Wolfe Society by right of the 18th Battery, descendants of the company which fought with General Wolfe at Quebec.

Anniversaries

Foundation Day (May 26): the day when two permanent companies were formed at Woolwich in 1716. Before this the cumbersome Train of Artillery, with its civilian drivers and part-time gunners, served the Artillery role with great inefficiency.

Customs

A Regimental Standard is kept for visiting Generals and Royalty, but has little significance in the accepted sense.

Mascot

Various unofficial mascots have been adopted over

the years, from an Edwardian tortoise, which 'didn't do much', to a sheep which attended all of the air raid alerts of World War 2 with its AA battery.

Dress distinctions

A blue dress cap with a scarlet band, mounted with the Regimental badge, the 'cap badge gun'. Collar badges: a grenade with *Ubique*. The stable-belt is red with a blue central band and yellow centre stripe. Bandsmen traditionally wear a busby mounted with the grenade badge.

Marches

The Regimental Quick March is a melange of the traditional *British Grenadiers* and the former unofficial Regimental March *Voice of the Guns*. The Regimental Slow March was specially written by HRH the Duchess of Kent for the Regiment, and was officially accepted in 1836. The *Keel Row* and *Bonnie Dundee* are played at the end of Officers' Mess functions.

Nicknames

'The Five-Mile Snipers'.

'The Gunners': from the Regimental term for soldiers of private rank.

'The Heavy Gunners': the Regiment handles all guns in the medium and heavy ranges.

'The Square Buttons': a Horse Artillery term for the Regiment, from an old distinguishing feature in their respective uniforms.

Recruiting

Nationwide. RHQ: Woolwich.

The Grenadier Guards

Insignia

The Royal Cipher, reversed and interlaced.

The grenade fired proper: granted to the Regiment after Waterloo to commemorate its part in the defeat of the French *Grenadiers de la Garde*. The badge, bearskin and white plume were authorised by the Prince Regent in an Army Order of July 29, 1815, which made the 1st Guards a regiment of Grenadiers.

Honours

Tangier 1680, Namur 1695, Gibralter 1704–05, Blenheim, Ramillies, Oudenarde, Malplaquet, Dettingen, Lincelles, Egmont-op-Zee, Corunna, Barrossa, Nive, Peninsula, Waterloo, Alma, Inkerman, Sevastopol, Tel-el-kebir, Egypt 1882, Suakin 1885, Khartoum, Modder River, South Africa 1899–1902.

Marne 1914, Aisne 1914, Ypres 1914, 1917, Loos, Somme 1916, 1918, Cambrai 1917, 1918, Arras 1918, Hazebrouck, Hindenburg Line, France & Flanders 1914–18.

Dunkirk 1940, Mareth, Medjez Plain, Salerno, Monte Camino, Anzio, Mont Pincon, Gothic Line, Nijmegen, Rhine.

Anniversaries

A laurel wreath is placed on the Colour staff on all of the Regiment's major battle anniversaries, though 'Waterloo' and 'Inkerman' are held in special esteem.

Customs

A dispensation from the Loyal Toast.

The Freedom of London (gained by right of the 3rd Battalion in 1915).

The senior company has the honour of being the Sovereign's own company, and as such is privileged to find the guard for Coronations and State Funerals. This tradition goes back to Charles II, who decreed that the senior company of his 1st Guards would undertake duties as his personal bodyguard. The commander of the company is addressed 'Captain of the Queen's Company' irrespective of rank, and a special Royal Standard is carried, the Sovereign's personal gift to the company.

Bass-drummers are known in the Regiment as 'Time-beaters'; subalterns are addressed as 'Mister', although 2nd Lieutenants are *ensigns,* and full Sergeants are 'Gold Sergeants' from their chevrons' colour.

The custom for the Foot Guards to march 'at attention' past Aspley House after the death of the Duke of Wellington was continued by the Grenadiers longer than any other regiment, and black arm bands were worn by the Time-beater.

Mascot

None.

Dress distinctions

The bearskin with a white plume on the left. A blue dress cap with red band and piping, mounted with the grenade badge. Buttons are embossed with a

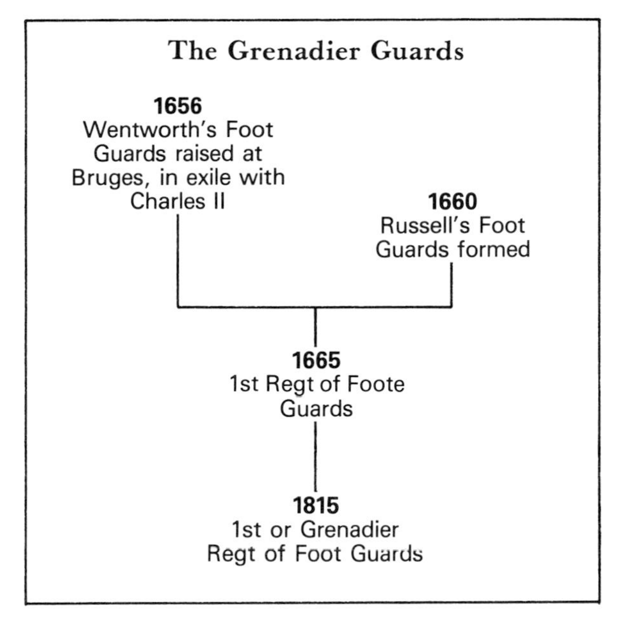

Above right *A sketch of Privates in the 1st Guards made before Waterloo.*

Below *The Grenadier company trooping the colour in 1814.*

Men of the 1st Battalion, Grenadier Guards, at RAF Sharjah in 1969. The Guards' universal use of the dress cap extends even to tropical kit.

Crown over the Royal Cipher reversed and interlaced, over a flaming grenade. The scarlet dress tunic is distinguished by a white collar grenade, and the Royal Cipher emblem on the shoulder straps. The stable-belt is of Guards pattern: equal stripes blue/red/blue.

Marches

The British Grenadier, the Regimental Quick March. *The Grenadiers' March,* this, and the Quick March, were universally played for the grenadier companies of the Army, but were adopted as Regimental marches by the Grenadier Guards in 1815. *The Grenadiers' March* is played only when marching into camp or barracks. The March from *Scipio,* written for the 1st Guards by Handel in 1726. *The Duke Of York's March,* adopted as a slow march during the colonelcy of the Duke of York in 1805. *Rule Britannia,* always played before the National Anthem at Tattoo in the 3rd Battalion to commemorate its service as marines in the Dutch Maritime War of the 1670s. The Battalion was disbanded in 1960, and Inkerman Company of the 2nd Battalion was authorised to continue its practices.

Nicknames

'The Bermuda Exiles': in 1890 the 2nd Battalion was posted to a penal station in the West Indies for refusing to parade at Wellington Barracks.

'The Bill Browns': an old name for the 3rd Battalion.

'The Coal-heavers': a nickname derived from the 17th century custom for officers of the 1st Guards to hire out their men to London's coal merchants. The 18th century term 'cropping drums' referred to drummers of the Foot Guards farmed out to play the *Point of War* at weddings.

'The Grannies': a Guards Division corruption of 'Grenadiers'.

'The Sandbags': the proud reputation of the 3rd Battalion after the Battle of Inkerman in 1854. The only colours carried in the Army on that day were those of the 3rd Battalion Grenadier Guards. These were passed from hand to hand until out of danger and became the rallying point for that part of the Battalion cut off in the Sandbag Battery.

'The Tow-rows': from the sung chorus of the Regimental Quick March: 'With a tow row, row row, row row, to the British Grenadier'.

Recruiting

England. RHQ: London.

The Coldstream Guards

Insignia

The Star of the Order of the Garter ensigned with the Crown. The Garter Star has appeared on the appointments of the Coldstream Guards since the 1680s.

The Sphinx superscribed 'Egypt'.

Nulli Secundus. The motto (Second to none) refers to the fact that the Coldstream is older than any other regiment of Foot Guards. The early title '2nd Regiment of Foot Guards' came into being because the Coldstream entered Royal service after the 1st Guards, but has never been recognised in the Regiment.

Honours

Tangier 1680, Namur 1695, Gibraltar 1704–05, Oudenarde, Malplaquet, Dettingen, Lincelles, Copenhagen 1807, Talavera, Barrossa, Fuentes d'Onor, Nive, Waterloo, Alma, Inkerman, Sevastopol, Egypt 1882, Tel-el-kebir, Suakin 1885, Modder River, South Africa 1899–1902.

Retreat from Mons, Marne 1914, Aisne 1914, Ypres 1914, 1917, Loos, Somme 1916, 1918, Cambrai 1917, 1918, Arras 1918, Hazebrouck, Hindenburg Line.

Dunkirk 1940, Mont Pincon, Rhineland, North-West Europe 1940, 1944–45, Sidi Barrani, Tobruk 1941, 1942, Tunis, Salerno, Monte Ornito, Italy 1943–45.

Anniversaries

St George's Day (April 23): recognised as the Regimental Day.

Customs

The Freedom of London.

A dispensation from the Loyal Toast.

A crimson State Colour, emblazoned with the Garter Star, Sphinx and battle honours borne at the time of the Colour's presentation by King William IV: 'Lincelles', 'Talavera', 'Barrossa', 'Peninsula', and 'Waterloo'. 'Lincelles' was awarded only to the three senior Regiments of Foot Guards.

Mascot

A goose which attached itself to the Regiment in Quebec in 1838 was brought back to London, and delighted the populace by parading with his battalion at the old Portland Street Barracks.

Dress distinctions

The bearskin with a red plume on the right side. The plume varies in height according to rank. A blue dress cap fashioned with a white band and piping, mounted with the Regimental badge, 'the Cap Star'. Buttons are worn in pairs and stamped with the Garter Star in circular form. A rose emblem is worn on the shoulder straps.

Marches

Milanollo, the Regimental Quickstep. The March from Mozart's *Figaro*.

Nicknames

'The Coleys': Guards Division slang for 'The Coldstreamers'. The term 'Coldstream' began as a Regimental nickname in 1660, when the corps began its epic march from the border stronghold at Coldstream to restore order in London. The townspeople of London naturally referred to the strangers in their midst as 'The Coldstream Regiment'. The

Above *Men of the Coldstream Guards' light company holding the gate at Hougoumont during the Battle of Waterloo.*

Below *1660, and Monck's Regiment give a salute to the newly restored King Charles II.*

The Coldstream Guards

1650
Monck's Regt of Foote

|

1661
Enters the King's service as the Lord General's Regt of Foote Guards

|

1670
2nd or 'Coldstream' Guards

|

The Coldstream Guards

The band and drums, 1930. Note the distinctive custom of wearing the Garter Star on the pack.

Regiment's founder, General George Monck, was created The Lord General for his services to the Crown and his Regiment went under that name until 1670, when Monck died and the byname 'Coldstream' came into more formal use.

'The Lilywhites': a common term for regiments which sport items of white in their uniform. The Coldstreamers are distinguished from other Guards regiments by a white cap band.

'The Nulli Secundus Club': a Regimental society for officers, from the motto. The question of seniority is important in the Guards, and the ancient customs tied up with orders of precedence are slow to disappear. The Coldstream has been accused of refusing to march directly behind the Grenadiers, with a preference for bringing up the rear; but when this is done the Regiment is merely exercising the ancient right of second senior regiment to guard the rear (or left flank), a point of honour as jealously guarded as the senior regiment's privilege to lead a column of march and parade on the right flank.

Recruiting

England, with a preference for those counties passed through during the Regiment's famous journey from Coldstream to London in 1660. RHQ: London.

The Scots Guards

Insignia

The Star of the Order of the Thistle.

The Royal Arms of Scotland ensigned with the Crown: borne on the Colours of the 1st Battalion with the motto *En ferus hostis*.

The Thistle and Red and White Roses conjoined, ensigned with the Crown: borne on the Colours of the 2nd Battalion with the motto *Unita Fortior*.

A lion rampant with scroll inscribed *Intrepidus*.

The Sphinx superscribed 'Egypt'.

Honours

Namur 1695, Dettingen, Lincelles, Talavera, Barrossa, Fuentes d'Onor, Nive, Peninsula, Waterloo, Alma, Inkerman, Sevastopol, Tel-el-kebir, Egypt 1882, Suakin 1885, Modder River, South Africa 1899–1902.

Retreat from Mons, Marne 1914, Aisne 1914, Ypres 1914, 1917, Festubert 1915, Loos, Somme 1916, 1918, Cambrai 1917, 1918, Hindenburg Line, France & Flanders 1914–18.

Quarry Hill, Rhineland, North-West Europe 1944–45, Gazala, Medenine, Djebel Bou Aoukaz 1943, North Africa 1941–43, Monte Camino, Anzio, Italy 1943-45, Tumbledown Mountain, Falkland Islands, 1982.

Anniversaries

St Andrew's Day (November 30).

Customs

The Regiment's Colonel has always been a Prince of the Blood, or a distinguished soldier, a situation begun in 1642, when Charles I commissioned Archibald, 1st Marquess of Argyll, to raise the corps.

A crimson State Colour is carried in addition to the usual pair of Colours. The first State Colour was presented by Queen Victoria at Windsor Castle in 1889.

On St Andrew's Day the haggis is piped around the Battalion before dinner.

Mascot

None.

Dress distinctions

The bearskin with no plume. In 1831 the Foot Guards followed the example of the Grenadier Guards and adopted bearskins for all ranks. Those of the Grenadiers and Coldstream were distinguished by plumes of Regimental choice, but the 3rd Guards, being the most junior, and therefore

Representatives of the Scots Guards at Waterloo in 1965 for the 150th anniversary of the battle.

Left *The Scots Guards' light company in 1846.*

Below left *A full Scot's Guards' company at the Colour Trooping Ceremony in London.*

'centre of the line', chose to wear no plume at all. A blue dress cap with a red/white/blue diced band, mounted with the Star of the Order of the Thistle badge. A patch of Royal Stewart tartan is worn on the khaki cap, and behind the badge on the khaki beret. The scarlet full dress coat is distinguished by a white thistle embroidered on the collar. Buttons are worn in threes to denote the Regiment's precedence in the Foot Guards. The stable-belt is of Guards pattern: equal stripes blue/red/blue. Pipers are dressed in kilts of Royal Stewart, with a white Highland purse; stockings of red and green marl, and feather bonnets with a red over blue hackle.

Marches

Highland Laddie, the Regimental Quickstep. *Garb of Old Gaul*, the Regimental Slow March.

Nicknames

'The Jocks' or 'Jock Guards'.

'The Kiddies': before 1900 the Scots Guards were the junior regiment of Guards.

Recruiting

Scotland. RHQ: London.

The Irish Guards

Insignia

The Royal Cipher within the Collar of the Order of St Patrick ensigned with the Crown.

Honours

Retreat from Mons, Marne 1914, Aisne 1914, Ypres 1914, 1917, Festubert 1915, Loos, Somme 1916, 1918, Cambrai 1917, 1918, Hazebrouck, Hindenburg Line.

Norway 1940, Boulogne 1940, Mont Pincon, Neerpelt, Nijmegen, Rhineland, North-West Europe 1944–45, Djebel Bou Aoukaz 1943, North Africa 1943, Anzio.

The Irish Guards handing over the old colours at a presentation of new colours at Windsor.

The Irish Guards

1900
Raised by an Army order on the wishes of Queen Victoria to commemorate the bravery shown by her Irish regiments in South Africa

Anniversaries
St Patrick's Day (March 17).

Customs
Shamrocks are worn by all members of the Regiment on St Patrick's Day.

Mascot
The Regiment has been allowed to keep a succession of Irish Wolfhound mascots since 1902, each one named after an ancient Irish chieftian. On the St Patrick's Day parade the mascot is led forward to receive a wreath of shamrock. Queen Elizabeth The Queen Mother has presented shamrocks to the Battalion on London duties since 1928.

Dress distinctions
The bearskin with a plume of St Patrick's blue on the right side. A blue dress cap with a green band and piping, mounted with the Regimental badge, the Star of the Order of St Patrick, inscribed *Quis separabit* MDCCLXXXIII (1783 — the year in which the Order was instituted). The full dress scarlet tunic is distinguished by a white shamrock collar emblem. Buttons are worn in groups of four to signify the Regiment's precedence in the Foot Guards. The stable-belt is of Guards' pattern: blue/red/blue. Pipers are dressed in dark green with kilts of plain saffron serge, and a green caubeen fashioned with a blue hackle.

Marches
St Patrick's Day, the Regimental Quickstep. *Let Erin Remember*, the Regimental Slow March.

Nicknames
'The Micks': a term of endearment for the Regiment used by the rest of the Army.

'The Bog-rats': a Guards Division term alluding to the Regiment's national geographic feature.

'Bob's Own': a name from the Regiment's early days, with Lord Roberts as its first Colonel.

Recruiting
Ireland. RHQ: London.

The Welsh Guards

Insignia
A dragon passant with the motto *Cymru-Am-Byth* ensigned with a Crown.

A leek within the Garter ensigned with the Crown.

Honours
Loos, Givenchy, Flers-Courcelette, Morval,

Left *Northern Ireland. Welsh Guardsmen in two styles of Guards' headgear: the khaki beret, and the stiffened khaki peaked cap.*

Below *Welsh Guards marching through. The colours are carried in the centre of the column for safety.*

Pilckem, Poelcappelle, Cambrai 1917, 1918, Bapaume 1918, Canal du Nord, Sambre.

Defence of Arras, Boulogne 1940, Mont Pincon, Brussels, Hechtel, Fondouk, Hammam Lif, Monte Ornito, Monte Piccolo, Battaglia, Falkland Islands, 1982.

Anniversaries

St David's Day (March 1).

Customs

No Loyal Toast. The senior company of the Regiment is known as The Prince of Wales's.

Mascot

None.

Dress distinctions

The bearskin with a white/green/white plume on the left side. A blue dress cap with a black band, mounted with the leek badge. The scarlet full dress coat is distinguished by a white leek embroidered on the collar and shoulder straps. Buttons are worn in

The Welsh Guards

1915
Raised in London by a Royal
Warrant of King George V

groups of five: the Welsh Guards were the fifth regiment of Foot Guards to be raised. The stable-belt is of Guards pattern: blue/red/blue.

Marches

Rising Of The Lark, the Regimental Quickstep. *Men Of Harlech*, the Regimental Slow March.

Nicknames

'The Daffy Taffs': a Guards Division term.

'The Foreign Legion': a reference to the formation of the Regiment in 1915, when Welshmen were drawn from other Guards regiments to fill the ranks.

'The Jam Boys': a name given to the Prince of Wales' Company after the Second World War, when extra rations were requested to compensate for its members' extra height. The Quartermaster is reported to have unsympathetically recommended an extra spoonful of jam. After an inspection by Prince Charles in 1980 the company became known as 'The Prince of Wales's'.

Recruiting

Wales. RHQ: London.

The Royal Scots (The Royal Regiment) (1st Foot)

Insignia

The Royal Cipher within the Collar of the Order of the Thistle, with the badge appendant.

The Sphinx with 'Egypt'.

Honours

Tangier 1680, Namur 1695, Blenheim, Ramillies, Oudenarde, Malplaquet, Louisburg, Havannah, Egmont-op-Zee, St Lucia 1803, Corunna, Busaco, Salamanca, Vittoria, St Sebastian, Nive, Peninsula, Niagara, Waterloo, Nagpore, Maheidpore, Ava, Alma, Inkerman, Sevastopol, Taku Forts, Pekin 1860, South Africa 1899–1902.

Le Cateau, Marne 1914, 1918, Ypres 1915, 1917, 1918; Loos, Somme 1916, 1918, Arras 1917, 1918, Lys, Struma, Gallipoli, 1915, 1916, Palestine 1917, 1918.

Defence of Escaut, Odon, Aart, Flushing, Rhine, North-West Europe 1940, 1944–45, Gothic Line, Italy 1944–45, Kohima, Burma 1943–45.

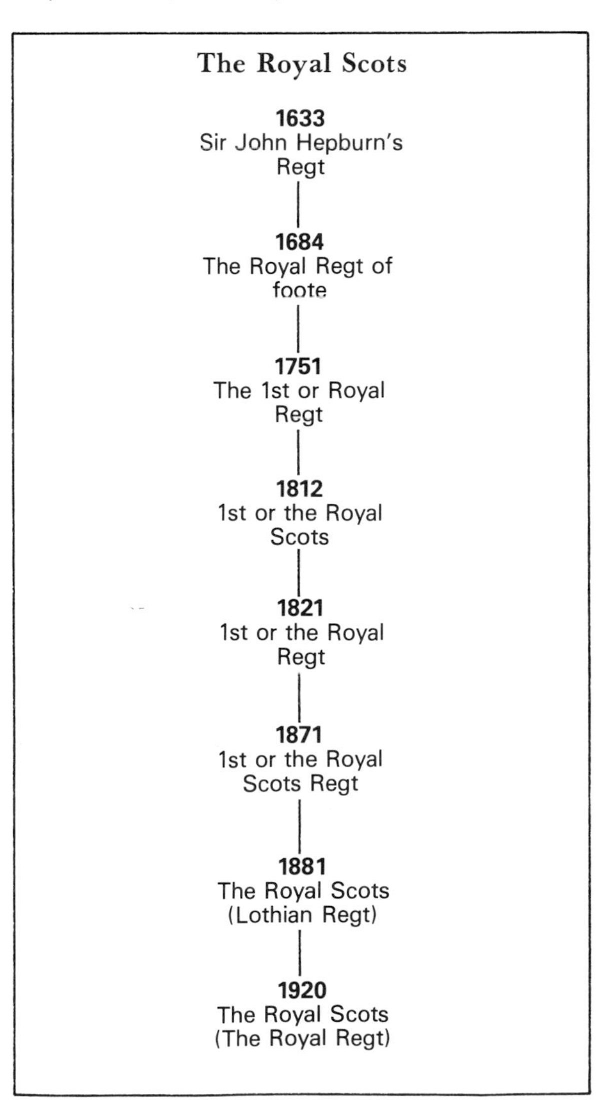

"Pontius Pilate's Bodyguard."
S.P.Q.

Above left *1902. Royal Scots officers wearing the new kilmarnock bonnet with black cock's feathers.*

Left *Cartoon of 'Pontius Pilate's Bodyguard'.*

Above *A musketeer of Dumbarton's Regiment in 1670.*

Anniversaries

Foundation Day (March 28): the Royal Scots hold the enviable boast of being the oldest regiment in the British Army and the senior regiment of infantry. This distinction is commemorated on March 28, the anniversary of the day in 1633 when Sir John Hepburn raised the corps under a warrant of the Privy Council of Scotland, for service in France.

Customs

After the toast to the Sovereign's health it was normal to make another to the Regiment's Colonel-in-Chief HRH The Princess Royal, at which the pipers would enter to *Princess Mary's March*. The tune *Lochaber No More* is played at Lights Out.

Mascot

None.

Dress distinctions

A blue glengarry with diced band and black cock's feathers, mounted with the Regimental badge, the Star of the Order of the Thistle with St Andrew and Cross on a red ground in the centre. Trews of Hunting Stewart tartan (authorised to the Regiment in 1901 in respect of its seniority). Bandsmen wear trews of No 8 tartan. Pipers were permitted the Royal Stewart tartan in 1933 on the occasion of the Regiment's tercentenary. The kilt is worn with a white hair sporran supporting two long black tassels; with a sporran badge of St Andrew and Cross within a thistle wreath.

Marches

Dumbarton's Drums, the Regimental Quick March is reckoned to be the Army's oldest, as witness Pepys in 1667: 'After meeting with the Corps in Rochester, here in the streets I did hear the Scotch March by the drums before the soldiers, which is very odde'. *Garb Of Old Gaul*, the Slow March. When Royalty is present the march *Daughters Of The Regiment* is substituted in honour of Queen Victoria, who was born in 1819, when her father, the Duke of Kent, was Colonel of the 1st Foot.

Nicknames

'Pontius Pilate's Bodyguard': a curious name which is said to go back to the Regiment's earliest days, the years spent fighting in the service of France. An argument is said to have developed between the officers of Hepburn's and the *Regiment d'Picardy* over the question of seniority and it transpired that *La Picardy* was descended from the Roman legion which kept watch over the tomb of Christ. At this the Scots rashly stated that had they been on guard they would not have fallen asleep, suggesting that history might have taken another direction.

'The Right of the Line': as the senior regiment of infantry the Royal Scots have the right to parade on the right flank of all other infantry regiments.

Recruiting

The Lothians and that part of Borders which was Peebleshire. RHQ: Edinburgh Castle.

The Queen's Regiment (2nd, 3rd, 31st, 35th, 50th, 57th, 70th, 77th, 97th, 107th Foot)

Insignia

A dragon within the Garter surmounted by the Prince of Wales' Plume: the main badge of the Regiment is emblazoned in the centre of the Regimental Colour surrounded by a wreath of Tudor roses; this marks the origin of the Regiment in the reign of Elizabeth I. The dragon comes from the Arms of Queen Elizabeth and was granted to the Buffs by Queen Anne in 1707, to be worn as a constant reminder of the Regiment's beginnings in the Trained Bands of London, which went off to fight in the service of the Dutch in 1572. The Garter is taken from the badge of the Royal Sussex Regiment, and the Plume from that of the Middlesex.

The cipher of Queen Catherine, reversed and interlaced: this cipher is borne on the Third Colour of the Queen's Royal Regiment in honour of Queen Catherine (of Braganza), the wife of Charles II, after whom the Regiment was named.

The Paschal lamb superimposed upon a crowned Garter Star: the badge of the Queen's Royal Surreys combined the Paschal lamb of the Queen's (Royal West Surrey Regiment) with the Garter Star (minus the Arms of Guildford) of the East Surrey Regiment. The lamb is the oldest of all regimental badges, and is thought to have been adopted by the old Queen's during their time in Tangier (1662–1684). It may have been taken up as a Christian symbol in the fight against the Barbary Moor, or for its Portuguese origins, to cement the link with Catherine of Braganza.

The White Horse of Kent with motto *Invicta*: the ancient emblem of the county of Kent was adopted by the Queen's Own Royal West Kent Regiment from the county militia, and eventually became the main badge of the Queen's Own Buffs.

The Roussillon Plume superimposed by the Garter Star and Cross: the Garter of the Knights of England was confirmed to the 35th Regiment in 1879 through a connection with a former Colonel, Charles Lennox, 4th Duke of Richmond KG. The Roussillon Plume goes back to the Battle of Quebec, where the 35th helped to obliterate the French Regiment *Royal Roussillon*. In their advance to pursue the French left flank the victorious red coats siezed the Regiment's fallen Standard for their own and a facsimile of the *Roussillon's* magnificent hat plume was later incorporated into the insignia of the 35th. The Garter and the Plume combined to form the badge of the Royal Sussex Regiment.

The Coronet and cipher of the Duke of Cambridge surmounted by the Prince of Wales' Plume: the badge of the Middlesex Regiment took its shape

'The Tangierenes': an officer for Tangier in 1680.

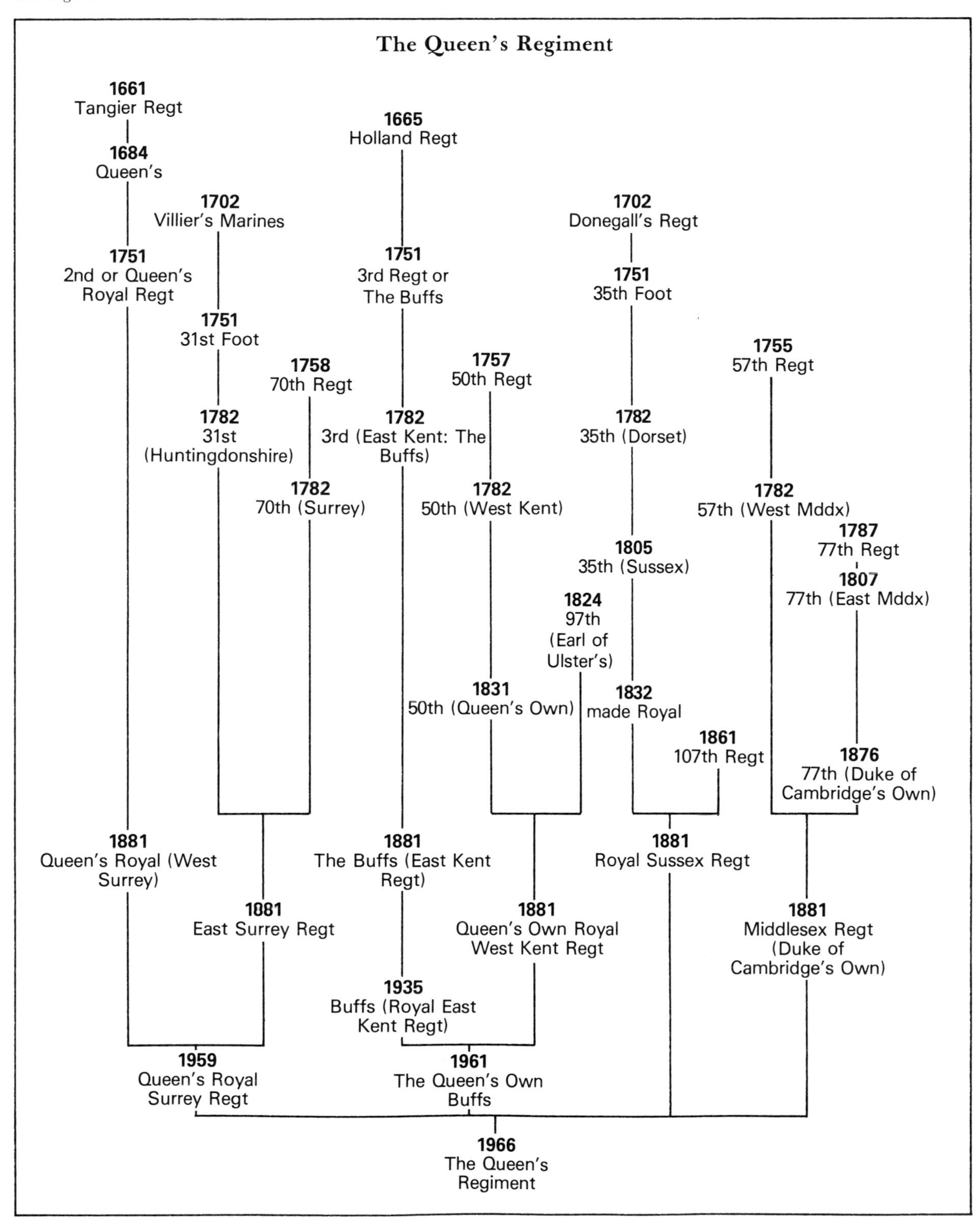
The Queen's Regiment
1661
Tangier Regt
1684
Queen's
1702
Villier's Marines
1665
Holland Regt
1702
Donegall's Regt
1751
2nd or Queen's
Royal Regt
1751
3rd Regt or
The Buffs
1751
35th Foot
1751
31st Foot
1758
70th Regt
1757
50th Regt
1755
57th Regt
1782
31st
(Huntingdonshire)
1782
3rd (East Kent: The
Buffs)
1782
35th (Dorset)
1782
70th (Surrey)
1782
50th (West Kent)
1782
57th (West Mddx)
1787
77th Regt
1805
35th (Sussex)
1807
77th (East Mddx)
1824
97th
(Earl of
Ulster's)
1831
50th (Queen's Own)
1832
made Royal
1861
107th Regt
1876
77th (Duke of
Cambridge's Own)
1881
Queen's Royal (West
Surrey)
1881
The Buffs (East Kent
Regt)
1881
Royal Sussex Regt
1881
East Surrey Regt
1881
Queen's Own Royal
West Kent Regt
1881
Middlesex Regt
(Duke of
Cambridge's Own)
1935
Buffs (Royal East
Kent Regt)
1959
Queen's Royal
Surrey Regt
1961
The Queen's Own
Buffs
1966
The Queen's
Regiment

Above *On exercise in Westphalia.*

Above right *Buglers of the 1st Middlesex ('The Die-hards') sound the Last Post and Reveille on the battlefield of Albuhera, May 16 1964.*

Below *Queensmen on observation duty, Cyprus, 1982.*

from the cipher of the titular head combined with the Plume, Coronet, and motto of the Prince of Wales. The latter was conferred on the 77th Regiment in 1810 in recognition of its recent campaigns in India.

The Naval Crown superscribed '1 June 1794': awarded to the Queen's Royal West Surreys in 1909 in respect of the part played by the Regiment in the naval victory known as 'The Glorious First of June'.

The Sphinx with 'Egypt': formerly borne on the Colours of the Queen's Royal West Surrey and the Queen's Own Royal West Kent; the badge was awarded in 1802 to the 2nd and 50th Regiments.

Unconquered I Serve: the Regimental motto takes its form from the Queen's Own Royal West Kent's *Invicta* (Unconquered) and the Middlesex Regiment's *Ich dien* (I Serve).

Honours

Tangier 1662–80 (2nd); Namur 1695 (2nd); Gibraltar 1704–05 (31st/35th); Blenheim, Ramillies, Malplaquet (3rd); Dettingen (3rd/31st); Louisburg, Quebec 1759 (35th); Guadaloupe 1759 (3rd); Martinique 1762, St Lucia 1778 (35th); Seringapatam (77th); Maida (35th); Vimiera, Corunna (2nd/50th); Douro (3rd); Talavera (3rd/31st); Albuhera (3rd/31st/57th); Badajoz (77th); Almaraz (50th); Salamanca (2nd); Vittoria (2nd/3rd/31st/50th/57th); Afghanistan 1839 (2nd); Punniar (3rd/50th); Moodkee, Sobraon, (31st/50th); Inkerman (50th/57th/77th); Sevastopol (3rd/31st/50th/57th/77th/97th); Lucknow (97th); Taku Forts (2nd/3rd/31st); New Zealand (50th/57th/70th); South Africa 1879 (3rd/57th); Nile

1884–85 (Sussex/QORWK); Burma 1885–87, (Queens); Chitral (Buffs); Relief of Ladysmith (Queens/E Surrey/Mddx); Relief of Kimberley (Buffs); South Africa 1899–1902 (common to all).

Mons (E Surrey/QORWK/Mddx); Marne 1914 (E Surrey/ Mddx); Aisne 1914 (Buffs); Ypres 1914, 1915, 1917, 1918, (Queens/Sussex/QORWK); Hill 60 (QORWK); Festubert 1915 (Queens); Somme 1916, 1918 (common to all); Albert 1916, 1918 (E Surrey/Mddx); Vimy 1917 (QORWK); Cambrai 1917, 1918 (E Surrey/Mddx); Hindenburg Line (Buffs/Sussex/Mddx); Italy 1917–18 (Sussex/ QORWK); Macedonia 1915–18 (Buffs/E Surrey/ Mddx); Gallipoli 1915 (Queens/Sussex/QORWK); Gaza (QORWK); Jerusalem (Buffs/Mddx); Palestine 1917–18 (Queens/Sussex); Defence of Kut al Amara (QORWK); Mesopotamia 1915–18 (Queens); North-West Frontier India 1915, 1916, 1917 (Sussex).

Dunkirk (E Surrey/Mddx); Normandy Landing (Mddx); North-West Europe 1940, 1944–45 (Queens/Mddx); Abyssinia 1941 (Sussex); Omars, Alem al Halfa (Sussex); El Alamein (Queens/ Buffs/Sussex/QORWK/Mddx); Longstop Hill 1943 (E Surrey); North Africa 1940–43, (Sussex); Sicily 1943 (Buffs/E Surrey/Mddx); Salerno (Queens); Sangro (E Surrey/QORWK); Anzio (Queens/Buffs/Mddx); Cassino (E Surrey/ QORWK); Italy 1943–45, (E Surrey); Malta 1940–42, (QORWK); Hong Kong (Mddx);

The 31st at the Battle of Moodkee, December 18 1845.

Band of the Queen's Own Buffs in Canada, 1963. The Drum Major's sash is buff with a blue roundel for the White Horse of Kent badge.

Above *Lord Mayor's show 1982. D Company (Sutton and Camberwell).*

Below *Band of the Queen's Division beating retreat 1983.*

Bottom *At the Worthing Freedom Parade.*

Malaya 1941–42 (E Surrey); Defence of Kohima (QORWK); Burma 1943–45 (Sussex).

Korea 1950–51 (Mddx).

'Tangier 1662–80' is shared only with the Blues & Royals.

'Douro' is a rare battle honour made famous by the Buffs' passage of the Douro River in the Peninsula War.

'Punniar' was awarded to only three British regiments and was unique in the infantry to the Queen's Own Buffs.

Anniversaries

Albuhera Day (May 16): The battle of Albuhera, in 1811, involved three of the Queen's founding Regiments, and was commemorated in the Buffs and Middlesex Regiment. The day culminates with the Middlesex 'Die-hard Ceremony' in which a toast is drunk to the immortal memory of all who have died in the Regiment's name. The battle is remembered for the appalling losses sustained by the 57th (West Middlesex) Regiment in a horrific fire-fight, and the Buffs caught in the open by enemy light horse.

Sobraon Day (February 10): 'Sobraon' was the chief battle honour of the East Surreys and February 10 was observed in the Regiment as Sobraon Day. 1 Queen's perpetuate the custom on this day of the Sergeants taking custody of the Colours. This is done as a tribute to Sergeant McCabe of the 31st and his gallantry in taking up the Regimental Colour to carry the momentum of attack on to the Sikh camp. The custom is common to the Staffordshire and the Duke of Edinburgh's Royal Regiment.

Ypres Day (April 23): the St George's Day battle at Ypres is remembered in the 1st Battalion for the bravery displayed by the 1st and 2nd Battalions of the East Surrey Regiment in the first gas attacks of World War 1.

The Glorious First of June: the former Regimental day of the Queen's Royal West Surreys celebrates the victorious naval engagement of 1794, in which companies of the 2nd Foot took part. The largest detachment served on board Admiral Howe's flagship *Queen Charlotte*.

Salerno Day (September 9): Salerno Day is honoured in 1 Queen's to commemorate the combined part played by six territorial battalions of the Queen's Royal West Surreys on Sicily in 1943.

December 20: the day in 1941 when the remnants of the 2nd East Surreys and 1st Leicestershire were united to make 'The British Battalion' in Malaya. A toast is drunk to its memory in 1 Queen's today.

Corunna Day (January 16): Corunna is remembered in 2 Queen's for the bravery of Charles Napier and Charles Stanhope, who

A grenadier of the 50th leaving his village for his Regiment and the Crimea.

Lieutenant Latham of the Buffs fighting for the King's Colour at Albuhera. He survived his hideous wounds and lived to become a folk hero of his Regiment.

together led the 50th in to clear the village of Elvina, to the personal praise of Sir John Moore. None of these men escaped from Corunna with the army and a toast to 'The Corunna Majors' is now made on the anniversary of the battle.

Sevastopol Day (September 8): the Battle for Sevastopol is commemorated in 2 Queen's to mark the joint services of the 50th and 97th Regiments in the trenches before the town.

Quebec Day (September 13): the former Regimental Day of the Royal Sussex is celebrated now in 3 Queen's to honour the conduct of Otway's Regiment (the 35th) at the Battle for Quebec in 1759. The Royal Sussex Regiment's membership of the Wolfe Society is maintained by the Queen's.

Customs

The Third Colour: the mess of 1 Queen's is the lodging-place for the old Third Colour of the Queen's Royal Regiment. The Queen's have always had a sea-green Colour bearing the cipher of Queen Catherine, and honour it in the belief that it was a personal gift from her to the Regiment. Although the original was lost in a fire the Queen's have repeatedly tried to get permission to carry a replica in the ranks; George IV agreed to this, but the order was soon rescinded. Only once, on King's Birthday Parade 1927 in Hong Kong, was this rule broken.

The Salt Ceremony: an old custom of the East Surrey Regiment is perpetuated by each officer on first dining: salt is taken from a special cellar which contains a fragment of the 31st's buff Regimental Colour inside its cover. The buff cloth is revealed when salt is taken, and the officer is then reminded of his responsibilities to the Regiment.

The Loyal Toast: the Toast is drunk seated in the Queen's, with each member and guest responding to the proposal by turn. This ritual was used by the Royal Sussex Regiment and harks back to its beginnings as the Earl of Donegall's in 1702. The Regiment was raised in Belfast and spent long periods aboard ship during its first year as an amphibious force 'to make descents upon the land as occasion requires'. The habit of drinking the sovereign's health seated is a naval custom picked

Presentation of new bugles to the Middlesex Regiment. The device on the drums is that of the coronet and cypher of the Duke of Cambridge.

up by the officers during this time and the individual response to the Toast was devised by the Colonel to test his officers' fealty to the throne.

The Naval Connection: the Queen's has strong links with the Royal Navy through its founder Regiments. The East Surreys were raised as a regiment of marines in 1702 and maintained an association with the Royal Marines throughout its history. The mess mallet of 1 Queen's is made from the timbers of the ship on which the 2nd Foot fought in 1794, the *Queen Charlotte*. The *Charlotte*'s descendant, HMS *Excellent*, continues the association between ship and Regiment and received permission, in 1925, to share the Regiment's March *Braganza*.

As a result of the 50th Regiment's marine duty in an engagement with the French off Ushant in 1778, men of the Queen's Own Royal West Kent Regiment were often piped to dinner and officers of the corps wore navy blue string gloves and lanyards in battle dress.

Mascot

None.

Dress distinctions

A blue dress cap with a scarlet band and piping, mounted with the Regimental badge, a dragon within the Garter surmounted by the Prince of Wales' plume. The side hat is blue with scarlet piping. Collar badges: the White Horse of Kent set upon the Garter Star, superimposed upon the Roussillon Plume. Buttons are embossed with the crowned Garter Star embracing the Paschal lamb. Battalion lanyards are worn: blue in the 1st and 2nd Battalions, and Royal Dutch orange in the 3rd. Orange facings were worn by the 35th from 1702 to 1832, when the Regiment gained its Royal achievement. The stable-belt is blue.

Marches

Soldiers Of The Queen, the Regimental Quick March is taken from the patriotic song composed in 1895. *The Caledonian*, the Regimental Slow March has been inherited from the Middlesex Regiment. It was introduced to the 57th by Colonel Campbell, who commanded the Regiment from 1780 to 1806. *Braganza/Lass o'Gowrie*, the Battalion Quickstep 1 Queen's combines the former marches of the Queen's Royal West Surreys and the East Surreys respectively. *Braganza* was sanctioned to be used by the Queen's Royal West Surreys in 1903, a Portuguese tune solicited by the Regiment to replace the March *Old Queen's*, which was disallowed to the Queen's after the Aldershot Review of 1882 because of its distorted version of the National Anthem. *Old Queen's* is played now only on Guest Nights in the Officers' Mess. *Huntingdonshire*, the Battalion Slow March 2 Queen's comes from the East Surrey Regiment; the 31st was affiliated to Huntingdonshire for recruiting purposes between 1782 and 1881. *The Buffs/A Hundred Pipes*, the Battalion Quick March 2 Queen's combines the former marches of the Buffs and Royal West Kent Regiment respectively. *Men Of Kent*, the Battalion Slow March 2 Queen's was previously shared by both Kent Regiments. *Royal Sussex/Lass Of Richmond Hill*, the Battalion Quickstep 3 Queen's. *Roussillon*, the Battalion Slow March 3 Queen's (formerly the Royal Sussex Regiment). *Sussex By The Sea,* an unofficial march of the Royal Sussex Regiment.

Nicknames

'The Blind Half-hundred': a sobriquet of the 50th (West Kent) Regiment in the Egyptian campaign of 1801, when many of its number suffered from the effects of ophthalmia.

'The Buffs': originally a nickname of the 3rd Foot, in use from about 1708, after their 'flesh-coloured' facings. The word gradually crept into the Regiment's title and became official in 1751. As other regiments were raised, and allotted buff facings, the nickname varied to 'Old Buffs'.

'The Celestials': the 97th Regiment, from the peculiar shade of its blue facings.

'The Die-hards': the proud name of the Middlesex Regiment originated at the Battle of Albuhera, where the 57th lost 80 per cent of its effectives in a terrible fire-fight. At the height of the slaughter, Colonel Inglis fell and refused to be carried to the rear; his immortal words, 'Die hard, 57th, die hard!' served to inspire generations of Middlesex men in all theatres of war.

'The Dirty Half-hundred': a name acquired by the 50th Regiment at the Battle of Vimiero in 1808, where, the day being hot and the fighting furious, the black dye ran out of coat cuffs when men wiped their sweating brows.

'The Glasgow Greys': the 70th Regiment was raised in Glasgow in 1756 and sported grey coat facings until 1768, when a change was made to black.

'Kirke's Lambs': a sobriquet of the Queen's Regiment under Percy Kirke at the time of the Monmouth Rebellion (1685), when its notorious handling of suspects was anything but lamb-like. The name came from the Paschal lamb emblem worn by the Regiment on its grenadiers' caps and appointments.

'The Mids': the Middlesex Regiment.

'The Mutton Lancers': the Queen's Royal Regiment, from its cap badge, the Paschal lamb with halo and banner of St George.

'The Nutcrackers': a boastful reputation of the Buffs, supposedly from their skill at cracking French heads in the Peninsula War.

'The Orange Lillies': a nickname given to the 35th Regiment after Quebec, from its orange Regimental Colour and the *fleur-de-lys* of a captured French colour.

'The Pork and Beans': cockney rhyming slang for The Queen's.

'The Pot hooks': the 77th Regiment, from the shape of the numerals.

'The Resurrectionists': a reputation gained by the Buffs following their amazing recovery back to full strength after their losses at Albuhera.

'The Sleepy Queen's': the Queen's Royal Regiment allowed the French garrison of Almeida to slip through a blockade during the Peninsula War.

'The Tangierenes': the Tangier Regiment (later the Queen's Royal Regiment) formed at Putney in 1661 to supply the garrison for the Port of Tangier, newly acquired by Charles II in the marriage treaty for Catherine of Braganza.

Recruiting

Greater London, Kent, Sussex and Surrey. RHQ: Howe Barracks, Canterbury.

The King's Own Royal Border Regiment (4th, 34th, 55th Foot)

Insignia

The Royal Cipher within the Garter, all within a laurel wreath: the cipher was authorised to be displayed on the Colours of the 4th or King's Own Regiment in 1751. The laurel was awarded to the 34th Regiment for its outstanding rearguard action at the Battle of Fontenoy in 1745.

The Lion of England: the Lion appeared on the Colours of the King's Own in the early 18th century and is believed to be a personal award from William III to the Regiment for being the first to rally to his cause in 1688.

The Dragon superscribed 'China': conferred on the 55th Regiment for service in the Opium War of 1842.

Honours

Namur 1695, Gibraltar 1704–05 Guadaloupe 1759 (4th); Havannah (34th); St Lucia 1778 (4th/34th); Corunna (4th); Albuhera, Arroyo dos Molinos (34th); Badajoz, Salamanca (4th); Vittoria (4th/34th); St Sebastian (4th); Pyrenees, Nivelle (34th); Nive (4th/34th); Orthes (34th); Peninsula (4th/34th); Bladensburg, Waterloo (4th); Alma, Inkerman (4th/55th); Sevastopol (4th/34th/55th); Lucknow (34th); Abyssinia, South Africa 1879 (4th); Relief of Ladysmith, South Africa 1899–1902, (KORR/Border).

Marne 1914, (KORR); Ypres 1914, 1915, 1917, 1918 (KORR/Border); Langemarck 1914, 1917 (Border); Somme 1916, 1918, Arras 1917, 1918 (KORR/Border); Messines 1917, 1918 (KORR); Cambrai 1917, 1918 (Border); Macedonia 1915–18, Gallipoli 1915–16 (KORR/Border); Mesopotamia 1916–18 (KORR).

Afghanistan 1919.

Dunkirk 1940, Arnhem 1944 (Border); North-West Europe 1940, 1944 (KORR/Border); Defence of Habbaniya, Merjayun (KORR); Tobruk 1941 (Border); Tobruk Sortie, North Africa 1942

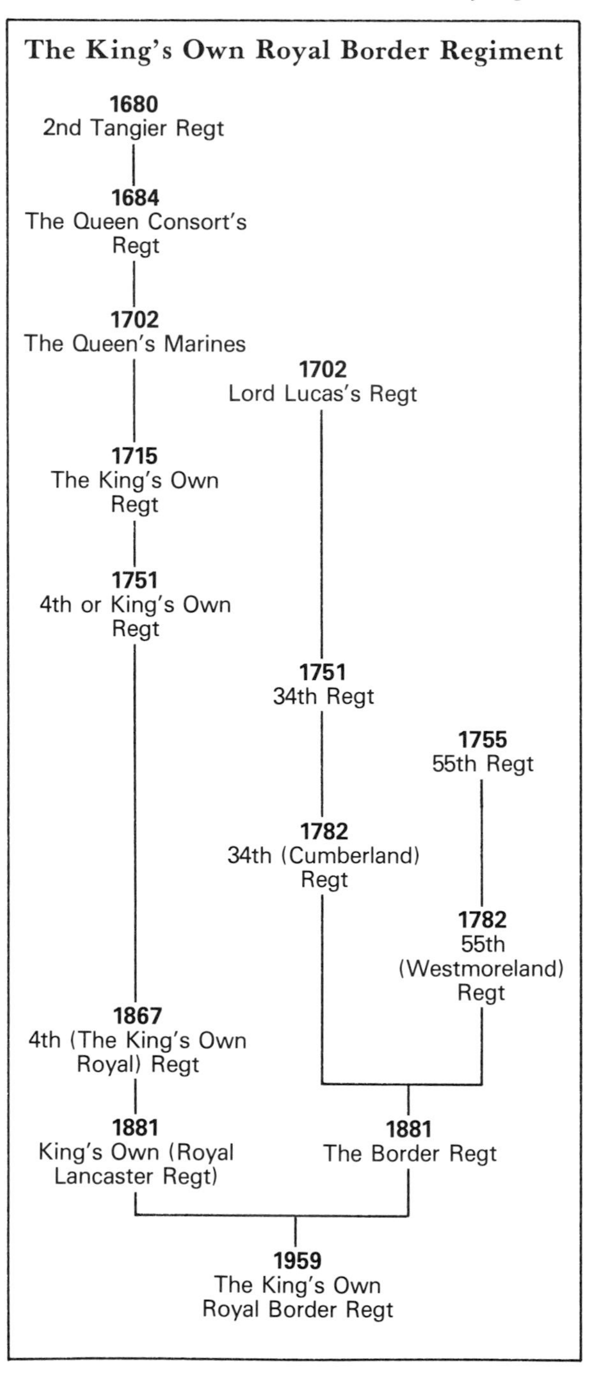

Above left *Simkin's impression of the Border Regiment drums and colours, 1893.*

Left *The Drum Major in the full dress uniform of the Corps of Drums, 1983.*

Arroyo Day, 1982. March Past of the 1st Battalion.

1982. Drummers in period dress present the French drums captured at the Battle of Arroyo dos Molinos in 1811.

(KORR); Landing in Sicily (Border); Montone, Lamone Bridgehead, Malta 1941–42 (KORR); Imphal Myinmu Bridgehead, Meiktila, Chindits 1944, Burma 1943–45 (Border).

'Abyssinia' tells of the Regiment's participation in Napier's expedition of 1868 to Magdala, where a bandsman in the 4th King's Own discovered the great King Theodore's Drum. This trophy was divided between three Regiments on the expedition: the King's Own, Duke of Wellington's and 3rd Dragoon Guards. These Regiments came together at Bulford in 1952, and the Drum was exhibited complete again.

Anniversaries

Arroyo Day (October 28): the Battle of Arroyo dos Molinos was but a backwater in the British Army's glorious list of Peninsula successes, but is memorable for the resounding defeat of the French 34th Regiment by its opposite number, the 34th (Cumberland) Regiment. The British 34th afterwards received permission to commemorate its unique battle honour with a red and white cockade, worn in imitation of those of the French 34th. The Border Regiment was able to continue this privilege in its Maltese Cross badge, the centre of which was halved red and white. It is the custom on Arroyo Day to combine the former practices of the founding Regiments: officers and Sergeants wear red roses in their caps, as the King's Own have done for St George's Day since 1900, and a wreath of red roses is carried on the Colour. The French drums

China dragon collar badges of the 55th Regt 1874.

captured in the battle are paraded by drummers in period uniform and then trooped in slow time to the band's rendition of *La Marseillaise*.

Customs

The Loyal Toast: both founder Regiments were required to drink the Loyal Toast, but neither did so in the conventional manner. When in the County Palatinate of Lancaster an old rule of the King's Own is invoked whereby the Queen's health is proposed 'The Queen, the Duke of Lancaster'.

Officers of the Border Regiment used the naval custom of drinking the Toast seated, a hangover from 1702, when the 34th was raised for service with the Fleet.

The Wolfe Society: the Regiment's right to membership of the Wolfe Society is by the King's Own, in which Wolfe served his Captaincy (1744).

Mascot

None.

Dress distinctions

A blue dress cap with a scarlet band and piping, mounted with the Regimental badge on a red diamond backing. A blue side hat with red flaps and peak, piped yellow (gold for officers). Buttons are embossed with the Border Regiment's Dragon inscribed 'China'. A glider arm badge (gold for officers and yellow for other ranks) is worn as a battle honour. The 1st Battalion Border Regiment was the first unit to go into action by glider (1st Airborne Division's invasion of Sicily, 1943). The stable-belt is blue (as are the facings) with a gold centre strip. Musicians wear a white marine-style helmet in full dress, a picturesque reminder of the Regiment's marine history, particularly during the Duke of Marlborough's time when both the 4th and 34th had seagoing experience. The helmets were adopted around 1970, and authorised to the KORBR in 1978.

Marches

The Regimental Quick March opens with a few bars from the *March Of The French 34th Regiment*, followed by *John Peel*, an old Cumbrian hunting air from the Border Regiment. This is followed by two Scottish airs: *Lass o'Gowrie* (55th) and *Corn Riggs Are Bonny*. *Trelawney (Song Of The Western Men)*, the Regimental Slow March has been played in the King's Own since the turbulent days of James II's reign, when Regimental loyalties leaned more towards the imprisoned Bishop Trelawney than to the King.

Nicknames

'Barrell's Blues': the 4th or King's Own under the Hon William Barrell, who assumed the Colonelcy in 1734. The name referred to the blue breeches and coat facings evident in a Royal regiment at this period, but was regarded more as a fighting reputation. The Regiment distinguished itself at Culloden and Falkirk Muir, and carried the unofficial device 'Culloden' on its Colours.

'The Cattle Reavers': the Border Regiment (a reference to the bandit pursuits of Border Country people in the Middle Ages).

'The Harry Lauders': rhyming slang for The Borders.

'The Lions': the King's Own, from their cap badge.

Recruiting

Cumbria and northern Lancashire. RHQ: Carlisle Castle.

The Royal Regiment of Fusiliers (5th, 6th, 7th, XXth Foot)

Insignia

St George and the Dragon within the Garter: the

Old regimental silver of the Northumberland Fusiliers, with an antique St George and dragon.

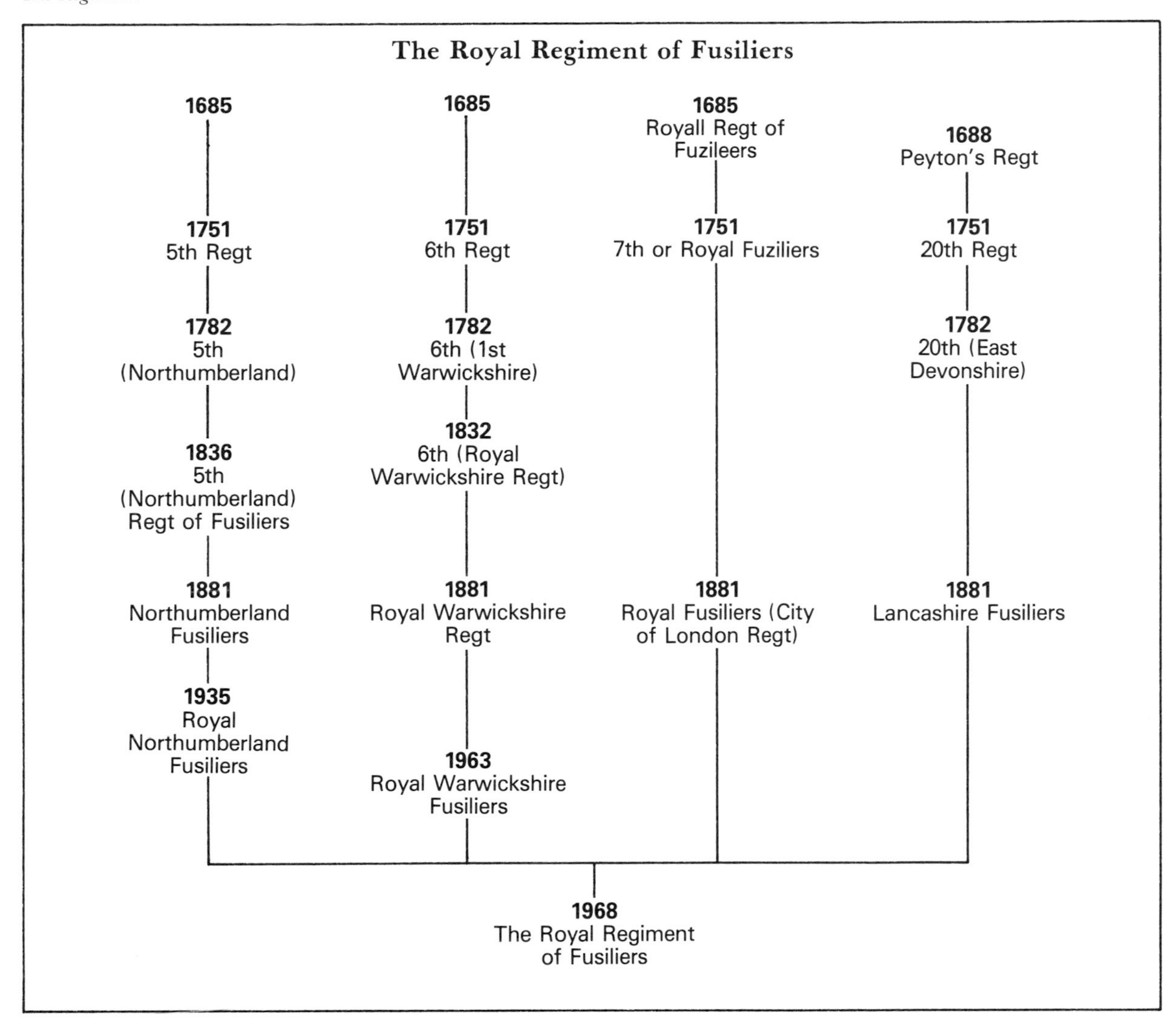

The Lancashire Landing, Gallipoli, April 25 1915.

Harry Payne's version of the 20th at Minden.

emblem of England was adopted by the English Brigade in Dutch service, and worn until 1685, when the unit was recalled to England by James II and its regiments established as the 5th and 6th in line. The badge was preserved for the Colours of the 5th Foot, and subsequently the dress and appointments of the Northumberland Fusiliers. The crest is embraced by the Minden wreath from the Lancashire Fusiliers.

The United Red and White Rose slipped ensigned with the Royal Crest: adopted in 1674 by the English Brigade in Dutch service. The emblem was borne by the Brigade to show its allegiance to England and was worn for difference 'slipped', that is, torn from the main stock.

An antelope gorged with a ducal coronet with rope flexed over the back: as one of the 'Six Old Corps' the 6th Foot was permitted the privilege of displaying on its Colours and appointments a Regimental emblem. The antelope from the Arms of Henry VI was adopted, and later became the official badge of the Royal Warwickshire Regiment. An old tradition of the Warwickshires has it that the device came from a Moorish banner, taken by the 6th at Saragossa in 1707.

The White Horse of Hanover: the ancient symbol of the Royal Fusiliers.

The Red Rose of Lancaster: the badge is emblazoned on the Regimental Colour to represent the Lancashire Fusiliers.

The Sphinx superscribed 'Egypt': awarded to the 20th Regiment in 1802 and worn by the Lancashire Fusiliers embossed to their grenade badge.

Honours

Namur 1695 (6th/7th); Dettingen, Minden (20th); Wilhelmstahl, St Lucia 1778 (5th); Martinique 1794, 1809 (6th/7th); Egmont-op-Zee, Maida (20th); Rolica (5th/6th); Vimiera, Corunna (5th/6th/20th); Talavera, Busaco (7th); Ciudad Rodrigo (5th); Badajoz (5th/7th); Albuhera (7th); Salamanca (5th/7th); Vittoria (common to all); Pyrenees (6th/7th/20th); Nivelle (5th/6th); Orthes (common to all); Toulouse (5th/7th/20th); Peninsula (common to all); Niagara, South Africa 1846–47, 1851–53 (6th); Alma, Inkerman, Sevastopol (7th/20th); Lucknow (5th/20th); Kandahar 1880 (7th); Afghanistan 1878–80 (5th/7th); Atbara (RWR); Khartoum (NF/RWR/ LF); Relief of Ladysmith (RF/LF); Modder River (NF); South Africa 1899–1902 (common to all).

Mons (NF/RF); Marne 1914 (NF); Aisne 1914, 1918 (LF); Ypres 1914, 1915, 1917, 1918 (common to all); St Julien (NF); Somme 1916, 1918 (common to all); Arras 1917, 1918 (RWR/RF/LF); Passchendaele (LF); Cambrai 1917, 1918 (RF/LF); Lys (RWR); Hindenburg Line (RWR/RF/LF); Piave (NF/RWR); Struma (NF/RF); Macedonia 1915–18 (LF); Landing at Helles (RF/LF); Suvla (NF); Sari Bair (RWR); Gallipoli 1915–16 (LF); Egypt 1915–17 (RF); Baghdad (RWR).

Defence of Escaut (RWR/LF); Dunkirk 1940 (RNF/RF); Normandy Landing (RWR); Caen (RNF/RWR/LF); Rhineland (RNF); Bremen, North-West Europe 1940, 1944–45 (RWR); Keren (RF); Defence of Tobruk (RNF); Medjez el Bab (LF); North Africa (RF); Sangro (LF); Mozzagrogna, Salerno, Anzio (RF); Cassino II (RNF/RF/LF); Gothic Line (RF); Malta 1941–42 (LF); Kohima (LF); Burma 1943–45 (RWR/LF).

Imjin (RNF); Korea 1950–53 (RNF/RF).

'Albuhera' marks the battle in which Myers'

St George's Day in the Northumberland Fusiliers, 1895. Note the attached roses.

The mascot leads out a company on Buckingham Palace duty.

A fusilier on duty in Northern Ireland.

Fusilier Brigade, which included two battalions of the 7th Royal Fusiliers, made its famous charge to save Hoghton's Brigade. The Regiment suffered greatly in the fighting, but managed to recapture a tattered pair of Colours which belonged to the Buffs and, in returning them to the Regiment, created a lasting bond between the two. May 16 was a common day of celebration in the Buffs and the Royal Fusiliers.

'Ciudad Rodrigo' commemorates the engagement at nearby El Bodon, too small itself to be considered for a battle honour, but memorable for the fellowship forged between the 5th and 77th Regiments. September 25 was kept as El Bodon Day in the Northumberland Fusiliers before amalgamation.

'Pyrenees' covers the daring charge made by the 6th Regiment at Echelar, described by Wellington as 'the most gallant and the finest thing I have ever witnessed'.

'Alma' is significant in RRF history for the intrepid assault on the Russian redoubts by the 7th Royal Fusiliers under Colonel Lacey Yea. The Russian-pattern drums carried in the RRF were inherited from the Royal Northumberland Fusiliers, who, curiously, did not take part in the Crimean War.

'Inkerman' was an important battle honour in the Lancashire Fusiliers and November 5 was reserved in that corps as Inkerman Day.

'Gallipoli' has always been associated with the Lancashire Fusiliers. On Gallipoli Day (April 25), the fusiliers remember the many who fell in the ill-fated landings and the 'Six VCs won before breakfast' by the Lancashire Fusiliers. The Ship's bell from HMS *Euryalus* was kept by the Regiment to sound time in barracks.

'Normandy Landings' was a prominent battle honour in the Royal Warwickshire and June 6 was kept as Normandy Day in solemn memory of the Regiment's losses in the assault on the German stronghold at Lebissey.

Anniversaries

St George's Day (April 23): the Regimental Day celebrates the 1968 union of the four English fusilier Regiments as the RRF. St George's day used to be the chief day of celebration in the Northumberland Fusiliers and is observed today, true to the ideals of that Regiment, with drums, Colours and headgear

3rd Battalion band and Corps of Drums.

Ceremony of the Keys, Gibraltar. Note the saw-tooth edging to the drums, and the broad trouser stripes.

all bedecked in red and white roses. This celebration began in 1836, when the 5th was awarded its unique battle honour 'Wilhelmstahl' and created a regiment of Fusiliers to confirm its right to the old custom of wearing fur caps taken from French grenadiers captured in the battle. A gosling green silk Colour, emblazoned with the Regiment's badge and motto, was allowed to be paraded once a year on St George's Day to mark the capture of an enemy banner at Wilhelmstahl in 1762. This, the 'Drummer's Colour', is kept by each Battalion in turn and paraded by that Battalion on St George's Day.

Minden Day (August 1): roses are worn on Minden Day in the tradition of the Lancashire Fusiliers, who were wont to celebrate the prestigious battle anniversary with elaborate ritual. The age-old rose-eating ceremony, which supports the belief that soliders picked and wore roses on the battlefield, is also perpetuated in the RRF.

A laurel wreath device was awarded to the 20th Regiment after the battle, to be displayed on the Regimental Colour as a testament of their extreme gallantry in the fray. This is now incorporated in the badge of the RRF.

Customs

The Loyal Toast: the right to ignore the ritual associated with the Loyal Toast comes from the 7th Royal Fusiliers and their privileged connections with King William IV and his family. The King dined regularly with the Regiment and granted his one and only dispensation from the Toast in 1835.

The Wolfe Society: James Wolfe was in command of the 20th Regiment from 1750 to 1758.

Mascot

'Bobby', an Indian blackbuck, is descended from a long line of blackbucks maintained by the Royal Warwickshire Regiment. The first was adopted by the 6th Regiment whilst serving in India in 1871, to complement the Regimental badge. The mascot is kept in the charge of a Buck leader and is cared for by each Battalion in turn.

Dress distinctions

A blue beret mounted with a grenade badge and red over white hackle. Officers and Warrant Officers are issued with the Royal pattern peaked dress cap. The grenade badge is common to all fusilier regiments, and the RRF pattern is based on that worn by the Royal Fusiliers, with the Crown in the centre. The design on the grenade is St George and the dragon, taken from the badge of the Northumberland Fusiliers, embraced by the 'Minden wreath' of the Lancashire Fusiliers.

The beret hackle relates to the hackle worn on the side of the full dress sealskin cap, and has been a feature of fusilier dress since 1946. Before amalgamation, the Royal Fusiliers had an all-white hackle of ancient origin, the Royal Warwickshire a blue/orange hackle (from 1963) and the Lancashire Fusiliers one of primrose yellow awarded in 1900 for conspicuous service at the Battle of Spion Kop. The handsome red over white hackle sported by the RRF was inherited from the Royal Northumberland Fusiliers and originated in an encounter with the French on the Island of St Lucia in 1778, where the 5th cunningly overcame great odds and plundered the enemy of its white plumes. These were granted to the 5th as a Regimental distinction, and when white plumes became standard wear for all infantry regiments, in 1830, the 5th chose to adopt one of red and white — the colours of St George. In full dress the hackle is worn on the right side of the sealskin cap in the style of the Royal Fusiliers. Buttons are stamped with the antelope device of the Royal Warwickshire Regiment.

No 1 dress trousers are worn with a broad scarlet stripe down the outer seams after the fashion of the Royal Artillery. This distinction came from the Royal Fusiliers, whose officers wore it as a symbol of the link between the two Regiments begun in the reign of James II. The Royal Fusiliers were raised by the King to guard his Train of Artillery in the Tower of London; their name originated with the matchless fuzil carried by officers and men of the Regiment in their duties with the volatile artillery. The stable-belt is striped equally crimson/yellow/crimson.

Marches

The British Grenadier, the Regimental Quick March is common to all regiments that wear the grenade badge and was authorised, in 1835, to be played before any other regimental march. *Rule Britannia*, the Regimental Slow March can be attributed to the Northumberland Fusiliers, whose practice it was to play the march on special occasions in commemoration of their landing on the Island of Martinique in 1693. *Blaydon Races*, (Royal Northumberland Fusiliers). *Warwickshire Lad/Saucy Sixth*, (Royal Warwickshire Fusiliers). *Fighting With The 7th Royal Fusiliers. The Minden March* (Lancashire Fusiliers).

Lord Dartmouth, founder of the Royal Regiment of Fuzileers, and Master General of the Ordnance, 1685.

Nicknames

'The Calcutta Home Guard': a derisory allusion to the 1st Royal Warwicks' peaceful posting to India during the Second World War.

'The Dutch Guards': the 6th Regiment began life in the pay of Holland, and came to England in 1688 with the army of William of Orange.

'The Elegant Extracts': the name was given to the fashion-conscious fops who flocked to join the *avant garde* fusiliers in 1685.

'The Fighting Fifth': the 5th (Northumberland) Regiment, from a remark made by Wellington during the Peninsula War: 'The ever fighting, often tried, but never failing Fifth'.

'The Goat Boys': the Royal Warwickshire Regiment, in deliberate mockery of its antelope cap badge.

'Guise's Geese': John Guise was Colonel of the 6th Foot from 1738 to 1765, and his Regiment was reputed to have followed him anywhere.

'Kingsley's Stand': the 20th Regiment (Kingsley's) at the Battle of Minden in 1759. The name derives from the Regiment's desire to stand in line despite its heavy losses and the Commander-in-Chief's order for them to stand down. Also 'The Minden Boys'.

'The Old and Bold': a general term used to describe old and venerable units of the Army, but particularly the 5th Regiment; said to have originated in the Peninsula War. Also 'The Old Fifth'.

'The Saucy Sixth': the 6th Regiment of Foot.

'The Shiners': the 5th Regiment was so described at an inspection of its dress and turnout in Ireland 1769. The name was a source of great pride, and was used by the Royal Northumberland Fusiliers in more recent times.

'The Warwickshire Lads': the Royal Warwickshire Regiment.

'The Young Fusiliers': the 20th Regiment was brigaded with the fusiliers for the Pyrenean campaign of 1813, and thereby acquired the name, which anticipated their conversion to a regiment of fusiliers by 68 years.

Recruiting

Northumberland, Lancashire, Warwickshire, West Midlands and Greater London. RHQ: HM Tower of London.

The King's Regiment (Manchester and Liverpool) (8th, 63rd, 96th Foot)

Insignia

The White Horse of Hanover superimposed upon the fleur-de-lys: the Horse of Hanover was granted to the 8th Foot in 1714 when King George I came to the throne and approved that the Regiment should in future be styled 'The King's. The fleur-de-lys was probably adopted by the 63rd Regiment in 1815 to commemorate its service on the former French island of Guadaloupe.

The Royal Cipher surmounted by the Crown: as a Royal Regiment, the 8th was allowed to display a Royal badge on its Colours from 1751.

The Sphinx superscribed 'Egypt': awarded to the 8th and the Queen's German Regiment in 1802 in recognition of their part in the Egyptian campaign of 1802. The Queen's Germans were formed as a regiment in 1798 and placed as the 96th Foot in 1818 shortly before they were disbanded. The 96th Regiment reformed in 1824 at Manchester and, in 1874, was permitted to display the honours won by their predecessors, the Sphinx and 'Peninsula'.

Honours

Blenheim, Ramillies, Oudenarde, Malplaquet, Dettingen (8th); Guadaloupe 1759, Egmont-op-Zee (63rd); Peninsula (96th); Martinique 1809 (8th/63rd); Guadaloupe 1810 (63rd); Niagara (8th); New Zealand (96th); Alma, Inkerman, Sevastopol (63rd); Delhi 1857, Lucknow, Peiwar Kotal (8th); Afghanistan 1878–80 (8th/63rd); Egypt 1882 (MR); Burma 1885–87 (Kings); Defence of Ladysmith, South Africa 1899–1902 (Kings/MR).

Mons (MR); Retreat from Mons, Marne 1914,

Mess silver.

Silver drums of the Manchester Regiment (left) and the King's Liverpool (right). The drummers' scarlet tunics are faced in deep green.

Aisne 1914 (Kings); Ypres 1914, 1915, 1917, 1918 (Kings/MR); Givenchy 1914 (MR); Festubert 1915, Loos (Kings); Somme 1916, 1918 (Kings/MR); Arras 1917, 1918, Scarpe 1917, 1918 (Kings); Hindenburg Line, Piave, Macedonia 1915–18, Gallipoli, Megiddo, Baghdad (MR).

Afghanistan 1919 (Kings).

Dyle, Defence of Arras (MR); Normandy Landing (Kings); Caen, Lower Maas, Roer, Reichswald (MR); Cassino II, Trasimene Line, Tuori (Kings); Gothic Line (MR); Capture of Forli, Rimini Line (Kings); Malta 1940 (MR); Athens (Kings); Kohima (MR); Chindits 1943 (Kings).

Anniversaries

Blenheim Day (August 13): the principal battle honour 'Blenheim' records the heavy casualties incurred by the 8th Foot in the early part of the battle, despite which the Battalion went on to stop the French Guards' escape, and took some 1,000 prisoners.

Guadaloupe Day (June 10): observed in honour of the 63rd Regiment's part in the expeditionary force sent to besiege the French West Indies, and the capture of Guadaloupe in 1759.

Inkerman Day (November 5): kept to honour the tenacity of the 63rd in forcing the Russian rout at

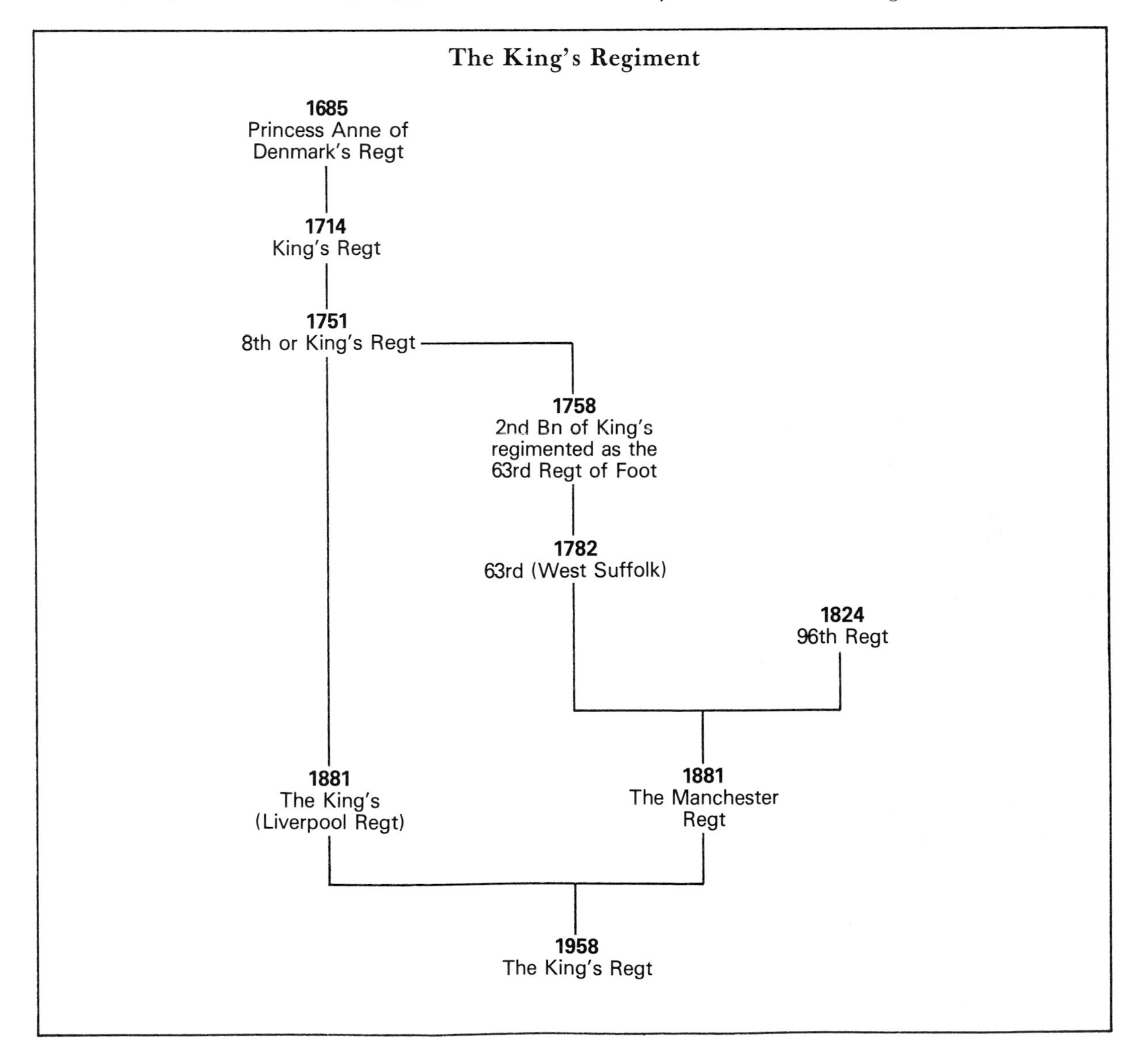

Inkerman, despite heavy losses among the officers. One of the Battalion Colours carried in the action is now in the possession of 1st King's.

Delhi Day (September 14): on this day in 1857 the Army breached and stormed the Delhi defences. The 8th Regiment lost 50 men before reaching the breach, and then followed six days of bloody street fighting before the mutineers abandoned the city.

Ladysmith Day (February 28): the anniversary recalls a day in the defence of Ladysmith and the stoic resistance put up by 16 men of the Manchester Regiment in a remote corner of Caesar's Camp. For 16 hours the little band fought continuously and by nightfall only two remained alive.

Somme Day (July 1): the official first day on the Somme anniversary is commemorated, although this is secondary to the advance of 1st/5th King's on August 8. The King's suffered fearful losses in the six-month battle.

Francilly-Selency Day (April 2): the celebration of the 2nd Battalion Manchesters' capture of a battery of German 77mm guns at Francilly in 1917.

Kohima Day (May 15): the Manchesters' Machine Gun Battalion in the Relief of Kohima and the King's 'Chindits' are commemorated on this day.

March 16 is kept to honour the Regiment's hard-fought engagements at Cassino, Gioiella, Touri, River Morano and Fiori.

Customs

Private soldiers hold the rank of Kingsman.

Mascot

None.

Dress distinctions

A blue dress cap with a scarlet band and piping, mounted with a fleur-de-lys badge superimposed by the Horse of Hanover. The fleur-de-lys was worn

The Colour Party, with details of the Regiment's Colours and honours obligingly set out behind.

by the 63rd Regiment until 1881, when they became 1st Battalion of the Manchester Regiment and then the Arms of the City of Manchester was adopted as the Regimental cap badge. This was derided as 'The tram-conductor's badge', and replaced with the fleur-de-lys in 1923. A maroon side hat with a green tip. Collar badges: as the cap badge. Lanyards of deep green. The deep green facings of the old 63rd were restored to the Manchesters, with their old badge, in 1923. The stable-belt is deep green with a central maroon stripe.

Marches

Here's To The Maiden/The Manchester, the Quick March of the King's Liverpool Regiment, *Here's To The Maiden,* comes from incidental music composed by Thomas Linley in 1777. *The Manchester* is an adaptation of two popular Neopolitan songs: *La Luisella* and *Fenesta Vascia. Lord Ferrers March,* the Regimental Slow March, is a *mélange* of *The English Rose* (King's) with an arrangement from the opera *Merrie England,* and *Farewell Manchester,* based on Felton's *Gavotte,* a piece written for harpsichord in 1728. *Zachmi Dil*, the March of the 2nd Battalion King's Liverpool Regiment was adopted in India from an old Pathan song which means 'The Wounded Heart'. It was the custom for this march to be played on Guest Nights to recall the days spent on the North-West Frontier. *The Young May Moon*, the Quickstep of the 2nd Battalion Manchester Regiment is an old Irish air from the comic opera *Robin Hood.*

Nicknames

'The Bendovers': the 96th Regiment, from the shape of its numerals. Also 'The Ups and Downs'.

'The Bloodsuckers': the 63rd Regiment, from the

Kingsmen relieve men of the Scots Guards on Public Duties in London, 1965. The two regiments fought together at Dettingen in 1743.

shape of its fleur-de-lys badge, which was thought to resemble a mosquito, or 'bloodsucker'. It is a favourite theory among Kingsmen that their badge was awarded for their former proficiency in killing Frenchmen. The name was common in the 18th century, however, for those with a taste for drawing blood without compunction.

'The Leather Hats': a name associated with men of the 8th Regiment, from their habit of taking leather tricorns from captured wounded Americans in the invasion of Lower Canada at the outbreak of the American War of Independence.

Recruiting

Merseyside and Greater Manchester. RHQ: TA Centre, Liverpool.

The Royal Anglian Regiment (9th, 10th, 12th, 16th, 17th, 44th, 48th, 56th, 58th Foot)

Insignia

The Castle and Key of Gibraltar upon an eight-pointed star: the Castle and Key formed the main body of the badges of three founding Regiments — the Suffolk, Essex, and Northamptonshire; whilst the star (minus the Maltese Cross and hart) is from the Bedfordshire & Hertfordshire Regiment.

The figure of Britannia: authorised to the 9th Regiment in 1799 and worn as the Regimental badge of the Royal Norfolk. The emblem is thought to have been awarded to the Regiment by Queen Anne in recognition of its gallantry at the Battle of Almanza, but there is no evidence for this supposition.

The Sphinx superscribed 'Egypt': awarded in 1802 to the 10th, 44th and 58th Regiments for service in the Egyptian campaign of the previous year. The Sphinx was later incorporated into the cap badge of the Essex Regiment, but the Lincolnshire Regiment, whose forebears had had to endure a 120-mile desert march to secure the honour, wore the Sphinx with no other device.

The Castle and Key superscribed 'Gibraltar 1779–83' with motto *Montis Insignia Calpe* underneath: awarded to the 12th, 56th, and 58th Regiments in 1836 for their part in the glorious defence of Gibraltar during the Great Siege of 1779 to 1783. The motto translates 'By the sign of the Rock'. The Essex Regiment used to observe February 6 as Gibraltar Day.

The Royal Tiger superscribed 'Hindoostan':

Below *1st Battalion Colour Party, Royal Anglian Regiment. The Colour is blue, but the Subalterns' colour-belts are yellow.*

Bottom *Drummers of the Royal Leicestershire Regiment in distinctive Tiger skins. The Royal Tiger badge was worn on the cap, and on the collar within the unbroken laurel wreath.*

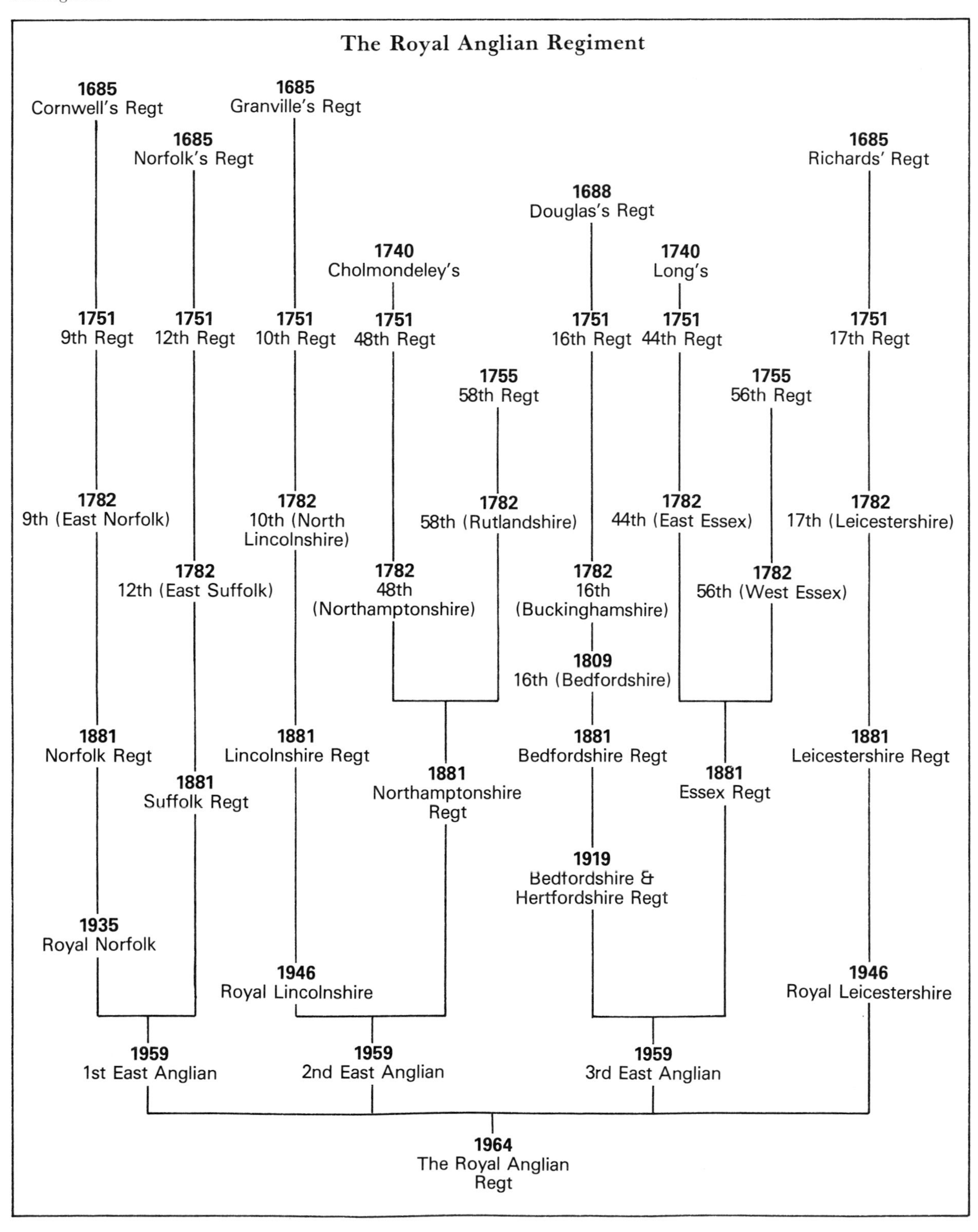
The Royal Anglian Regiment
1685
Cornwell's Regt
1685
Granville's Regt
1685
Norfolk's Regt
1685
Richards' Regt
1688
Douglas's Regt
1740
Cholmondeley's
1740
Long's
1751
9th Regt
1751
12th Regt
1751
10th Regt
1751
48th Regt
1751
16th Regt
1751
44th Regt
1751
17th Regt
1755
58th Regt
1755
56th Regt
1782
9th (East Norfolk)
1782
10th (North Lincolnshire)
1782
58th (Rutlandshire)
1782
44th (East Essex)
1782
17th (Leicestershire)
1782
12th (East Suffolk)
1782
48th (Northamptonshire)
1782
16th (Buckinghamshire)
1782
56th (West Essex)
1809
16th (Bedfordshire)
1881
Norfolk Regt
1881
Lincolnshire Regt
1881
Bedfordshire Regt
1881
Leicestershire Regt
1881
Suffolk Regt
1881
Northamptonshire Regt
1881
Essex Regt
1919
Bedfordshire &
Hertfordshire Regt
1935
Royal Norfolk
1946
Royal Lincolnshire
1946
Royal Leicestershire
1959
1st East Anglian
1959
2nd East Anglian
1959
3rd East Anglian
1964
The Royal Anglian Regt

Above left *Dusting off the royal-pattern cap for guard duty.* **Above right** *Adjutant in No 1 dress, and Drum Major inspecting the Corps of Drums. Note the Spinx collar badges which denote the 2nd Battalion. The Drum Major's sash reads 'Duchess of Gloucester's Own Royal Lincolnshire and Northamptonshire. Note the absence of drummers' shoulder wings in this Regiment.*

awarded to the 17th Regiment in 1825 'as a lasting testimony to the exemplary conduct of the corps during its service in India from 1804 to 1823'. The badge was worn without embellishment on the caps of the Royal Leicestershire Regiment.

An Eagle within the Garter: the Napoleonic Eagle of the Essex Regiment is borne within the Garter of the Bedfordshire Regiment and commemorates the capture of a regimental Eagle of the French 62nd by the 44th Regiment at the Battle of Salamanca in 1812.

Honours

Namur 1695 (16th/17th); Blenheim, Ramillies, Oudenarde, Malplaquet (10th/16th); Dettingen (12th); Louisburg (17th/48th/58th); Quebec 1759 (48th/58th); Minden (12th); Martinique 1762 (17th/48th); Havannah (9th/17th/48th/56th); Martinique 1794 (9th/44th/58th); Seringapatam (12th); Corunna (9th); Talavera, Albuhera (48th); Badajoz (44th/48th); Salamanca (9th/44th/58th); Vittoria (9th/48th/58th); Nivelle (48th/58th); Peninsula (9th/10th/44th/48th/58th); Bladensburg, Waterloo, Ava (44th); Ghuznee 1839, Khelat (17th); Cabool 1842, Moodkee, Ferozeshah (9th); Sobraon (9th/10th; Goojerat (10th); New Zealand (12th/58th); South Africa 1851–53 (12th); Inkerman (44th); Sevastopol (9th/17th/44th/48th/56th); Lucknow (10th); Taku Forts (44th); Afghanistan 1878–80 (9th/12th/17th); Nile 1884–85 (Essex); Tirah (Nthptn); Atbara, Khartoum (Lincs); Paardeberg (Norfk/Lincs/Essex); Defence of Ladysmith (Leics); South Africa 1899–1902 (common to all).

Mons (Norfk/Lincs/Bedfd/Nthptn); Le Cateau (Suffk/Essex); Marne 1914 (Norfk/Lincs/Bedfd/Essex/Nthptn); Aisne 1914, 1918 (Leics/Nthptn); Ypres 1914, 1915, 1917, 1918 (common to all); Neuve Chapelle (Lincs/Leics/Nthptn); Loos (Lincs/Bedfd/Essex/Nthptn); Somme 1916, 1918 (common to all); Arras 1917, 1918 (Suffk/Essex/Nthptn); Cambrai 1917, 1918 (Suffk/Bedfd/Leics/Essex); France & Flanders 1914–18 (Bedfd/Leics): Macedonia 1915–18 (Suffk); Gallipoli 1915–16

Above left *Back on the Rock. Men of the 6th Battalion tread in the footsteps of their Regimental forebears in Gibralter.* **Above right** *The Corporal's brassard shows him to be part of the Regimental display unit.*

(Essex); Gaza (Norfk/Suffk/Bedfd/Essex/Nthptn); Palestine, Mesopotamia 1914–18 (Leics).

Dunkirk 1940 (Lincs/Suffk/Bedfd); Normandy Landing (Norfk/Lincs/Suffk); Brieux Bridgehead (Norfk); Venraij (Norfk/Suffk); North-West Europe 1940, 1944–45 (Norfk/Bedfd/Leics/Essex/Nthptn); Tobruk 1941 (Bedfd/Essex); Defence of Alamein Line (Essex); Salerno (Lincs/Leics); Anzio (Nthptn); Cassino I–II (Bedfd/Essex/Nthptn); Gothic Line (Lincs/Leics); Italy 1943–45 (Bedfd/Leics/Nthptn); Crete (Leics); Singapore Island (Norfk/Suffk); Malaya 1941–42 (Leics); Yu (Nthptn); Ngakyedauk Pass (Lincs); Imphal (Suffk/Nthptn); Chindits 1944 (Bedfd/Leics/Essex); Burma 1943–45 (Norfk/Lincs/Suffk/Nthptn).

Korea 1951–52, (Norfk).

'Dettingen' records the services of the 12th Foot, placed in the centre of King George II's front line in the Battle of Dettingen (1743). The King granted the Regiment the privilege of wearing a laurel leaf on the anniversary of the battle in recognition of their escorting him safely throughout. In later times the Suffolk Regiment altered the custom to that of wearing a rose on Dettingen Day.

'Mons' is remembered for the 'Mons Drum' of the Bedfordshire Regiment. The instrument was thrust into the care of a local peasant woman during the Mons offensive for safety. It was later 'rescued' and accorded a place of honour in the Regiment.

'Arras' was commemorated every year in the Essex Regiment before amalgamation on March 28.

'Singapore Island' marks the fall of Singapore in 1941, where the Cambridgeshire TA buried its regalia to avoid capture. The Battalion drums were recovered later and always paraded in silence as a solumn tribute to the men of East Anglia who never returned from Malaya. The drums are now in the care of the Suffolk Regimental Museum.

'Malaya 1941–42' was the hard-won battle honour of the Royal Leicestershire, whose 1st Battalion suffered such heavy casualties in the jungle campaign that its remnant was ordered to join forces with the similarly-depleted East Surreys in order to operate as an effective unit.

Anniversaries

Almanza Day (April 25): the former Regimental Day of the Royal Norfolk Regiment is observed by 1RAR to honour the sterling 9th and its heroic attempts to reverse the battle's fate.

Minden Day (August 1): the chief battle anniversary of the Suffolk Regiment has always been celebrated with the wearing of red and yellow roses. 1RAR maintains this custom of the 'Minden regiments' and every member of the Battalion wears a red and yellow 'Minden' flash on his sleeve.

Sobraon Day (February 10): 2RAR maintain the Royal Lincolns' Regimental Day to commemorate the gallant 10th's noted parade-like advance on the Sikh guns at Sobraon in 1846. Their cool discipline was much admired by the enemy artillerymen, but the guns inflicted a heavy toll on the redcoat lines before the antagonists were able to close.

Talavera Day (July 27): the Regimental Day of the Northamptonshires is perpetuated in 2RAR to commemorate the celebrated manoeuvre of the 48th Regiment to plug a gap in Wellington's line at Talavera in 1809. The Duke's despatch gave mention to the episode: 'The battle was certainly saved by the advance, position, and steady conflict of the 48th Regiment'. Officers of the Northamptonshire Regiment would drink to the memory of the gallant 48th from the 'Talavera Cup'.

Salamanca Day (July 22): the Essex Regiment kept this day as a tribute to the Irish-raised 2nd Battalion 44th Regiment, whose doughty warriors captured the Regimental Eagle of the French 62nd at Salamanca in 1812. The Battalion was disbanded at the close of the Napoleonic Wars, but the Essex Regiment continued to preserve its memory by playing a medley of Irish airs at *Reveille* on St Patrick's Day.

Blenheim Day (August 13): the other anniversary celebrated in 3RAR is that formerly observed by the Bedfordshire & Hertfordshire Regiment.

Royal Tiger Day (June 25): the Regimental Day of the Royal Leicestershire Regiment marks the day in 1825 when George IV conferred the Royal Tiger emblem, superscribed 'Hindoostan', on the 17th (Leicestershire) Regiment in recognition of its services to the crown in India, where it fought 'up country' against the warrior Gurkha.

Customs

Once a year on a special Guest Night in the Lincolnshire Regiment, a special toast was made to Charles Austin, Citizen of the USA. Austin regularly dined with the officers during the Regiment's stay in Yokohama between 1868 and 1871, and on his death left the balance of his property to 'HM 10th Lincolnshire Regiment in memory of 50 glorious years of friendship'.

The Wolfe Society: three of the founder Regi-

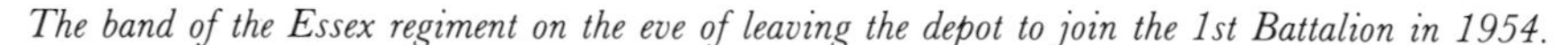

The band of the Essex regiment on the eve of leaving the depot to join the 1st Battalion in 1954.

Colour of Duroure's Regiment (the 12th Foot).

'The Steelbacks' at Laing's Nek, 1880, otherwise known as Majuba Hill. The 58th had the distinction, here, of being the last regiment to carry its colours in battle.

ments contributed their membership of the Wolfe Society to the RAR. The Suffolk Regiment was recognised for the Society by virtue of the fact that James Wolfe served with the 12th Foot as a subaltern and went with it to take part in the Battle of Dettingen. The Leicestershire and Northamptonshire Regiments fought together directly under Wolfe at the Siege of Louisburg in 1758. The Royal Leicestershire Regiment honoured the great General's memory by playing *Wolfe's Lament* on 1st Battalion church parade. On Guest Nights in the Officer's Mess a black crepe ribbon would be laid across the dining table: lozenge shaped in the 1st Battalion and rectangular in the 2nd, both designed to embrace the Regimental silver.

Mascot

None.

Dress distinctions

A blue dress cap with scarlet band and piping, mounted with the Regimental badge, the Castle and Key of Gibraltar upon an eight-pointed star. A blue side hat with scarlet peak and gold piping. A khaki beret mounted with a black flash for the badge. Collar badges are worn to Battalion pattern: 1RAR: the Castle of Gibraltar (Suffolks) superimposed by the figure of Britannia (Norfolks). 2RAR: the Sphinx with 'Egypt' (Lincolns) above a 'Talavera' scroll (Northamptons). 3RAR: the Imperial Eagle (Essex) within the Garter (Bedfords). Buttons are embossed with the Royal Tiger within an unbroken laurel wreath (Royal Leicestershire). A laurel wreath was conferred on the Regiment in an unbroken form to commemorate the January morning in 1777 when 250 men of the 17th Foot broke their way out of a cordon of 3,000 American troops under the command of General Washington at Princeton.

Lanyards are worn to Battalion pattern: 1RAR — yellow, from the facing colour restored to the Norfolks in 1905 and to the Suffolks in 1899; 2 RAR — black, from the former facings of the 58th Regiment; and 3RAR — rose purple, from the facing of the 56th Regiment, restored to the Essex in 1936. Prior to its disbanding in 1970 the 4th (Leicestershire) Battalion wore lanyards to grey/red/black. Pearl grey facings of the 17th were restored to the Leicestershire Regiment in 1931, and black was worn in the officers' full dress lace as a sign of mourning for General Wolfe.

The stable-belt is blue with a central scarlet band divided by a narrow yellow centre stripe. Members of the display unit wear a black brassard bearing the Regimental badge.

Marches

Rule Britannia/Speed The Plough, the Regimental Quick March combines the marches of the Royal Norfolk and Suffolk Regiments. *Rule Britannia* refers to the figure of Britannia worn as the Regimental badge of the Royal Norfolk Regiment. *The Northamptonshire*, the Regimental Slow March comes from the Northamptonshire Regiment and was known to the men of that corps as 'Hard Up'. *The Lincolnshire Poacher* (ex Lincolnshire and Northamptonshire Regiments). *The Duchess* (ex 2nd Battalion Suffolk Regiment). *Mandolinata* (ex Bedfordshire & Hertfordshire Regiment). *The Valse Destiny*, this march was regarded as sacred music in the Bedfordshire & Hertfordshire Regiment because of it being the last thing played by the 1st Battalion band before going off to war in 1914. *The Pilgrim's Hymn*, adopted for the Bedfordshire & Hertfordshire Regiment in 1941 in respect to Bedford's link with John Bunyan. *The Hampshires,* (ex the Essex Regiment). *A Hunting Call*, adopted by the Leicestershire Regiment in 1933 from the county militia, to replace *Romaika*, a Greek dance tune introduced to the 17th by a bandmaster transferred from the 64th Regiment.

Nicknames

'The Vikings': the nickname of 1RAR alludes to the Viking culture of Norfolk and Suffolk. It was probably created to compete with the inherited nicknames of the other Battalions.

'The Poachers': 2RAR, from its Lincolnshire content.

'The Pompadours': 3RAR: a legacy of the Essex Regiment, which inherited the name from the old 56th of Foot. The 56th were known as 'The Pompadours' from their unique rose purple facings, said to have been the favourite colour of Madame de Pompadour.

'The Black Cuffs': a name given to the 58th (Rutlandshire) Regiment during the Maori Wars of the 1840s, from their tunic facings. Before the advent of county affiliations in 1782 the 58th liked to be known as 'The Black Regiment'.

'The Charps and Dils': the 'Beds and Herts' (or Bedfordshire & Hertfordshire Regiment), from their time in India, where the Hindustani words

The raising of Douglas's Regiment (16th Foot) in 1688.

Men of the 10th (North Lincolnshire) Regiment spike Sikh guns at Sobraon.

charp (bed) and *dil* (heart) were used.

'The Cobblers': the Northamptonshire Regiment, from the county's boot and shoe industry.

'The Featherbeds': a clever jibe at the Bedfordshire Regiment's distinct lack of battle honours prior to the First World War.

'The Fighting Ninth': a reputation won by the 1st Battalion of the 9th Regiment at the Battle of Rolica, where its timely support of the 29th Regiment in a critical stage of the battle prompted a lasting friendship between the two Regiments.

'The Fighting Northamptons': the Northamptonshire Regiment upheld a consistently high fighting record.

'The Four and Eights': the 48th (Northamptonshire) Regiment, from its numerals.

'The Holy Boys': the 9th (East Norfolk) Regiment, from its Britannia badge, which was often mistaken for being the Virgin Mary in Spain during the Peninsula War. Another theory imputes the name to the men selling off their issue bibles.

'The Little Fighting Fours': the 44th (East Essex) Regiment, from the numerals carried on the soldiers' packs; probably a reference to the Battalion which carried off a French Eagle at Salamanca.

'The Old Dozen', or 'Old Twelfth': the 12th Regiment of Foot.

'The Peacemakers': another derisive name for the Bedfordshire Regiment relating to its small list of pre-1914 battle honours.

'The Silly Suffolks': a name inspired by the lines of slow-witted rural lads of Suffolk who filled the Battalions of their county Regiment in the early days of the First World War.

'The Steelbacks': a proud name owned to by one or two regiments in the days of the lash, when it was a point of honour among the grenadiers not to 'sing out' at the halberds. The 58th Regiment was recognised for using the name more than any other and the reputation was carried on by the Northamptonshire Regiment.

'The Tigers': of the five regiments that were awarded the Royal Tiger emblem for long years of service in India, only the Leicestershire wore the badge without embellishment and thereby gained the nickname.

'The Yellow-bellies': the Lincolnshire Regiment, from an old English name for a type of eel caught in the Fens.

'The Yellow Devils': a reputation gained by the Bedfordshire Regiment at Gallipoli, where they were picked out by a yellow flash on their helmets.

Recruiting

Lincolnshire, Leicestershire, Northamptonshire, Cambridgeshire, Norfolk, Suffolk, Bedfordshire, Hertfordshire and Essex. RHQ: Gibraltar Barracks, Bury St Edmunds.

The Devonshire and Dorset Regiment (11th, 39th, 54th Foot)

Insignia

The Sphinx with 'Marabout' superimposed upon the Castle of Exeter: the Devonshire Regiment adopted the Castle and Star from the county Militia in 1883, The Sphinx, from the badge of the Dorset Regiment, was awarded to the 54th in 1802.

The Castle and Key superscribed 'Gibraltar 1779–83' with the motto *Montis Insignia Calpe*: awarded to the 39th Regiment in 1836 in

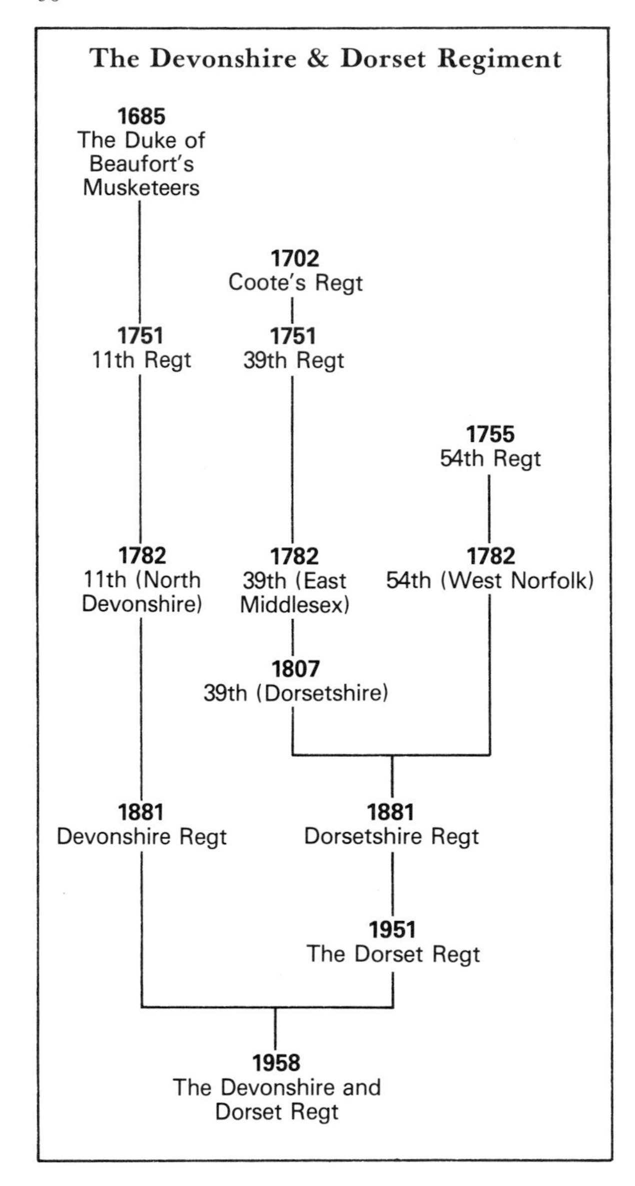

recognition of its part in the Great Siege of Gibraltar 56 years before. The emblem was borne on the Colours and appointments of the 39th until 1881, when it was combined with the 54th's Sphinx to create the Dorset Regiment badge.

The Sphinx with 'Marabout': the battle honour 'Marabout' was granted to the 54th Regiment in 1840 to commemorate its single-handed capture of Fort Marabout at the entrance to the harbour of Alexandria on August 21 1801. The 'Marabout Gun', a prize taken in the battle, is the centrepiece of the Dorset Military Museum.

Semper fidelis: the motto of the Devonshire Regiment (Always faithful).

Primus in Indis: the motto of the Dorset Regiment (First in India) relates to the 39th Regiment and its proud claim of being the first of His Majesty's regiments to serve in India (1757).

Honours

Dettingen (11th); Plassey, Martinique 1794 (39th); Marabout (54th); Albuhera (39th); Salamanca (11th); Vittoria (39th); Pyrenees, Nivelle, Nive, Orthes (11th/39th); Toulouse (11th); Peninsula (11th/39th); Ava (54th); Maharajpore, Sevestopol (39th); Afghanistan 1879–80 (11th); Tirah (Devon/Dorset); Defence of Ladysmith (Devons); Relief of Ladysmith, South Africa 1899–1902 (Devon/Dorset).

Mons, Marne 1914 (Dorset); La Bassée 1914 (Devons); Ypres 1915, 1917 (Devon/Dorset); Loos, Somme 1916, 1918, Bois des Buttes (Devons); Hindenburg Line (Devon/Dorset); Sambre (Dorset); Vittorio Veneto, Doiran 1917, 1918 (Devons); Suvla, Gaza (Dorset); Palestine 1917–18 (Devons); Shaiba, Ctesiphon, Khan Baghdadi (Dorset); Mesopotamia 1916–18 (Devons).

St Omer–La Bassée (Dorset); Normandy Landing, Caen (Devon/Dorset); Arnhem 1944, Aam, Geilenkirchen (Dorset); Rhine, North-West Europe 1944–45 (Devons); Landing in Sicily (Devon/Dorset); Regalbuto (Devons); Malta 1940–42 (Devon/Dorset); Imphal (Devons); Kohima, Mandalay (Dorset); Myinmu Bridgehead, Burma 1943–45 (Devons).

'Plassey' is unique to the Regiment. June 23 was set aside in the Dorset Regiment for the celebration of Clive's victory at Palasi in 1757, where 300 men of the 39th, together with 2,000 native troops, defeated an enemy force 50,000 strong. A silver-headed Drum Major's staff, presented to the 39th by the Nawab of Arcot for its gallantry at Palasi, is still in the possession of the Dorset Military Museum.

'Salamanca' is important in Devonshire Regimental history for the legendary advance of the 11th against the guns of the French rearguard. The battle, which all but destroyed the Battalion, was always commemorated by the Devons on July 22.

'Regalbuto' was won by the 2nd Devons and 1st Dorsets in a five-day battle in the hills above Regal-

Above right *A romanticised painting of the 39th at Plassey in 1757.*

Right *Painting of the charge of the 1st Devons at Wagon Hill, January 6 1900.*

The epic of the Sarah Sands, *November 11 1857.*

buto in Sicily (1943). July 29 was reserved for its celebration in the Devonshire Regiment.

'Imphal' was remembered by the Devonshire Regiment as Nippon Hill Day (April 11). Nippon Hill was the key position in the Japanese line of defence on the Tamu Road in Burma, that was taken by the 1st Devons in 1944 and held despite all attempts to dislodge them.

'Kohima' was commemorated in the Dorset Regiment every year on May 13.

Anniversaries

Amalgamation Day (May 17): the D&D was formed in 1958 and Foundation Day is celebrated each year with a reunion at Exeter. All of the Regiment's major parades are scheduled to take place on the nearest convenient date to Amalgamation Day.

Wagon Hill Day (January 6): the battle for Ladysmith is commemorated in the way of the Devonshire Regiment, with Warrant Officers and Sergeants invited to the Officers Mess for the evening.

Bois des Buttes Day (May 27): the bloody encounter in which the 2nd Devons were awarded a unit *Croix de Guerre avec Palme* is remembered for the tenacity of the men, who, although completely surrounded in an area where gas and shellfire had annihilated their supporting units, defeated all enemy attempts to advance. The Battalion put up a splendid resistance to the German drive on Paris in 1918 and gained much prestige for its Regiment, but lost its Colonel, 22 officers and 528 men in the process.

Sarah Sands Day (November 11): in 1857 a Battalion of 54th men set sail for India to reinforce the army engaged in putting down the Mutiny and a great fire broke out on their troop-ship SS *Sarah Sands*, when 800 miles from Mauritius. It became obvious that the fire would spread to the powder magazine and the crew, already close to mutiny, took to the boats, and left it to soldiers and their wives and children, to fight the flames. This was done with great courage and the fire was brought under control after 18 hours. On a command of

'The Janners' training in Northern Ireland, 1983.

Queen Victoria a general order was issued, to be read out at the head of every regiment in the Army, commending 'The remarkable gallantry and resolution' of the Regiment. Sarah Sands Day is usually celebrated with a tough ten-mile inter-platoon march and shoot competition (the Sarah Sands Gallop).

Customs

The Duke of Kent's Punch Bowl: when HRH Prince Edward, 1st Duke of Kent, took over the Governorship of Gibraltar in 1802, his harsh discipline proved so unpopular that two Regiments of the garrison marched on the Residence intent on his assassination. His life was saved, however, by the timely intervention of the 54th Regiment, who scattered the mutineers with a volley. The Prince remembered the Regiment's loyalty with a gift in constant use in the mess, and serves to mark the link with successive Dukes of Kent, who traditionally become Colonel-in-Chief of the Regiment. It was a custom of the Dorset Regiment to drink a Bumper Toast to the memory of the 1st Duke.

The French Toast: the custom of drinking a toast to the French Army after the Loyal Toast originated in the Devonshire Regiment and the *Croix de Guerre* bestowed by the French Government for the remarkable stand of the 2nd Battalion at Bois des Buttes.

Mascot

None.

Dress distincitons

A blue dress cap mounted with the Regimental badge on a green backing: the Castle of Exeter superimposed by a Sphinx inscribed 'Marabout'. At the top the motto *Semper fidelis* and, below, *Primus in Indis*. The side hat is grass green (piped gold for officers) with blue flaps. Buttons are stamped with the Prince of Wales' Plume (the Regiment is part of the Prince of Wales' Division). Lanyards of grass green (Sergeants and above). The *Croix de Guerre* ribbon is worn by all ranks as an arm badge. The

Regimental drummers at Tidworth Tattoo in 1973 in the white helmet and the junior drummers' dress cap. The helmet is distinguished by a green pagri today. The second rank shows musicians of the 13th/18th Hussars.

stable-belt is grass green with a tawny orange centre strip. Bandsmen and drummers wear a white pith helmet personalised with a green puggaree. Their scarlet coats are faced in green, a Regimental colour restored to the Dorsets in 1904 and the Devons in 1905. The 'champion' Duke of Kent's Platoon is distinguished by a red and green (*Croix de Guerre*) lanyard in No 2 Dress.

Marches

Widdecombe Fair/Maid of Glenconnel/We've Lived And Loved Together, the Regimental March is a composition of the founder Regiments' marches. *The Maid of Glenconnel.* is of Dorset origin, and was often played along with *Farmer's Boy*, the common march of the Wessex regiments. *Widdecombe Fair* and *We've Lived And Loved Together* were the marches of the Devonshire Regiment; the latter dates from 1812 and took the nickname 'Turnips' from a substituted lyric to that effect.

Nicknames

'The Janners': a modern Regimental nickname, from the local term for soldier.

'The Bloody Eleventh': a proud reputation earned by the 11th at Salamanca, where heavy losses were sustained in the evening assault on the French rearguard.

'The Flamers': a name acquired by the 54th Foot after an incident at the port of New London in 1781, where 12 American privateers were burnt by the redcoats.

'The Green Linnets': the 39th Regiment, from its green facings.

'The Popinjays': the 54th Regiment: an 18th century term for their facing colour, popinjay green.

'Sankey's Horse': from an episode in 1707, when the 39th were unceremoniously bundled on mules in order to get them to Almanza in time for the battle.

'Daft and Dozy': a term applied by other regiments as a translation of the D&D insignia, which the wearers see as 'Death and Destruction'.

Recruiting

Devon and Dorset. RHQ: Wyvern Barracks, Exeter.

The Light Infantry (13th, 32nd, 46th, 51st, 53rd, 68th, 85th, 105th, 106th, Foot)

Insignia

The bugle horn stringed: the emblem which went to form the basis of all modern light infantry badges was first adopted at the outset of the Napoleonic Wars by the light company of each regiment and those regiments converted whole to light infantry or rifles. Its form relates to the hunting horn carried by woodsmen of the 18th century, on whom the rapid movements of the light infantry were founded.

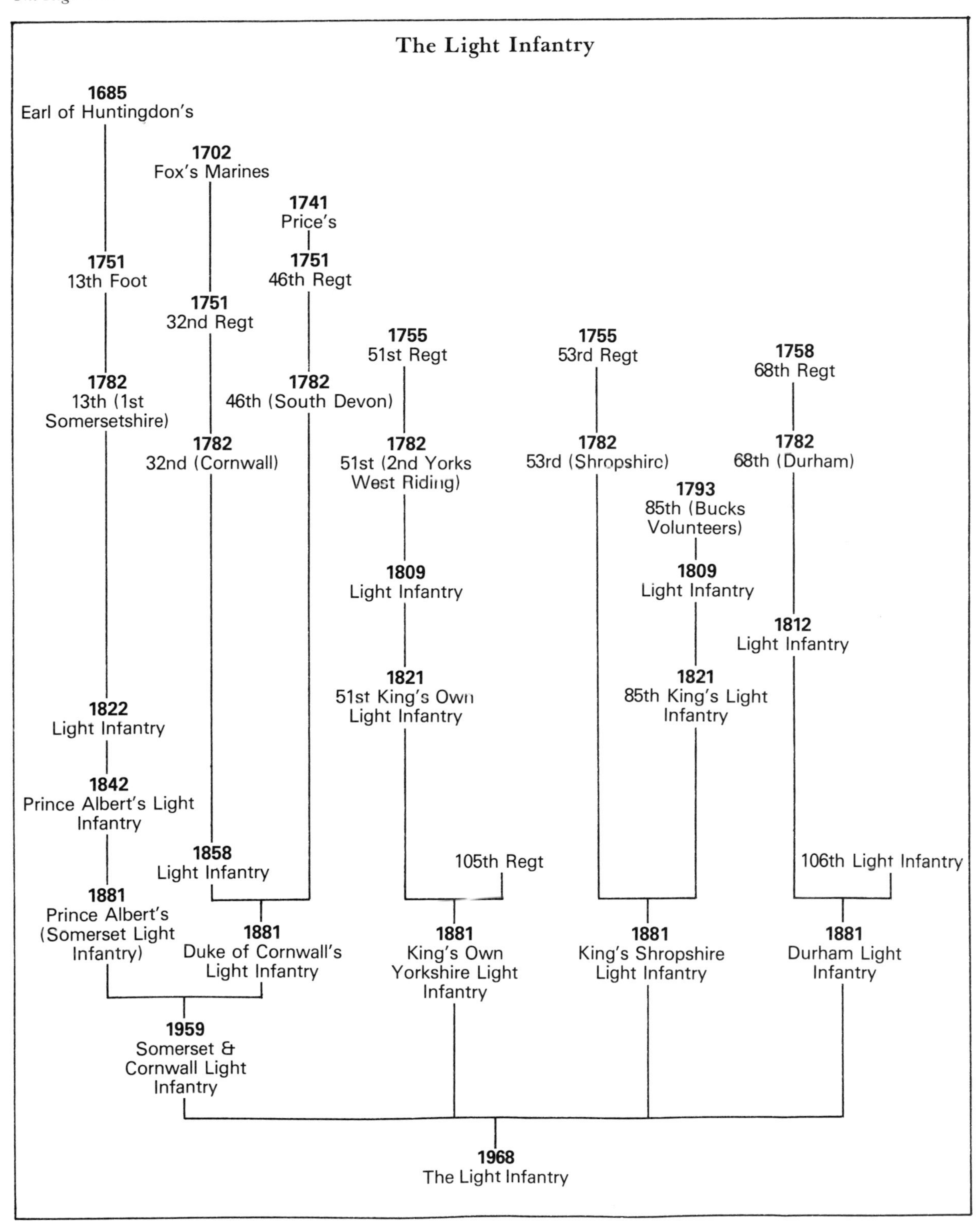
The Light Infantry
1685
Earl of Huntingdon's
1702
Fox's Marines
1741
Price's
1751
13th Foot
1751
46th Regt
1751
32nd Regt
1755
51st Regt
1755
53rd Regt
1758
68th Regt
1782
13th (1st Somersetshire)
1782
46th (South Devon)
1782
32nd (Cornwall)
1782
51st (2nd Yorks West Riding)
1782
53rd (Shropshire)
1782
68th (Durham)
1793
85th (Bucks Volunteers)
1809
Light Infantry
1809
Light Infantry
1812
Light Infantry
1821
51st King's Own Light Infantry
1821
85th King's Light Infantry
1822
Light Infantry
1842
Prince Albert's Light Infantry
1858
Light Infantry
105th Regt
106th Light Infantry
1881
Prince Albert's (Somerset Light Infantry)
1881
Duke of Cornwall's Light Infantry
1881
King's Own Yorkshire Light Infantry
1881
King's Shropshire Light Infantry
1881
Durham Light Infantry
1959
Somerset & Cornwall Light Infantry
1968
The Light Infantry

Above left *The double past is intrinsic to the Light Division.*

Left *The band and Corps of Bugles.*

Above *Light Infantry reception, Shrewsbury.*

The Sphinx superscribed 'Egypt': awarded to the 13th Regiment in 1802 for its part in the campaign in Egypt of the previous year.

The Mural Crown superscribed 'Jellalabad': awarded to the 13th Regiment in 1842 in recognition of its epic defence of Jellalabad on the North-West Frontier of India. The device was worn in conjunction with the bugle horn to form the badge of the Somerset Light Infantry. The embattled Crown was originally presented by the ancient Romans to the soldier who first carried the ramparts of a besieged city.

Aucto Splendore Resurgo: the motto of the 85th Regiment (Rise again with increased splendour) appertains to the fact that previous regiments existed with the same number.

Cede nullis: the motto of the King's Own Yorkshire Light Infantry (Yield to none) comes from the old 105th Regiment.

Faithful: a prefix motto conferred upon the 68th Regiment after its successful campaign against the Caribs of Antigua in 1764. The privilege is said to have been withdrawn in 1780 due to pressure from other regiments jealous of the distinction.

Honours

Gibraltar 1704–05, Dettingen (13th/32nd); Minden (51st); Nieuport, St Lucia 1796 (53rd); Corunna (32nd/51st); Fuentes d'Onor (51st/85th); Salamanca (32nd/51st/53rd/68th); Vittoria (51st/53rd/68th); Pyrenees (32nd/51st/68th); Nivelle (32nd/51st/53rd); Orthes (32nd/51st/68th); Peninsula (32nd/51st/53rd/68th/85th); Bladensburg (85th); Waterloo (32nd/51st); Afghanistan 1839 (13th); Inkerman (68th); Sevastopol (13th/46th/68th); Persia (106th); Lucknow (32nd/53rd); New Zealand (68th); Pegu, Ali Masjid (51st); S Africa 1878–80 (13th); Afghanistan 1878–80 (51st/85th); Burma 1885–87 (SLI/KOYLI); Modder River (KOYLI); Paardeberg (DOCLI/KSLI); Relief of Ladysmith (SLI/DLI); South Africa 1899–1902 (common to all).

Mons (DOCLI/KOYLI); Le Cateau (KOYLI); Aisne 1914, 1918 (SLI); Messines 1914, 1917, 1918 (KOYLI/DLI); Ypres 1914, 1915, 1917, 1918 (common to all); Hooge (DLI); Somme 1916, 1918 (common to all); Albert 1916, 1918 (SLI); Arras 1917, 1918 (common to all); Passchendaele (DOCLI); Cambrai 1917, 1918 (common to all); Havrincourt (KOYLI); Doiran 1917, 1918 (DOCLI/KSLI); Jerusalem (KSLI); Palestine 1917–18, Tigris 1916 (SLI).

Afghanistan 1919 (DLI).

Norway 1940 (KOYLI/KSLI); Dunkirk 1940 (DLI); Normandy Landing (KSLI); Fontenoy le Pesnil (KOYLI); Hill 112 (SLI/DOCLI); Gheel (DLI); North-West Europe 1940, 1944–45 (common to all); El Alamein, Mareth (DLI); Argoub Sellah (KOYLI); Primosole Bridge (DLI); Sicily 1943 (KOYLI); Salerno (KOYLI/DLI); Anzio (KOYLI/ KSLI); Cassino II (SLI/DOCLI); Italy 1943–45, (SLI/KSLI); North Arakan (SLI); Kohima (DLI); Burma 1942, 1943–45 (KOYLI).

Korea 1951–53 (KSLI/DLI).

'Minden' was celebrated in the King's Own Yorkshire Light Infantry on August 1, and its members wore a white rose in the cap to remind them of the story of their forebears wearing roses in the battle. The Minden wreath (of bay and laurel) was carried on the Regimental Colour.

'Nieuport' was unique to the King's Shropshire Light Infantry and commemorates the gallant defence of that town by the 53rd Regiment in October 1793. The garrison won acclaim for its tenacious stand, which held off a besieging force of 12,000 French troops for ten days.

'Bladensburg' was won by the 85th in America in 1814. A Colour of the James City Light Infantry

The Siege of Badajoz, in which Joseph Dyas of the 51st earned great approbation for his untiring attempts to lead the forlorn hope into the breeches. In 1908 the 1st KOYLI revived the toast to 'Ensign Dyas and His Stormers'.

and a Guidon of the James City Light Dragoons were taken in the battle and now reside in the Shropshire Light Infantry Museum.

'Inkerman' was observed by the Durham Light Infantry every November 5.

'Lucknow' was an important battle honour for the Duke of Cornwall's Light Infantry and November 17 was set aside each year to commemorate the 32nd's dogged defence of the city, for which it was rebadged as a regiment of light infantry. The privations of the siege were such that the officers were forced to conserve what little wine they had to toast the Queen's health on her birthday, a custom which led the Regiment thereafter to make the Loyal Toast on the Sovereign's birthday only.

'Paardeberg' was special to the 2nd Battalion King's Shropshire Light Infantry and February 27 was kept by the unit as Paardeberg Day.

'Hooge' was the subject of a Regimental Day in the Durham Light Infantry (August 9 1915).

'Anzio' (May 14) was the Regimental Day of 1st Battalion King's Shropshire Light Infantry.

'Dominica' is an honour of the Regiment not displayed on the Colours. It represents the defence of the Island in 1805 against a superior French force and was awarded solely to the 46th Regiment.

Anniversaries

Salamanca Day (July 22): the Regimental Day of the Light Infantry is held to celebrate the 1812 battle in which the 32nd, 51st, 53rd and 68th Regiments took part. The anniversary was not previously celebrated by any of the founder Regiments, but represents a time of great glory for these units, many of which were converted to light infantry during the Peninsula War.

Customs

Sergeants' sashes are worn over the left shoulder (see dress distinctions). Officers of the Somerset Light Infantry wore a cavalry pattern mess vest (see under 'Pearce's Dragoons' in the 'Nicknames' section).

White roses are worn in the headgear of all ranks on Minden Day, a former custom of KOYLI.

Officers of the DLI and KSLI were absolved of the need to drink the Loyal Toast, a privilege maintained by the Light Infantry today. This privilege was bestowed upon the 85th in 1821, after members of the Regiment had saved the King from a mob at the Theatre Royal in Brighton.

Mascot

None.

Dress distinctions

A rifle green beret mounted with the bugle horn badge. Officers and senior NCOs wear a dress cap of the same colour. The badge is coloured red in the area between bugle and strings in compliance with the custom of the Duke of Cornwall's Light Infantry to wear their badge on a red backing. This symbolised an old privilege of the 46th Regiment, whose drummers and light companymen were allowed to sport red pom-poms in their headgear in honour of a daring attack made on the American camp at Brandywine in 1777. The Light Company of the 46th was reputed to have worn red feathers in their caps after the battle as a sign to the enemy that they alone were responsible for the raid. A rifle-green side hat. Stable-belts and lanyards are rifle-green. Bandsmen and buglers wear green regimentals, with black belts, and busbies fashioned on the pattern adopted by the rifle regiments in the 1870s. These were first worn in the Light Infantry in 1973. Officers and warrant officers wear the 'Inkerman' chain from a black shoulder-belt. Sergeants wear this legacy of the Durham Light Infantry from their scarlet sash. Sergeants' sashes are worn from the left shoulder and knotted on the right hip, a unique Regimental custom confirmed solely to the 13th (Somerset) Light Infantry in 1865. Sergeants of the 13th have always worn their sashes of rank in the manner used by officers. Theorists have attributed this to a privilege supposedly granted to the Sergeants of the Regiment for taking over the duties of their officers killed in battle, notably Killiecrankie in 1689 or Culloden in 1746. Officer casualties among Hastings Regiment, at the former, and Pulteney's, at the latter, however, do not support this. Blue facings were inherited from the SLI, KOYLI, and KSLI. The Somerset Light Infantry was authorised to wear the colour in 1842 on becoming 'Prince Albert's' and continued to be the only non-Royal regiment to boast blue facings. The 51st and 85th Regiments came by their blue facings in 1821, when King George IV dubbed them both 'King's Light Infantry'.

Marches

The Light Infantry, the Regimental March. *Silver Bugles*. *Prince Albert/Trelawney* (Somerset & Cornwall Light Infantry). *With A Jockey To The Fair/Minden March* (King's Own Yorkshire Light Infantry). *Old Towler/Daughter Of The Regiment* (King's Shropshire

Ensign to the Colour receives the Queen's Colour from the RSM.

'The Red Feathers'. A light company man of the 46th Regiment wearing the red cap feather, 1780.

Left *Colours dipped in Royal salute, 2 LI, 1983.*

Above *'Pearce's Dragoons'.*

Below left *No 2 dress; note the black waist-belts and the Sergeant's left-shoulder sash with its attached chain.*

Light Infantry). *The Light Barque* (Durham Light Infantry). *Keel Row* and *Moneymusk*, together, form the Regimental Double Past (DLI).

Nicknames

'The Bleeders': an unenviable name owned to by the 13th Regiment prior to their posting to the North-West Frontier in 1842, where their image quickly improved to hero status.

'The Docs': the Duke of Cornwall's Light Infantry, from its initials.

'The Elegant Extracts': the 85th (Bucks Volunteers) in 1811, when its officers were dispersed to other regiments on the orders of the Duke of York for internal bickering. The 'Elegant Extracts' were the officers summoned from other corps to fill the vacuum.

'The Faithful Durhams': a name given to the Durham Light Infantry with respect to their old motto *Faithful*.

'The Honeysuckers': a reputation atttracted by honey-poachers of the 53rd Regiment during the Peninsula War.

'The Illustrious Garrison': a term of acclaim won by the 13th Regiment in the defence of Jellalabad in 1842. Also 'Jellalabad Heroes'.

'The Koylis': the King's Own Yorkshire Light Infantry, from its initials.

The 'Lacedemonians': the 46th Regiment, from a reputed outbreak of Lacedemonian discipline in one of its early Colonels.

'Murray's Bucks': the 46th Foot, about 1745.

'The Old Five and Threepennies': the 53rd Regiment, from its numerals.

'Pearce's Dragoons': the 13th Foot *circa* 1706, when the Regiment was told off for mounted service under Colonel Pearce to offset the shortage of cavalry in Spain. Colonel Barrymore returned to England with his officers to re-raise the 13th, whilst 'Pearce's Dragoons' went on to distinguish themselves in their new role until destroyed at Almanza in 1707. Officers of the Somerset Light Infantry began the singular practice of wearing cavalry pattern mess dress to commemorate this episode in the Regiment's history.

'The Red Feathers': the 46th Foot, from the cap feathers worn by the light company to signify its part in a night raid on the American camp at the Brandywine in 1777.

'The Red Regiment': Napoleon's term for the 53rd (Shropshire) Regiment, whose 2nd Battalion spent a long period with him on St Helena. The name comes from the Regiment's facings, which was also to lead to the name 'The Brickdusts'.

'The Sets': the Somerset Light Infantry.

Recruiting

Durham, South Yorkshire, Shropshire, Somerset, Avon and Cornwall. RHQ: moved from Shrewsbury to Peninsula Barracks, Winchester in 1983.

The Prince of Wales's Own Regiment of Yorkshire (14th, 15th Foot)

Insignia

The White Rose of York superimposed upon an eight-pointed star: the badge adopted by the East Yorkshire Regiment in 1881. The Prince of Wales' Plume: granted to the 14th Regiment in 1876, when the Prince of Wales (later King Edward VII) presented new Colours to the 1st Battalion in India and asked for the Regiment to be known in future as The Prince of Wales's Own. The White Horse of

Top *The 14th at Waterloo. The youthful appearance of the 3rd Battalion committed it to garrison duty, until a representation was made to Lord Hill, whereupon the Duke of Wellington inspected the unit and declared it fit to join battle with the French.*

Above *Imphal Day, when the Regimental Colour is garlanded with a wreath of white roses. The drummers' uniform is distinguished by white facings.*

Below *Sergeants in No 1 dress.*

Hanover with motto *Nec aspera terrent*: conferred on the 14th Regiment by King George III in 1765 as a token of his pleasure at the turn-out of its guard detachments at Windsor and Hampton Court in the same year. The grenadiers were permitted to retain the Horse on the new bearskin caps being adopted by the Army and officers of the Regiment began to incorporate the design in their cap badge in 1816.

The Royal Tiger superscribed 'India': bestowed on the 14th Regiment in 1838 for continuous service in India between the years 1807 and 1831. The device was carried on the Colours and buttons of the West Yorkshire Regiment.

Honours

Namur 1695 (14th); Blenheim, Ramillies, Oudenarde, Malplaquet, Louisburg, Quebec 1759, Martinique 1762, Havannah, St Lucia 1778, Martinique 1794, 1809 (15th); Tournay, Corunna (14th); Guadaloupe 1810 (15th); Java, Waterloo, Bhurtpore, Sevastopol, New Zealand (14th); Afghanistan 1879–80 (14th/15th); Relief of Ladysmith (W Yorks); South Africa 1899–1902 (W Yorks/E Yorks).

Aisne 1914, 1918, (E Yorks); Armentières 1914 (W Yorks/E Yorks); Neuve Chapelle (W Yorks); Ypres 1915, 1917, 1918 (W Yorks/E Yorks); Loos, Somme 1916, 1918, Arras 1917, 1918 (E Yorks); Cambrai 1917, 1918 (W Yorks/E Yorks); Villers Brettoneux, Lys, Tardenois, (W Yorks); Selle (E Yorks); Piave, (W Yorks); Doiran 1917, (E Yorks); Suvla (W Yorks); Gallipoli 1915 (E Yorks).

Dunkirk 1940, Normandy Landing, Odon, Schaddenhof, North-West Europe 1940, 1944–45, (E Yorks); Keren (W Yorks); Gazala (E Yorks); Defence of Alamein Line (W Yorks); El Alamein, Mareth, Sicily 1943 (E Yorks); Pegu 1942, Yenangyaung 1942, Maungdaw, Defence of Sinzweya, Imphal, Bishenpur, Meiktila, Sittang 1945 (W Yorks); Burma 1942–45, (E Yorks).

Anniversaries

Quebec Day (September 13): the chief battle honour of the East Yorkshire Regiment is celebrated every year in the traditions of that Regiment, with a wreath of white roses carried on the Colour. The black edging on certain items of PWO dress follows the black mourning line worn in East Yorkshire officers' full dress in memory of General Wolfe. The Regiment's annual representation to the Wolfe Society is carried on by the PWO today.

Imphal Day (June 22): the principal anniversary of the West Yorkshire Regiment is maintained to commemorate the raising of the Siege of Imphal by the 1st and 2nd Battalions in Burma 1944. The day is doubly important in being the PWO birthday:

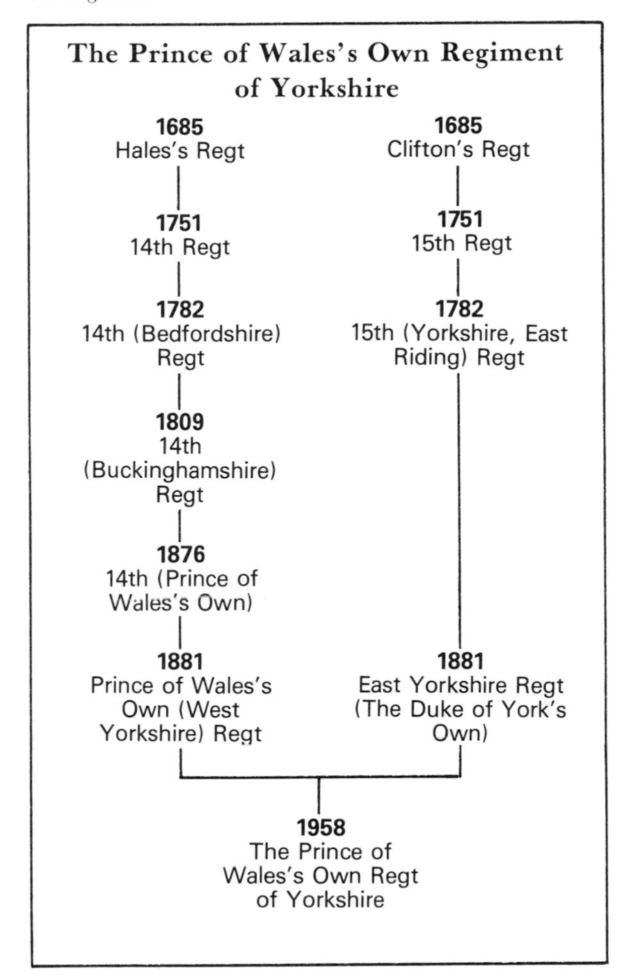

both founder Regiments were raised on June 22 1685.

Customs

It was usual in the East Yorkshire Regiment for the Mess President to both propose and second the Loyal Toast, a celebration of a dinner at which the second-in-command proved to be too inebriated to perform his duties.

Subalterns of the East Yorkshire Regiment who carried a Colour on parade for the first time were expected to pay 'footing' afterwards in the Sergeants' Mess.

Mascot

The East Yorkshires kept a dog mascot for many years.

Dress distinctions

A blue dress cap mounted with the Horse of Hanover badge. A buff side hat piped in black, with maroon flaps and peak. Buff was the facing colour of the West Yorkshire Regiment. Collar badges: an eight-pointed star with the White Rose of York on a black ground in the centre. Buttons are embossed with the Plume and motto of the Prince of Wales. The stable-belt is maroon, with a central yellow stripe and black edges.

Barrack dress showing the khaki beret. This type of beret became popular with regiments of the King's Division at the close of 1983.

Marches

Ca Ira/Yorkshire Lass, the Regimental Quick March combines the former marches of the West Yorkshire *(Ca Ira)* and East Yorkshire *(The Yorkshire Lass)*. *Ca Ira* has an interesting history and is unusual in being the only march gained in battle: Famars, May 23 1793. Confronted with the French revolutionaries' chant, and their clear advantage in the entrenched camp, Lieutenant Colonel Doyle (14th) rallied his

Above *The Battle of Famars, May 23 1793.*

Left *The 'Yorkys' passing York Minster in a Freedom March, 1981. Note the ski troops in white at the rear of the procession.*

men with the exclamation 'Come along my lads, let's break the scoundrels to their own damned tune, drummers, strike up *Ca Ira*!' And so, to the Revolution Song, the 14th went forward and successfully stormed the camp at Famars. When the Duke of York came to hear the story he bade the 14th to adopt the air as its rightful march. *Von England*, the Regimental Slow March is based on the March *The XVth von England*, first used by the 15th Regiment in the 1790s. Other marches played by the Regiment on occasions of review include *Three Quicksteps* from the 18th century (15th Foot), the 'troop' *Duke of York* (East Yorks) and *God Bless The Prince Of Wales*.

Nicknames

'The Yorkys': a modern, self-styled name.

'Calvert's Entire': a byname for the 14th Regiment during the years of 1806 and 1826, when it went under command of Sir Harry Calvert, a colourful squire who influenced the Regiment's county title to be changed from Bedfordshire to

Buckinghamshire. The name is believed to have come from a contemporary brewer of the same name, who was wont to call his beer 'Calvert's Entire'.

'The Iron-footed Bastards': the proud nickname of the 2nd Battalion East Yorkshire Regiment in 1880; inspired by a 250-mile slog to Kandahar in extremely hot weather.

'The Poona Guards': another sobriquet picked up by the 2nd East Yorkshires in India (1875–86).

'The Powos': the Prince of Wales's Own (West Yorkshire Regt), from its initials.

'The Snappers': a 'Snapper', in 18th century parlance, was a man who carried a firearm, but the East Yorkshires attributed their nickname to an incident at the Battle of Brandywine in 1777, where the Regiment's dwindling ammunition was distributed to its marksmen, while the remainder of its men had to run from tree to tree harmlessly 'snapping' their firelocks at the enemy.

Recruiting

West and central Yorkshire and North Humberside. RHQ: Imphal Barracks, York.

The Green Howards (19th Foot)

Insignia

The cipher of HRH Alexandra, Princess of Wales, interlaced with the Dannebrog inscribed with the date 1875, the Roman numerals *XIX* below and the whole surmounted by the Coronet of the Princess: granted to the 19th Regiment in 1875 at an inspection by Princess Alexandra. A request was made by the Princess at the same time for the corps to be named after her.

Honours

Malplaquet, Belleisle, Alma, Inkerman, Sevastopol, Tirah, Relief of Kimberley, Paardeberg, South Africa 1900–02.

Ypres 1914, 1915, 1917, Loos, Somme 1916, 1918, Arras 1917, 1918, Messines 1917, 1918,

'Green Howards' drummer in full dress; his scarlet tunic is distinguished by facings of grass green.

Valenciennes, Sambre, France & Flanders 1914–18, Vittorio Veneto, Suvla.

Afghanistan 1919.

Norway 1940, Normandy Landing, North-West Europe 1940, 1944–45, Gazala, El Alamein, Mareth, Akarit, Sicily 1943, Minturno, Anzio.

'Malplaquet' is recognised as being the bloodiest of Marlborough's battles and the 19th is prominent in history for its part in the fierce fighting that went on in and around the woods of Sart.

Anniversaries

Alma Day (September 20): the battle in which the 19th made its reputation at the defence of the Great Redoubt is celebrated in the Regiment every year with great pageantry. The colours and Russian

drums are trooped before the battalion ahead of the Corps of Drums.

Customs

The Regiment upholds a strong link with the Norwegian Royal Family.

Drums of the Russian Minsk and Vladimir regiments, captured at the Alma, are paraded on all occasions of Regimental importance.

Mascot

None.

Dress distinctions

A blue dress cap mounted with the Regimental badge, the Danish Cross interlaced with the cipher of Princess Alexandra; above, her Coronet. A khaki beret was adopted in 1983. A grass green side hat with blue flaps, piped in gold. Lanyards, facings, badge backings and stable-belt of grass green, the latter with a central white stripe. The green facings of the 19th were restored to the Regiment in 1899.

Left *Private Lyons winning his VC in the Crimea.*

Below *The 1912 squad at the Royal Tournament dressed as 'Green Howards' of 1743.*

The Champion Rifle (or King Olav) Company is distinguished by an unofficial arm badge: a crowned *O* on *V*.

Marches

The Bonnie English Rose, the Regimental Quickstep was adopted in 1868 and endorsed to the Regiment in 1881. *Maria Theresa*, the Slow March dates back to 1742 and Colonel Howard's diplomatic mission to Austria, where the Empress presented him with the score for this march which bears her name.

Nicknames

The Regiment's present title 'Green Howards' began as a nickname around 1744, when it went on campaign alongside another of the same name — Howard's. Both Regiments were told to distinguish between themselves, and this they did by their facing colours: thus, the 19th became 'The Green Howards' and the 3rd Foot was known as 'Howard's Buffs'.

Recruiting

North Yorkshire and Cleveland. RHQ: Richmond.

The Royal Highland Fusiliers (21st, 71st, 74th Foot)

Insignia

The monogram *HLI* surmounted by the Crown upon a grenade with the motto *Nemo nos impune lacessit*: the monogram of the Highland Light Infantry was used, within a bugle horn, to form the centre of that Regiment's badge. The Royal Scots Fusiliers wore the grenade badge with the Royal Arms superimposed. The motto (We are not provoked with impunity) was formerly used by both Regiments in one form or another.

The Royal Cipher surmounted by the Crown.

The Castle and Key superscribed 'Gibraltar 1780–83' with the motto *Montis Insignia Calpe*: granted to the Highland Light Infantry in 1909 to mark the part played by the 2nd Battalion 73rd Highland Regiment (later the 71st) in the Great Siege of Gibraltar.

An elephant superscribed 'Assaye': awarded to the 74th (Highland) Regiment with an Honorary Colour in 1803 as a testament to its devoted service at the Battle of Assaye. The device was eventually incorporated into the badge of the Highland Light Infantry.

Honours

Blenheim, Ramillies, Oudenarde, Malplaquet, Dettingen, Belleisle (21st); Hindoostan, Carnatic, Sholingur (71st); Mysore (71st/74th); Seringapatam (74th); Martinique 1794 (21st); Cape of Good Hope 1806, Rolica, Vimiera, Corunna (71st); Busaco (74th); Fuentes d'Onor (71st/74th); Ciudad Rodriogo (74th); Almaraz (71st); Badajoz, Salamanca (74th); Vittoria, Pyrenees (71st/74th); Nivelle, Nive (71st); Orthes (74th); Toulouse, Peninsula (71st/74th); Bladensburg (21st); Waterloo (71st); South Africa 1851–53 (74th); Alma, Inkerman (21st); Sevastopol (21st/71st); Central India (71st); South Africa 1879 (21st); Tel-el-kebir, Egypt 1882 (HLI); Burma 1885–87, Tirah (RSF); Modder River (HLI); Relief of Ladysmith

Far left *The Royal Scots Fusiliers in 1910. The singular uniform relied on a combination of fusilier cap, Scottish doublet (scarlet), and trews of Black Watch tartan.*

Left *A Highland Light Infantry officer, 1900. The only Highland regiment not to wear the kilt eventually became part of the Lowland tribe.*

Below left *Presentation of a new Assaye Colour in Germany, 1982. Escort to the old colour completing the troop through the remainder of the battalion.*

Above right *Piper George Clark of the 71st played his company on when wounded in the groin. His defiance was echoed in his words 'Deil ha' may saul, if ye shall want music'. Vimiera, 1808.*

Right *Fusiliers in Patrol Order, Belfast, 1983.*

(RSF); South Africa 1899–1902 (RSF/HLI).

Mons (RSF/HLI); Marne 1914 (RSF); Ypres 1914, 1915, 1917, 1918 (RSF/HLI); Loos (HLI); Somme 1916, 1918, Arras 1917, 1918 (RSF/HLI); Lys (RSF); Hindenburg Line (RSF/HLI); Doiran 1917, 1918 (RSF); Gallipoli 1915–16, Palestine 1917, 1918 (RSF/HLI); Mesopotamia 1916–18 (HLI).

Archangel 1919 (HLI).

Ypres–Comines Canal (RSF); Odon (RSF/HLI); Falaise (RSF); Scheldt (RSF/HLI); Walcheren, Reichswald (HLI); Rhine (RSF/HLI); Bremen (RSF); North-West Europe 1940, 1944–45, Keren, Cauldron (HLI); Landing in Sicily (RSF/HLI); Garigliano Crossing (RSF); Greece 1944–45 (HLI); North Arakan, Pinwe (RSF).

'Inkerman' was a battle commemorated by the Fusiliers to honour the men of the 21st and their gallant defence of 'The Barrier', a stone breastwork which had the distinction of being the only point not to change hands in the battle.

Anniversaries

Assaye Day (September 23): the Battle of Assaye (1803) was the keenest ever fought in India and is remembered in the RHF for the bloodbath in which the 74th Highlanders were all but destroyed as an effective unit. The Governor of India approved that the 74th and two other British regiments in the battle should receive an Honorary Colour with an

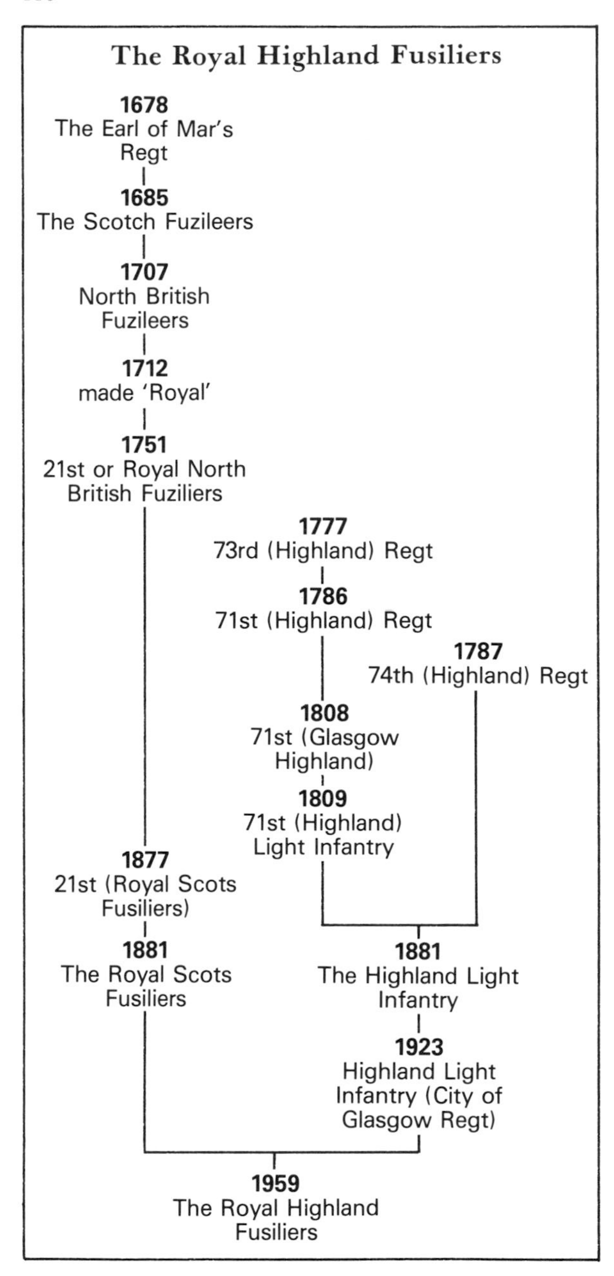

elephant and 'Assaye' honour emblazoned thereon. The buff Honorary Colour is trooped on Assaye Day by a Quartermaster, an old custom of the Highland Light Infantry performed in honour of Quartermaster Grant, the senior surviving member of the 74th who led the remnant out of Assaye.

Customs

In 1879 the Royal Scots Fusiliers began their long-standing practice of playing hymns after the Last Post on Sundays. *Abide With Me* and *God Save The Queen* were always played.

Mascot

None.

Dress distinctions

A blue glengarry with diced band, mounted with the Regimental grenade badge. A white hackle is worn on other forms of headgear in the tradition of the Royal Scots Fusiliers. Collar badges are not worn. Trews of Mackenzie tartan (HLI). Pipers and drummers wear the (Earl of Mar's) Dress Erskine tartan, first granted to pipers of the Royal Scots Fusiliers on the 250th anniversary of the Regiment in 1928. Hunting Erskine was authorised for the whole Regiment in 1948. Pipers wear a white hair sporran with three long black tassels. The Drum Major wears the tall bearskin associated with fusilier officers' full dress. The Prince of Wales' plume worn on the colour belts, Drum Major's belt and pipers' cross-belts, comes from the pipers of the RSF, who bore the emblem from 1919 to perpetuate the memory of the 3rd (Militia) Battalion, which was disbanded in that year as 'The Prince Regent's Own'.

Marches

British Grenadiers (RSF) and *Whistle o'er The Lave o't* (HLI) — the Quick March. *Garb Of Old Gaul* (RSF) and *March Of The 21st Regiment* — the Slow.

Nicknames

'The Assaye Regiment': of the three British Regiments which fought at Assaye only the 74th was entitled to go by this nickname. Wellington referred to the 74th as 'My Fighting Regiment'.

'The Fusil Jocks': the Royal Scots Fusiliers.

'The Glesca keelies': a colloquialism for the Highland Light Infantry, meaning 'Glasgow toughs' or hard men.

'The Heroes of Vittoria': the 71st Regiment, is so named from its conduct at the Battle of Vittoria in 1813, with special reference to Piper McLaughlin, who is famous in Regimental folklore for his example to the men in the battles of the Peninsula War. At Vittoria he played his pipes to encourage his comrades, even though he was shot through both legs and had little time left to live.

'Marlborough's Own': the Royal Scots Fusiliers, after their distinguished service under the Duke of Marlborough, particularly at the Battle of Blenheim. The Scots Fuziliers held an enviable reputation in battle during the 18th century; legend has it that King George II approached Colonel Agnew at Dettingen with, 'I saw the *cuirassiers* in among your men this morning, Colonel', to which Sir Andrew is said to have replied, 'Oh aye, your Majesty, but they didna' get oot again'.

'Mar's Grey-breeks': the Scotch Fuziliers, raised by Charles Erskine, 5th Earl of Mar, were clothed at first in coarse grey breeches.

'The Pig and Whistle Light Infantry': the Highland Light Infantry, from their badge, which incorporated the elephant of the 74th (pig) and the bugle horn of the 71st (whistle).

'The Tortoise Warriors': the Kaffirs of the Amatola Mountains viewed the 74th in the war of 1851 as being similar to tortoises in their brown cotton jackets and Lamont tartan trews, which had a defined square sett.

Recruiting

Glasgow and that part of Strathclyde which was Ayrshire. RHQ: Glasgow.

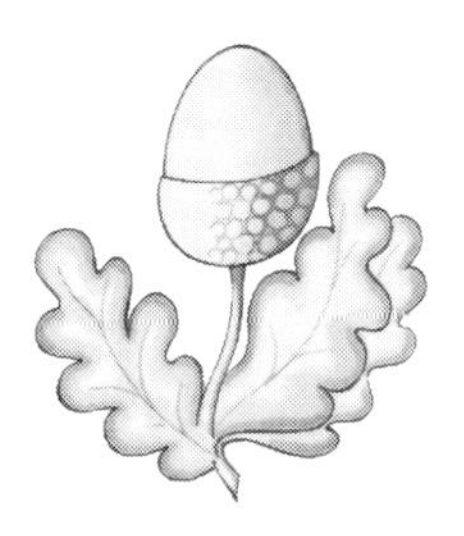

The Cheshire Regiment (22nd Foot)

Insignia

An acorn, leaved and slipped: the acorn and oak leaf, the ancient symbol of permanence and strength, probably derives as a Regimental badge from the Arms of the first Colonel, Henry Howard, 7th Duke of Norfolk, which included the supporter 'A horse bearing in its mouth an acorn sprig with two leaves'. Another legend has it that King George II bestowed the emblem on the Grenadier Company (detached from the Regiment) for saving him from enemy cavalry beneath an oak tree at the Battle of Dettingen in 1743.

Honours

Louisburg, Martinique 1762, Havannah, Meeanee, Hyderabad, Scinde, South Africa 1900–02.

Mons, Ypres 1914, 1915, 1918, Somme 1916, 1918, Arras 1917, 1918, Messines 1917, 1918, Bapaume 1918, Doiran 1917, 1918, Suvla, Gaza, Kut-al-Amara 1917.

St Omer–La Bassée, Normandy Landing, Capture of Tobruk, El Alamein, Mareth, Sicily 1943, Salerno, Rome, Gothic Line, Malta 1941–42.

'Louisburg' was fought by the Regiment (Whitemore's) as a whole and the Grenadier Company went on with Wolfe to Quebec in the following year. As a result the Cheshire is a member regiment of the Wolfe Society.

Anniversaries

Meeanee Day (February 17): the Regimental Day honours Sir Charles Napier's small field force which defeated an army of 30,000 Baluchis at Meeanee in 1843. Napier is said to have signalled his victory in one word, *Peccavi*, I have Scinde! The 22nd was the only British regiment present at the time of battle and much of the Regimental silver dates from this campaign. 'Meeanee', and the sister battle honours 'Hyderabad' and 'Scinde', are unique to the Cheshire Regiment in the British Army.

The 22nd at the Battle of Meeanee.

Oak leaves behind the cap badges determine the band of the Cheshire Regiment.

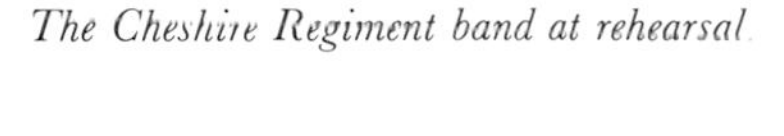

The Cheshire Regiment band at rehearsal.

Customs

Oak leaves are worn behind the cap badge on Regimental days and in the presence of Royalty, a custom confirmed to the Cheshires in 1933.

Mascot

None.

Dress distinctions

A blue dress cap mounted with the Regimental badge, an eight-pointed star with a circle and the acorn and oak leaves within. A blue side hat piped in buff. Collar badges: the acorn with oak leaf sprigs. The stable-belt is cerise and buff, its circular clasp fashioned with the numeral '22'. Buff facings are worn in full dress: the Regimental Colour of the 22nd was restored to the Cheshire in 1904. Oak leaves are worn in the cap or beret, originally on September 12, but now on all Regimental days.

Marches

Wha Wadna Fecht For Charlie, an old Jacobite song adopted in 1881 to reflect the Regiment's affiliation to Sir Charles Napier. *The 22nd Regiment Slow March 1772.*

Nicknames

'The Lightning Conductors': an old nickname which referred to the shape of the Regimental

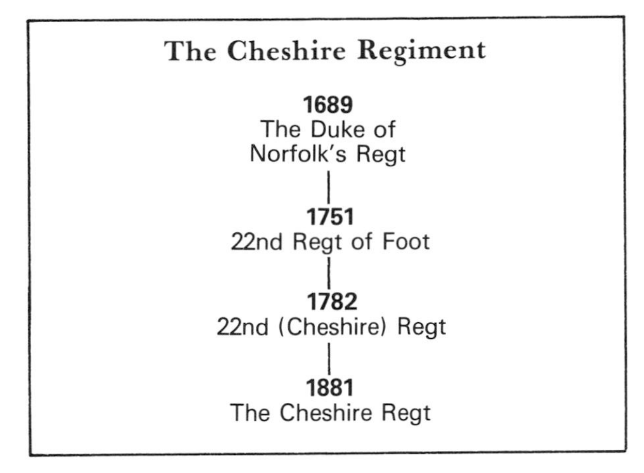

numeral displayed on the men's equipment. Also 'The Old Two-twos'.

'The Red Knights': a name which dates from the 1790s, when recruiting was poor, and the 22nd Regiment had to resort to enlisting boys from the poor house whom they clothed entirely in red. One of these orphans, John Shipp, was commissioned in the field.

Recruiting

Cheshire and Merseyside. RHQ: Chester Castle.

The Royal Welch Fusiliers (23rd Foot)

Insignia

The Prince of Wales' Plume: the device emblazoned in the centre of the Regimental Colour was first borne by the Regiment in the reign of George I, when it went under the name of The Princess of Wales' Regiment of Fuzileers.

The Red Dragon rampant: the ancient Welsh symbols of the Red Dragon and the Rising Sun are borne on the corners of the Regimental Colour.

The White Horse of Hanover: the emblem of the House of Hanover relates to the grenadier caps worn by the original regiments of fusiliers, which were embroidered with the White Horse of Hanover.

The Sphinx with 'Egypt': granted to the 23rd in 1802 for its part in the Egyptian campaign of the previous year.

Honours

Namur 1695, Blenheim, Ramillies, Oudenarde, Malplaquet, Dettingen, Minden, Corunna, Martinique 1809, Albuhera, Badajoz, Salamanca, Vittoria, Pyrenees, Nivelle, Orthes, Toulouse, Peninsula, Waterloo, Alma, Inkerman, Sevastopol, Lucknow, Ashantee 1873–74, Burma 1885–87, Relief of Ladysmith, South Africa 1899–1902, Pekin 1900.

Marne 1914, Ypres 1914, 1917, 1918, Somme 1916, 1918, Hindenburg Line, Vittoria Veneto, Doiran 1917, 1918, Gallipoli 1917, 1918, Egypt 1915–17, Gaza, Baghdad.

St Omer–La Bassée, Caen, Lower Maas, Reichswald, Weeze, Rhine, Madagascar, Donbaik, North Arakan, Kohima.

'Minden' is a proud battle honour, but the RWF does not celebrate its anniversary by wearing roses, as is normal among 'Minden regiments'.

'Albuhera' is synonymous with acts of great courage and extreme battalion casualities. The 23rd knew both these aspects of the battle in the charge of the Fusilier Brigade, which was described by Napier in moving terms: 'The Fusilier battalions struck by an iron tempest reeled and staggered like sinking ships. Suddenly and sternly recovering they closed with their terrible enemies and then was seen with what majesty the British soldier fights . . . ' The 23rd lost 333 men in the attack.

'Alma' is remembered for the courage of Sergeant O'Connor and Captain Bell, who distinguished themselves in the advance on the Russian redoubts. O'Connor won his VC when he took up the fallen Queen's Colour, and carried it through the shot and shell of battle. He received a battlefield commission and afterwards rose to the rank of Major General, and became Colonel of the Regiment. Captain Bell gained a VC for pointing an empty pistol at a Russian artillery team and forcing it to return with him to the British lines.

'Ashantee' is a rare battle honour, and 'Pekin 1900' (the Boxer Rebellion), unique.

Anniversaries

St David's Day (March 1).

Customs

The traditional Regimental Day of the RWF is

The Pioneer Sergeant is the only rank in the Army allowed to sport a full beard, the traditional symbol of his authority and skill.

Regimental goat and officers, 1892.

celebrated by all ranks wearing the leek and they who have not previously eaten one are required to do so. An officers' toast is made to 'Toby Purcell, His Spurs, and St David'. Purcell was the Regiment's second-in-command at the Battle of the Boyne in 1690; his spurs were handed down to be worn by successive seconds-in-command until 1842, when they were lost in a fire in Montreal.

The Leek ceremony is very old in the Regiment, and begins after dinner: the Regimental Goat is led around the table followed by a drummer, a fifer and the Drum Major carrying leeks upon a silver salver. The procession halts by the newest member, who stands on his chair with foot on table to consume a leek to a sustained drum roll. The Mess Sergeant is on hand to deliver a loving cup to the officer for another toast to St David.

The Loyal Toast is not made in the Regiment except on St David's Day, and officers and guests are not required to stand for the National Anthem. The custom has no solid origin, but is thought to have originated with the Prince Regent, who absolved the 23rd from the Toast because of the loyalty shown by the Regiment during the Mutiny at the Nore in 1797.

It is traditional on St David's Day for officers to ride in a five-mile steeplechase for the Red Dragon Cup.

Mascot

The Regimental Goat: the Regimental mascot idea is well established in the annals of the Army, and the Regimental Goat of the Royal Welch is the oldest recorded example; the 23rd fought at Bunker Hill in 1775 with a goat alongside them. Major Donkin wrote in his *Military Reflections* of 1777: 'The Royal Regiment of Welch Fuzileers has a privilegeous honour of passing in review preceded by a goat with gilded horns . . . the Corps values itself much on the ancientness of the custom'. The battalion goats have come from the Royal Herd since 1844, but wild herds from the mountains of North Wales have provided suitable offerings in more recent times.

Dress distinctions

A blue beret mounted with the Regimental badge

Right *The 23rd at Waterloo. Fur caps were probably not worn.*

Below *Goat and pioneers lead a recruiting march in 1958. The custom for fusilier regiments to keep ceremonial pioneers was authorised to the RWF in 1886.*

and white hackle. The badge is the grenade superimposed by the Prince of Wales' plume. Officers and warrant officers wear the royal pattern cap mounted with the grenade badge superimposed by the Welsh dragon. Collar badges: a plain grenade (officers' as their cap badge). Buttons are embossed with the Welsh dragon. Five black swallow-tail ribbons are worn from the rear of the

Fusiliers on the battlefield site of Waterloo in 1965. Note the white hackle and flash.

jacket collar in service dress. The 'flash' dates back to the reign of George III, when it was worn to protect the coat from the grease and powder used to dress the pigtail. These were abolished in 1808, but one battalion of the 23rd which was abroad at the time continued to wear the flash until its return to Portsmouth in 1834, where an inspecting General ordered its removal. At this, Colonel Harrison rode to London to receive permission from the King for its retention. The privilege was confined originally to officers and Sergeant Majors, but was extended to all ranks in 1900.

Full dress is worn by the pioneers, drums, and bandsmen: a scarlet tunic faced in blue, and a fusilier sealskin cap mounted with the Regimental cap badge and a white plume on the right. Pioneers wear white buff-leather aprons and gauntlets over the tunic.

Marches

British Grenadiers (Quick) and *War March Of The Men Of Glamorgan* (the Slow). Sousa's last march, *The Royal Welch Fusiliers,* was presented by the US Marine Corps in 1930 to mark the fellowship between the two units since 1900.

Nicknames

'The Nanny Goats': an old allusion to the Regiment's 'figurehead'.

Recruiting

North Wales. RHQ: Wrexham.

The Royal Welch Fusiliers

1689
Lord Herbert's Regt
|
1712
The Royal Regt of Welch Fuzileers
|
1714
The Prince of Wales's Own Royal Regt of Welch Fuzileers
|
1727
The Royal Welch Fuzileers
|
1751
23rd or Royal Welch Fuziliers
|
1881
The Royal Welsh Fusiliers
|
1920
The Royal Welch Fusiliers

Taffy III at Crickhowell. He was presented to the 1st Battalion in December 1982 from the Royal Herd at Whipsnade. The Goat Major is in full dress scarlet, his white helmet reminiscent of the tropical pattern worn by the 24th during the Zulu War.

The Royal Regiment of Wales (24th, 41st, 69th Foot)

Insignia

A silver wreath of immortelles with the Red Dragon superimposed: the wreath was bestowed upon the 24th Regiment by Queen Victoria in 1880 to mark the bravery shown in the 1st Battalion annihilated at Isandhlwana in 1879. It takes the form of silver immortelles and is always carried on the pikestaff of the Queen's Colour. The Welsh Dragon has graced Colours of the Welch Regiment since 1881.

The Royal Cipher.

The Rose and Thistle within the Garter, and the Crown over: the Union badge was borne on the colours and appointments of the 41st Regiment in the 18th century, when it was known as the Regiment of Invalids.

The Sphinx with 'Egypt': granted to the 24th Regiment in 1802, and worn on the dress and appointments until 1881, when it became the cap badge of the South Wales Borderers.

A Naval Crown superscribed '12th April, 1782': awarded to the Welsh Regiment in 1909 in recognition of the marine service endured by the 69th Foot in the naval battles of the Saints (1782) and St Vincent (1797).

Gwell Angau na chywilydd: the motto of the

Ensign Pennycuick standing over his father at Chillianwallah, January 13 1849.

The bodies of Lieutenants Coghill and Melvill, VC, discovered with the Regimental Colour at the Buffalo River, January 22 1879.

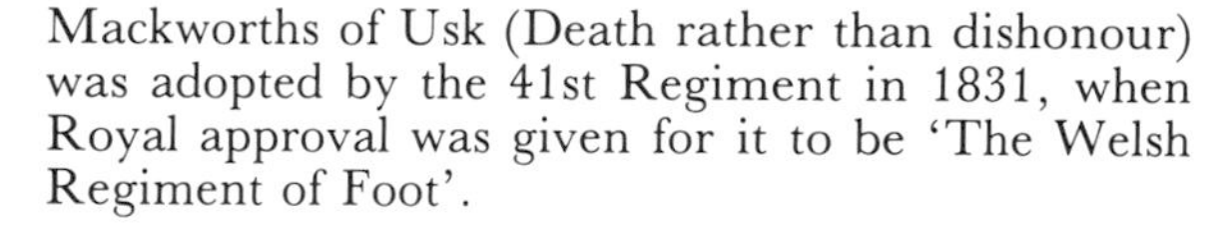

Mackworths of Usk (Death rather than dishonour) was adopted by the 41st Regiment in 1831, when Royal approval was given for it to be 'The Welsh Regiment of Foot'.

Honours

Blenheim, Ramillies, Oudenarde, Malplaquet (24th); Belleisle (41st); Martinique 1762 (41st/69th); St Vincent 1797 (69th); Cape of Good Hope 1806 (24th); India (69th); Talavera (24th); Bourbon (69th); Busaco, Fuentes d'Onor (24th); Java (69th); Salamanca (24th); Detroit, Queenstown, Miami (41st); Vittoria, Pyrenees, Nivelle (24th); Niagara (41st); Orthes, Peninsula (24th); Waterloo (69th); Ava, Candahar 1842, Ghuznee 1842, Cabool 1842 (41st); Chillianwallah, Goojerat, Punjaub (24th); Alma, Inkerman, Sevastopol (41st); South Africa 1877–79 (24th); Burma 1885–87 (SWB); Relief of Kimberley, Paardeberg (Welsh); South Africa 1899–1902 (SWB/Welsh).

Mons, Marne 1914 (SWB); Aisne 1914, 1918 (Welsh); Ypres 1914, 1915, 1917, 1918 (SWB/Welsh); Gheluvelt (SWB); Loos (Welsh); Somme 1916, 1918 (SWB/Welsh); Pilckem (Welsh); Cambrai 1917, 1918, Doiran 1917, 1918 (SWB); Macedonia 1915–18 (Welsh); Landing at Helles (SWB); Gallipoli 1915–16, Gaza (Welsh); Baghdad, Tsingtao (SWB).

Norway 1940, Normandy Landing, Sully, Caen (SWB); Falaise (Welch); Le Havre (SWB); Lower Maas, Reichswald (Welch); North-West Europe 1944–45, North Africa 1940-42 (SWB); Croce, Italy 1943–45, Crete, Canea (Welch); Mayu Tunnels, Pinwe (SWB); Kyaukmyaung Bridgehead, Sittang 1945 (Welch); Burma 1944–45 (SWB).

Korea 1951–52 (SWB).

Anniversaries

Rorke's Drift Day (January 22): the Regimental

Day of the South Wales Borderers is kept to educate the rank and file with the stirring story of the 24th and the Zulu War of 1879. The soldiers are shown relics of the war, and told how a single company held off the concerted attacks of 4,000 Zulus in the mission station at Rorke's Drift for two days and a night. Eleven VCs were won in the engagement. It is customary on Rorke's Drift Day for the Colours to be marched with the band and drums to the dining hall, where they are displayed for the rest of the day.

Inauguration Day (June 11): the RRW was formed by an amalgamation of the South Wales Borderers and the Welch Regiment on June 11 1969.

St David's Day (March 1).

Customs

Leeks are worn, and carried on the drums etc, on St David's Day, and all newly-appointed officers, Sergeants, and Privates take part in leek-eating ceremonies.

The 1st Battalion Welsh Regiment band was given to playing *Sun Of My Soul, Spanish Chant* and *The Vesper Hymn* at First Post on Sundays. The custom is believed to have originated in the 41st Regiment at the time of the Crimean War.

Mascot

The Regimental Goat: all battalions of the RRW go on parade with a goat, a custom first started by the 41st in the Crimean War, and by the 69th in 1873. The first goat to be presented by a Sovereign expired on the Nile Expedition of the same year (1886). Today's goats, officially all named Gwilym Jenkins, but called 'Taffy', are descended from a herd of Kashmir goats established at Windsor in 1828. On amalgamation with the South Wales Borderers, Taffy XII of the Welch became Taffy I of the new Regiment. Volunteer battalion goats are traditionally named 'Dewi' (3rd Battalion) and 'Sospan' (4th Battalion).

Dress distinctions

A blue dress cap with a scarlet band and piping, mounted with the Prince of Wales' Plume badge. Collar badges: a wreath of immortelles superimposed by the Dragon *rampant*. Buttons are stamped with the Welsh Dragon. The stable-belt is grass green with a broad white centre stripe edged in red. Full dress scarlet tunics are faced in grass green, the old Regimental colour of the 24th and 69th, restored to the SWB in 1905. The band and corps of drums wear, in addition, the tropical-pattern white helmet of the type used by the 24th in the Zulu War.

The 24th at Rorke's Drift, January 22 1879.

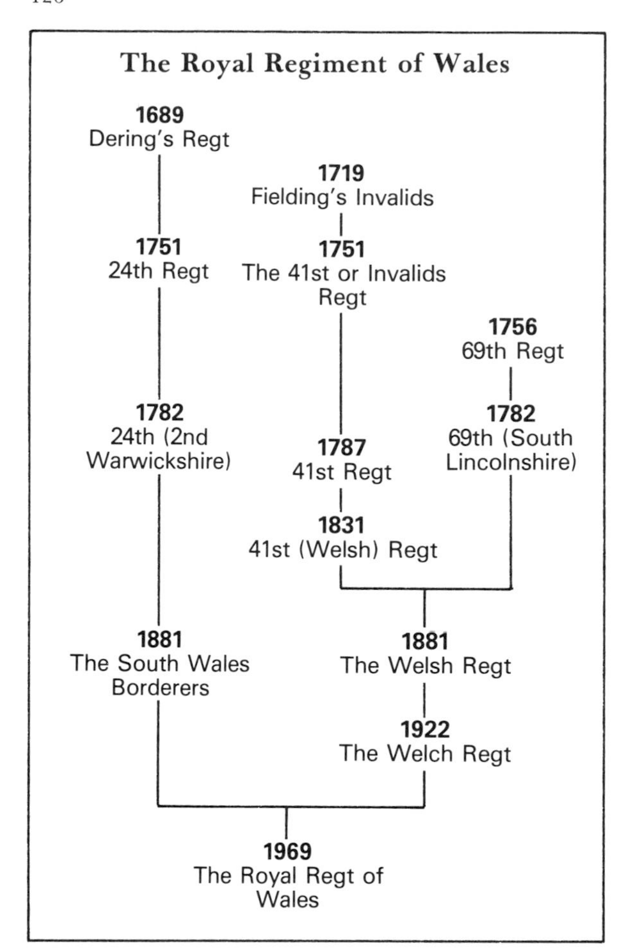

Marches

Men of Harlech, the Regimental Quick March (SWB). *Scipio*, the Regimental Slow March. *God Bless The Prince of Wales* (Welch). *Ap Shenkin* (Welch). *The Warwickshire Lad*, the old SWB march relates to the pre-1881 county designation of the 24th Regiment. *The Lincolnshire Poacher*, an old march of the 69th Regt, which was raised in Lincolnshire.

Nicknames

'The Old Agamemnons': from a remark made by Lord Nelson with reference to the 69th Regiment, part of which served aboard the *Agamemnon* at the Battle of St Vincent in 1797.

'The Swabs': the South Wales Borderers, from their cap badge, which bore the initials SWB.

Recruiting

South Wales. RHQ: Maindy Barracks, Cardiff.

The King's Own Scottish Borderers (25th Foot)

Insignia

The Castle of Edinburgh and motto *Nisi dominus frustra:* granted to the 25th Regiment in 1832 in recognition of an old title and honorary freedom of the City of Edinburgh. Leven's Regiment was raised in the city and became known as 'The Edinburgh Regiment' after its first blooding at Killiecrankie in 1689, where it behaved with exemplary fortitude, and received, by return, the right to recruit in the city by beat of drum and without need to consult the Lord Provost. The title was altered in 1782 after a 'petty quarrel' with the city elders over the privilege.

The Royal Crest and motto *In veritate religionis confido*: conferred on the Regiment in 1805 after the death of Colonel Lord Lennox, on the occasion of the 25th becoming The King's Own Borderers.

The White Horse of Hanover and motto *Nec aspera terrent*: authorised to the 25th Regiment by George III to be borne on the Regimental Colour with the Royal Crest in 1805.

The Sphinx with 'Egypt': awarded to the 25th Regiment in 1802 for its part in the Egyptian campaign of the previous year.

Honours

Namur 1695, Minden, Egmont-op-Zee, Martinique 1809, Afghanistan 1878–80, Chitral, Tirah, Paardeberg, South Africa 1900-02.

Mons, Aisne 1914, Ypres 1914, 1915, 1917, 1918, Loos, Somme 1916, 1918, Arras 1917, 1918, Soissonais-Ourcq, Hindenburg Line, Gallipoli 1915–16, Gaza.

Dunkirk 1940, Odon, Caen, Arnhem 1944, Flushing, Rhine, Bremen, Ngakyedauk Pass, Imphal, Irrawaddy.

Anniversaries

Minden Day (August 1): the 25th was one of six infantry regiments which stood against the might of the French cavalry at Minden, to gain the coveted battle honour. The KOSB follow the theory that roses were picked by the redcoats and worn in the fighting, and red roses are worn by all ranks on Minden Day.

Customs

Information not available.

Mascot

None.

Dress distinctions

A blue glengarry with a diced border, mounted with black cock's feathers and the Regimental badge, the Castle of Edinburgh upon St Andrew's Cross, within a thistle wreath; on two scrolls, the motto *In veritate religionis confido* (We trust in the truth of religion) above, and *Nisi dominus frustra* (Without the Lord all is in vain), below. Collar badges: the

The King's Own Scottish Borderers

1689
The Earl of Leven's or Edinburgh Regt

1751
25th or Edinburgh Regt

1782
25th (Sussex) Regt

1805
25th or King's Own Borderers

1881
The King's Own Borderers

1887
The King's Own Scottish Borderers

Minden Day. A Private in the RAPC assists in the distribution of roses, which the soldiers fit to their glengarries.

Left *KOSB types by Simkin, before the advent of the kilmarnock, 1893.*

Below left *A drawing of the King's Own Scottish Borderers' band in 1772.*

three-towered Castle (of Edinburgh) upon thistles. Buttons are embossed with the Royal Crest (the Lion and Crown). Trews of Leslie tartan. The Regiment made an appeal to Lord Leven for his help in having the family tartan authorised, which was done in 1898. Pipers wear the Royal Stewart tartan and a white hair sporran with three long black tassels.

Marches

Blue Bonnets O'er The Border, the Regimental March evokes the story of Piper Laidlaw at Loos in 1915. Laidlaw was famous for climbing on to the parapet of his trench at a critical moment in the battle to march up and down playing *Blue Bonnets* on the pipes. His act injected fresh courage into the Battalion. *The Standard On The Braes Of Mar* (the Slow).

Nicknames

'The KOSBs': from the Regiment's initials. The old favourite 'Kosbies' has fallen from favour in the Regiment.

'The Botherers': a corruption of 'Borderers'.

Recruiting

Borders, and Dumfries and Galloway (Berwickshire, Selkirkshire, Roxburghshire, Kirkcudbrightshire, Wigtonshire and Lanarkshire). RHQ: Berwick-upon-Tweed.

The Royal Irish Rangers (27th, 83rd, 86th, 87th, 89th, 108th Foot)

Insignia

An Irish Harp.

The Castle of Inniskilling with the flag of St

George: the symbol of the Protestant defence of Enniskillen in 1689 has been borne on the appointments of the 27th Foot since the early 18th century. After 1881 it was worn by the Royal Inniskilling Fusiliers stamped on the grenade cap badge.

An Irish Harp and Crown above a bugle horn: the badge of the Royal Ulster Rifles.

The Eagle and Coronet: the Imperial Eagle was used to personalise the grenade badge of the Royal Irish Fusiliers. The 87th Regiment had the distinction of being the first to capture a French Eagle standard in battle. The coronet was that of Princess Victoria. Queen Victoria approved the distinction to be used by the 89th Regiment on April 5 1866, when she presented new Colours to replace those received from her, as Princess Victoria, 33 years earlier.

The Harp and Crown: the former cap badge of the Royal Ulster Rifles was used as the badge of the North Irish Brigade (1951–68) before its Regiments amalgamated as the RIR in 1968.

Faugh a Ballagh: the Regimental motto (Clear the way!) is said to have originated among the 87th at the Battle of Barrossa in 1811.

The Sphinx superscribed 'Egypt': awarded in 1802 to the 27th, 86th, and 89th Regiments for their part in the Egyptian campaign of 1801.

Honours

Martinique 1762, Havannah, St Lucia 1778, 1796 (27th); India (86th); Cape of Good Hope 1806 (83rd); Maida (27th); Monte Video (87th); Talavera (83rd); Bourbon (86th); Barrossa (87th); Fuentes d'Onor (83rd); Java (89th); Tarifa (87th); Ciudad Rodrigo (83rd). Badajoz, Salamanca, Vittoria (27th/83rd); Pyrenees (27th); Nivelle (27th/83rd/87th); Niagara (89th); Orthes (27th/87th); Toulouse (27th/83rd); Peninsula (27th/83rd/87th); Waterloo (27th); Ava (89th); South Africa 1835, 1846–7 (27th); Sevastopol (89th); Central India (86th/108th); Tel-el-kebir, Egypt 1882 (RIF); Relief of Ladysmith (Innis/RIF); South Africa 1899–1902 (Innis/RIR/RIF).

Mons (RIR); Le Cateau (Innis/RIF); Marne 1914 (RIR/RIF); Messines 1914, 1917, 1918 (RIF); Ypres 1914, 1915, 1917, 1918 (Innis/RIR/RIF); Neuve Chapelle (RIR); Loos, Somme 1916, 1918 (Innis/RIR/RIF); Albert 1916 (RIR); Arras

Above right *Cpl William Hall of the 86th raising the King's Colour to the fury of French troops during the capture of Bourbon (Reunion) in 1810. The 86th became 'The Royal County Down Regiment' in honour of the conquest, with the added distinction of bearing the Irish Harp and Crown on its buttons.*

Right *Raising Tiffen's Regiment at Enniskillen in 1689.*

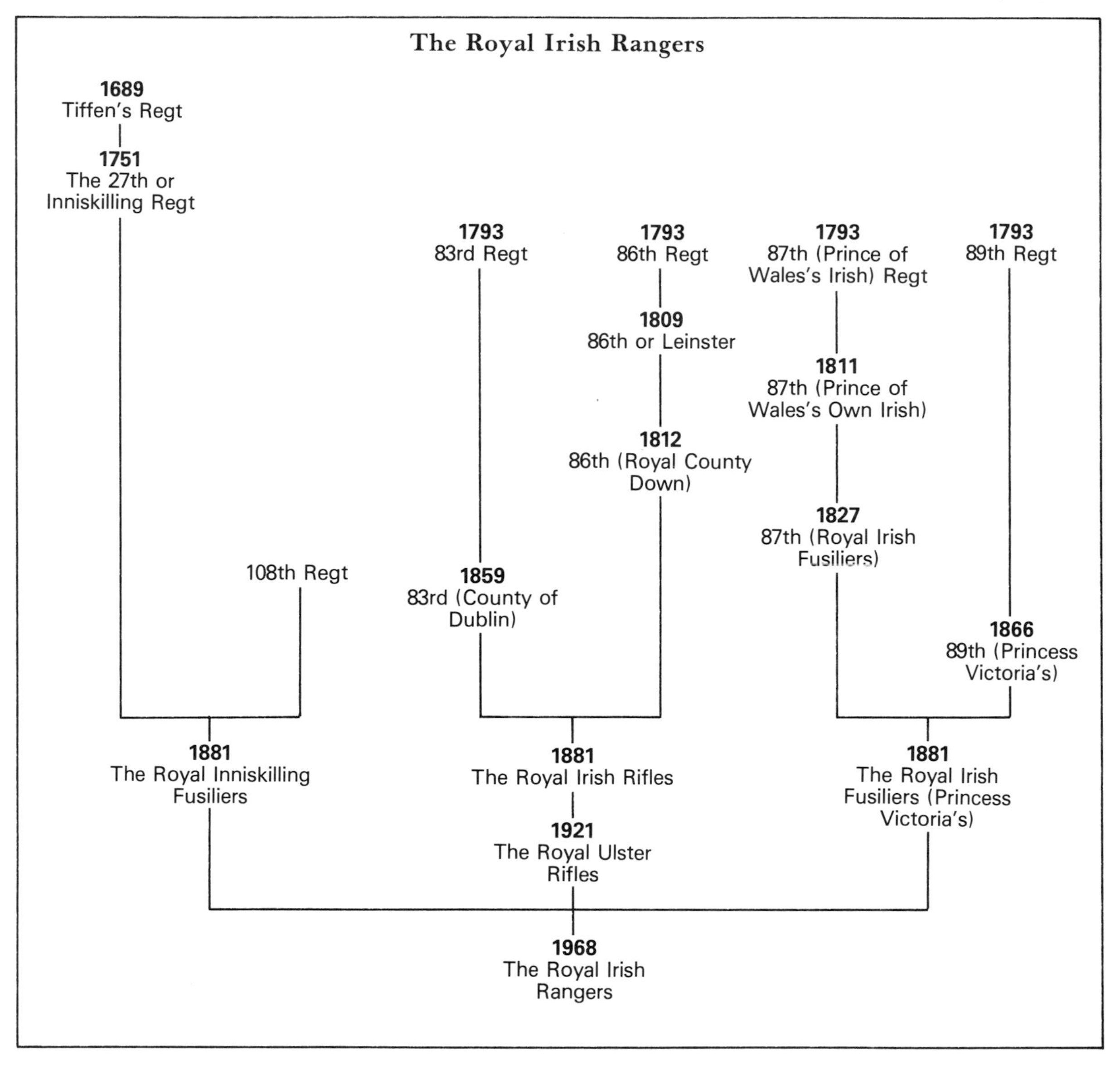

1917 (RIF); Cambrai 1917, 1918, Hindenburg Line, France & Flanders 1914–18 (Innis); Macedonia 1915–17 (Innis/RIF); Suvla (RIR/RIF); Gallipoli 1915–16 (Innis); Gaza, Jerusalem (RIR); Palestine 1917–18 (Innis/RIF).

Dyle, St Omer–La Bassée (RIF); Dunkirk 1940, Normandy Landing, Caen, Bremen (RUR); Bou Arada (RIF); Djebel Tanngoucha (Innis/RIF); North Africa 1942–43 (Innis); Centuripe (Innis/RIF); Sicily 1943 (Innis); Sangro (RIF); Garigliano Crossing, Anzio, Cassino II (Innis); Argenta Gap (RIF); Italy 1943–45, (Innis); Malta 1940 (RIF); Yenangyaung 1942, Burma 1942–43 (Innis).

Anniversaries

Barrossa Day (March 5): the anniversary of the Battle of Barrossa (1811) is celebrated to mark the capture of the Regimental Eagle of the French 8th

Above right *Faugh a Ballagh! The familiar silhouette of the charging Ranger.*

Right *Members of the Regiment's 'Saddle Club'.*

Sergeant Masterson seizing the Eagle with a cry of 'Be jabers, boys, I have the Cuckoo', Ensign Keogh having been killed in the attempt.

by Sergeant Masterson and Ensign Keogh of the 87th. The achievement was acknowledged by the Prince Regent, who moved that the 87th should, henceforward, be known as his Regiment and carry his emblem together with an Eagle within laurels.

Vesting Day (July 1): the day is observed to honour the amalgamation of the three Irish Regiments which went to make up the RIR in 1968, the mergers of the six founding Regiments in 1881, and the day, in 1916, when 18 battalions of the three Regiments fought together on the Somme.

Customs

In the Mess on Barrossa Day, brandy, cherry whisky, curacao and sherry are poured into the Barrossa Cup and passed around. This simple ceremony is done to commemorate the direct hit on the liquor wagon at Barrossa.

Mascot

Irish wolfhound adopted circa 1985.

Dress Distinctions

A piper green *caubeen* bonnet mounted with the crowned Harp badge and a piper green, cut-feather hackle. Collar badges: a three-towered castle beneath the inscription 'Inniskilling'. Buttons are black and embossed with the Harp. Piper green trousers are worn in No 2 dress. A stable-belt of piper green. Officers wear a black patent leather pouch-belt fashioned with the Barrossa Eagle. Pipers dress in a dark green tunic, cloak and stockings, and a saffron kilt overlaid with a small leather purse. The tunic has the special distinction of large looped piping down the front. Buglers wear the dark green regimentals of the band but with the Rifles' busby instead of the caubeen.

Marches

Killaloe, the Regimental Quick March. *Eileen Allanagh* (the Slow). *Rory O'More* (Royal Inniskilling Fusiliers). *Spring of Shellalagh* (Royal Inniskilling Fusiliers). *St*

Patrick's Day/Garryowen/Norah Creina/Barrossa Song (Royal Irish Fusiliers). *Off, Off, Said The Stranger* (Royal Irish Rifles). The band includes in its official repertoire the marches of the Irish regiments disbanded in 1922.

Nicknames

'The Aigle-catchers': a name acquired by the 87th after the capture of the French Eagle (*Aigle*) at Barrossa.

'Blayney's Bloodhounds': a reputation gained by the 89th in Ireland around 1800, from their relentless pursuit of rebels.

'The Faughs': the Royal Irish Fusiliers, from their unofficial motto *Faugh a Ballagh*.

'The Grey Inniskillings': the Royal Inniskilling Fusiliers were granted the right to wear a grey hackle on the fusilier cap in 1903 to commemorate the fact that Tiffen's Regiment, from Enniskillen, wore grey regimentals at the Battle of the Boyne.

'The Lumps': 2nd Battalion Royal Inniskilling Fusiliers, origin obscure.'Lump' in old English slang meant 'to beat'.

'The Skins' or 'Skillingers': the Royal Inniskilling Fusiliers.

'The Stackies': the Royal Ulster Rifles, from their dark green uniforms, which, when paraded together made them to resemble a host of chimney stacks.

Recruiting

Ireland. RHQ: Ballymena.

The Gloucestershire Regiment (28th, 61st Foot)

Insignia

Within a laurel wreath, upon a pedestal inscribed 'Egypt', the Sphinx: the Sphinx was awarded to both the 28th and 61st Regiments in 1802, but that of the 28th had the unique added distinction of the laurel wreath to commemorate the Regiment's celebrated feat of arms at the Battle of Alexandria.

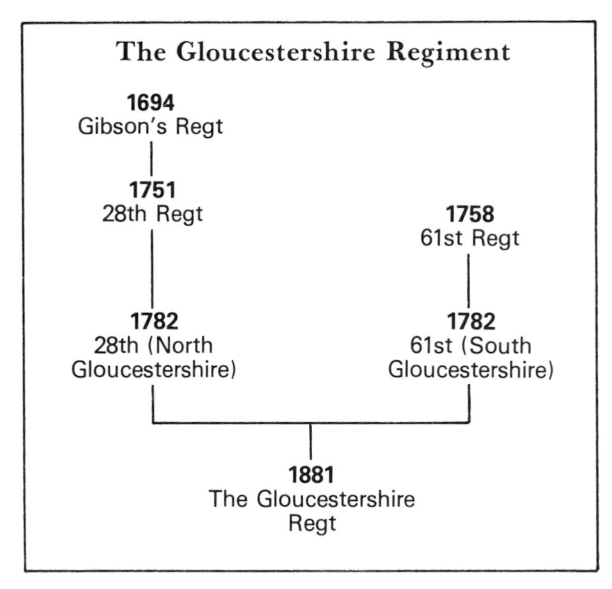

Honours

Ramillies, Louisburg, Quebec 1759 (28th); Guadaloupe 1759 (61st); Martinique 1762, Havannah, St Lucia 1778 (28th); Maida (61st); Corunna (28th); Talavera, Busaco (61st); Barrossa, Albuhera (28th); Salamanca (61st); Vittoria (28th); Pyrenees, Nivelle, Nive, Orthes, Toulouse, Peninsula (28th/61st); Waterloo (28th); Chillianwallah, Goojerat, Punjaub (61st); Alma, Inkerman, Sevastopol (28th); Delhi 1857 (61st); Defence of Ladysmith, Relief of Kimberley, Paardeberg, South Africa 1899–1902.

Mons, Ypres 1914, 1915, 1917, Loos, Somme 1916, 1918, Lys, Selle, Vittorio Veneto, Doiran 1917, Sari Bair, Baghdad.

Defence of Escaut, Cassel, Mont Pincon, Falaise, North-West Europe 1940, 1944–45, Taukyan, Paungde, Pinwe, Myitson, Burma 1942, 1944–45.

Imjin, Korea 1950–51.

'Quebec 1759' is remembered for the heroism of General Wolfe, who fell, mortally wounded, at the head of the 28th Regiment. The Gloucestershire is a member regiment of the Wolfe Society.

'Salamanca', of all the Peninsula battle honours, is borne with most pride. The 61st suffered more casualties than any other battalion engaged in the battle and, in the final assault, losses were such that it fell to Private soldiers to carry the Colours.

'Vittoria' is remembered, as with the 61st at Salamanca, as the battle in which the 28th sustained an extraordinary rate of casualties. It was probably after Vittoria, where the 28th had 17 officers wounded, that the Regiment's peculiar ritual for the Loyal Toast began. Only two officers were left to

The 28th fight back to back at Alexandria, March 21 1801.

attend dinner that night and, for the purposes of the Loyal Toast, they assumed the roles of Mess President and Vice President, but, instead of repeating the usual 'Gentlemen, The King', Mr Vice responded 'The King, Mr President'. This wording for the Toast is still used today.

Anniversaries

Back Badge Day (March 21): The Regimental Day takes its name from the unique practice of wearing a badge on the back of the cap in commemoration of an incident at the Battle of Alexandria on this day in 1801, in which the 28th, 42nd and 58th Regiments beat off a French attack on two fronts by turning their rear ranks back-to-back with the front ranks. An Army Order of 1955 granted the 1st Battalion special permission to fly a blue streamer from the pikestaff of the Regimental Colour on Back Badge Day. The streamer, in the hue of the US Citation ribbon, shows the word *Solma-ri*, and commemorates the Regiment's famous stand in the valley, of that name during the Battle of the Imjin River in 1951. Salamanca Day (July 22) is commemorated when possible with two privates forming the Colour escort in memory of privates Crawford and Coulson, whose lot it was to carry the colours on that day in 1812.

Customs

The time-honoured tradition of the 28th Regiment of wearing a badge on the back of its caps date to the Napoleonic Wars, when members of that corps began to fix the Regimental number in such a manner to celebrate the famous manoeuvre at Alexandria in 1801 (see above).

It was not until 1830 that the unofficial practice of the 28th was officially condoned, and then a diamond-shaped silver plate embossed with a Sphinx over '28' was authorised as a 'back badge'. This issue was soon sold off by the men for the silver value, however, and replaced with a simple brass

An impression of 'The Glorious Glosters' at Solma-Ri, April 1951.

oval plate pierced with '28', although bandsmen were expected to turn out in silver badges still.

When the 28th was paired with the 61st in 1881 the Regimental badge, a Sphinx within a laurel wreath, was worn on the back of the helmet. A larger version was struck after the First World War to mark the Regiment's back-to-back stand at Festubert, but this proved unpopular with the men and the small badge was re-adopted in 1935.

Mascot

None.

Dress distinctions

A blue dress cap mounted with the Sphinx on two twigs of laurel badge (front) and the Sphinx within a laurel wreath badge (back). The side hat is blue piped scarlet, with a primrose yellow tip. Collar badges: the Sphinx within a laurel wreath. Buttons are embossed with a lion and crown over an interlocking *G* and *R* within a laurel wreath. A US Presidential Citation (a blue rectangle edged in gold) is worn at the top of the sleeve to mark the award for the Regiment's bravery at the Battle of Imjin River.

Marches

The Kynegad Slashers, the Regimental March is based on a Leinster jig, and relates to an old nickname of the 28th. *The Silver-tailed Dandies* or *The 61st March*, the March takes its title from an old nickname of the 61st Regiment. *The Royal Canadian*, this March has been played since 1925 as a tribute to the Regiment's alliance with the Royal Canadian Regiment. *The Regimental Slow March*, the Slow incorporates the Regimental Call and a theme from the *61st March*. *Army Of The Nile*, the Battalion always comes on to parade to this march to mark the glorious service of both the 61st and 28th Regiments in the Egyptian campaign of 1801. *Salamanca Day*, a piece written for

the Corps of Drums as a tribute to the 61st at the Battle of Salamanca in 1812.

Nicknames

'The Glosters'.

The Back Numbers': a name given to the 28th Regiment from its custom for wearing the Regimental numerals at the back of its headgear. Also 'The Fore and Afts'.

'The Flowers of Toulouse': a poignant description of the 61st dead lying over the battlefield of Toulouse in 1814; their red coats picked out like poppies in the sun.

'The Glorious Glosters': the name probably derived from a newspaper headline reporting the Battle of the Imjin River in April 1951, when a Chinese Communist Army, 30,000 strong, crossed the river and attacked the British 29th Infantry Brigade. The Glosters fought back against impossible odds, but by the evening of the 24th were pushed back on a hill where they made a last stand

Left *A WRAC on detachment to the Gloucesters is granted the right to wear the back badge.*

Below *The 28th at Waterloo. The March* Wellington *is played by the band in tribute to the steadiness of the 28th's square at Waterloo and Quatre Bras.*

during the night. On the morning of April 25 the survivors made a desperate attempt to break out through the surrounding enemy. 526 men of the Battalion fell into Chinese hands and spent the rest of the war as prisoners of the enemy.

'Old Braggs': a famous name in the army of George II, dating back to 1734, when a colourful gentleman by the name of Philip Bragg began his long tenure of command in the 28th Foot.

'The Silver-tailed Dandies': the 61st Regiment, from its officers' penchant for wearing long, silver-laced coat tails during the Napoleonic Wars.

'The Slashers': this fearsome reputation of the 28th has two theories connected with its origin. One story has the men slicing off the ear of a magistrate (Thomas Walker) who was said to have deprived them of their rightful billet, in Canada in 1764, whilst the other cites the 28th fording a river during the Battle for White Plains in the American War of Independence. In this the grenadiers had to scramble up the far bank under fire and, finding the cliff wet and slippery, discarded their muskets, drew out their hangers (swords), and beat the Americans into submission to the cheers of the rest of the army. A 'slasher' in 18th century slang meant 'swash-buckler' or 'fighter', and it is possible that the 28th played on their notoriety to turn the name into one of a dashing nature.

Recruiting

Gloucestershire and Avon. RHQ: Gloucester.

Harry Payne's watercolour of 'The Capture of Derby I' by the 95th (Derbyshire) Regiment at the Siege of Kotah, March 30 1858.

The Worcestershire and Sherwood Foresters Regiment (29th, 36th, 45th, 95th Foot)

Insignia

A Maltese Cross charged with the Garter encircling a stag lodged on water, thereunder a plinth inscribed 'FIRM'. The whole upon an elongated star of eights: the Maltese Cross and stag were used to form the basis of the badge of the Sherwood Foresters. The elongated star of the Worcesters is similar to the Garter Star of the Coldstream Guards, and is displayed to symbolise a link between the two Regiments that began in 1694 when Colonel Farrington came from the Guards to raise the 29th Foot. Successive Colonels of the 29th also came from the Coldstream and the star is thought to have been adopted in the early 18th century.

Upon a pedestal inscribed 'FIRM' the Lion of the Royal Crest: an emblem of the Worcestershire Regiment first seen on the colours of the 36th Foot. The motto is believed to have been conferred on the 36th for its conduct at the Battle of Lauffeld, but was not displayed on the Colours until 1773.

A Maltese Cross charged in the centre with a stag lodged upon water within a wreath of oak: the

Badajoz Day, April 6 1964. The Sherwood Foresters' scarlet jacket ceremony to commemorate the capture of the fortress in 1812.

badge of the Sherwood Foresters incorporates facets of local significance: the oak of Sherwood Forest and the White Hart of Derbyshire.

A Naval Crown superscribed '1st June 1794': granted to the Worcestershire Regiment in 1909 in belated recognition of the part played by the 29th Foot in Lord Howe's famous naval victory off the Port of Brest in 1794.

Honours

Ramillies (29th); Louisburg (45th); Belleisle. Mysore, Hindoostan (36th); Rolica, Vimiera (29th/45th); Corunna (36th); Talavera (29th/45th); Busaco, Fuentes d'Onor (45th); Albuhera (29th); Ciudad Rodrigo, Badajoz (45th); Salamanca (36th/45th); Vittoria (45th); Pyrenees, Nivelle (36th/45th); Nive (36th); Orthes, Toulouse (36th/45th); Peninsula (29th/36th/45th); Ava (45th); Ferozeshah, Sobraon, Chillianwallah, Goojerat, Punjaub (29th); South Africa 1846–47 (45th); Alma, Inkerman, Sevastopol, Central India (95th); Abyssinia (45th); Egypt 1882, Tirah (SF); South Africa 1899–1902 (Worcs/SF).

Mons (Worcs); Aisne 1914, 1918 (SF); Ypres 1914, 1915, 1917, 1918, Gheluvelt (Worcs); Neuve Chapelle (Worcs/SF); Loos (SF); Somme 1916, 1918, Cambrai 1917, 1918 (Worcs/SF); Lys (Worcs); St Quentin Canal, France & Flanders 1914–18 (SF); Italy 1917–18, Gallipoli 1915–16 (Worcs/SF); Baghdad (Worcs).

Norway 1940 (SF); Mont Pincon, Seine 1944, Geilenkirchen, Goch, North-West Europe 1940, 1944–45, Keren (Worcs); Gazala (Worcs/SF); El Alamein, Tunis, Salerno, Anzio, Campoleone, Gothic Line, Coriano, Singapore Island (SF). Kohima, Mandalay, Burma 1944–45 (Worcs).

The WFR has inherited from the Sherwood Foresters their membership of the Wolfe Society, this as a direct result of the participation of the 45th Foot in the Siege of Louisburg in 1758.

Anniversaries

The Glorious First of June: the great naval victory of June 1 1794, in which the marine contingent was reinforced by the 29th Regiment, has long been a major reason for celebration with the Worcesters.

The storming of Badajoz, where Lieut McPherson of the 45th took off his coat to fly from the flag-pole in order to signal the success of the assault.

Alma Day (September 20): the Regimental Day of the Sherwood Foresters has always been held with the Battalion parading the Russian drums captured by men of the 95th Regiment at the Battle of the Alma in 1854. It was customary in the Foresters for the eldest serving soldier to carry the Regimental Colour on this day. WFR drums are still distinguishable by the dog-tooth edges of Russian Crimean pattern.

Gheluvelt Day (October 31): the timely advance of the Worcesters to hold the line at Gheluvelt, which effectively saved the flank of the BEF in 1914, is commemorated on this old Regimental Day of the Worcestershires.

Customs

A Regimental association is maintained with the Royal Anglians through an old campaigning friendship the Worcesters had with the Royal Lincolnshire and Royal Norfolk Regiments.

Until 1970, when the custom was taken up by Nottingham City Council at the Castle, the Sherwood Foresters upheld a strange practice on Badajoz Day (April 6), in which a red jacket was flown from the flag-pole. This ritual was to commemorate an incident during the Siege of Badajoz on April 6, 1812, in which Lieutenant McPherson of the 45th, after being wounded in a previous assault, succeeded in climbing a tower and tearing down the enemy flag. With no other flag to signal the achievement McPherson removed his own jacket and hoisted it up the flag-pole.

In 1784 an Army Order abolishing pouch insignia in the infantry made an exception for the 29th to continue with its star badge. The authorisation was confirmed in 1825 and 1838, and when the valise appeared in 1875 the star was borne on the flap in the style of the Coldstream Guards. This custom is kept alive in the Regimental band and drums today.

Certain officers wear swords at dinner (see 'Nicknames' section).

Mascot

Private Derby Ram comes from the Duke of Devonshire's estate in Yorkshire, and, on parade, wears a

BUTCHER'S HALL
Engrav'd Printed & Sold by PAUL REVERE BOSTON

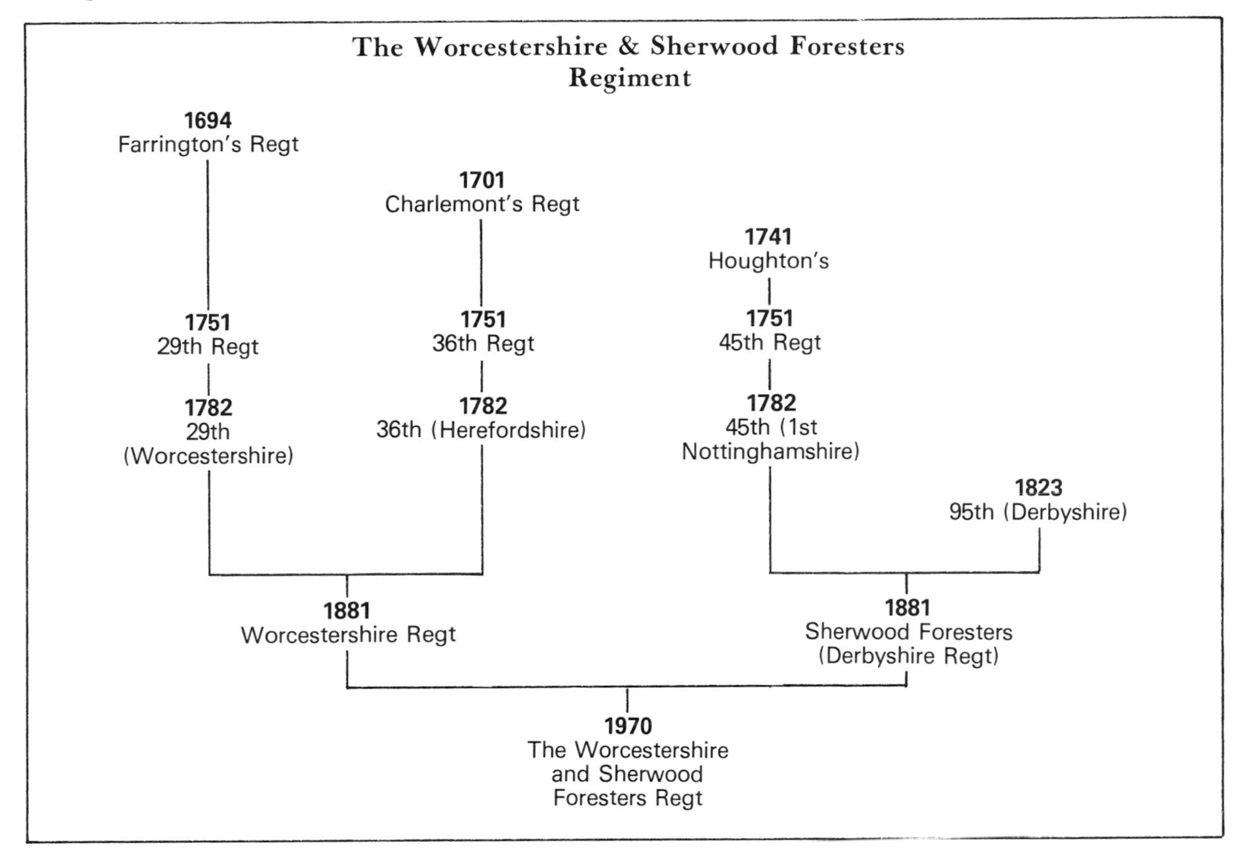

green coat emblazoned with the Regiment's battle honours and a replica of the Indian Mutiny medal awarded to Derby I, the first of the Foresters' long line of mascots. Private Derby is looked after by a Ram Major and Ram Orderly.

Dress distinctions

A blue dress cap mounted with the Regimental badge, the elongated star superimposed by a Maltese Cross and stag. Collar badges and buttons are stamped as the Regimental badge. The stable-belt is Lincoln green with a central maroon stripe. Full dress scarlet tunics sport the Lincoln green facings restored to the Sherwood Foresters in 1913.

Above far left *The Glorious First of June.*

Above left *The Worcesters at Gheluvelt.*

Left *The 'Boston Massacre'.*

Marches

Royal Windsor/Young May Moon (Quick), the former marches of the 29th and 45th Regiments; the *Windsor* was presented to the 29th by Princess Augusta in 1791 and the *May Moon* is said to have been adopted on the night march to join the siege at Badajoz in 1812. *The Duchess Of Kent* (Worcs) is the Slow March. *Hearts Of Oak* and *Rule Britannia* are played in tribute to the men of the 29th who sailed with Lord Howe on June 1 1794. *The Lincolnshire Poacher,* an old air of the 36th Regiment, is played before the Quickstep to honour the Worcesters' long campaigning fellowship with the Lincolnshire Regiment. *Derby Ram,* the former Quickstep of the Foresters, is based on an old Jacobite song.

Nicknames

'The Woofers': from initials WFR used by the Regiment.

'The Ever-sworded 29th': an old nickname related to an incident which took place in North America in 1746, in which officers of the 29th

Regiment were surprised at dinner by Indians. After this it became normal for officers of this Regiment to wear their swords at dinner, but in 1850 the custom was restricted to the Orderly Officer and Captain of the Week, an arrangement that has lasted to this day.

'The Guards of the Line': the Worcesters' association with the Coldstream Guards was highlighted in a memo from Horse Guards in 1877, which said: 'His Royal Highness, with a view to the assimilation . . . of the pouches of the 29th Regiment to those of the Guards, has approved of white ammunition pouches in lieu of black ones.'

'The Nails': a reference to the men of the 95th (Derbyshire) Regiment in the Indian Mutiny, from their reputation for being as hard as nails.

'The Old Stubborns'; a worthy title given to the 45th Regiment in battle during the Peninsula War, probably at Busaco or Talavera.

'The Rams': the Sherwood Foresters, from their familiar ram mascot.

'The Saucy Greens': the 36th Foot, from its high Irish content and the colour of its facings.

'The Vein-openers': a name which goes back to the 'Boston Massacre' of 1770, in which a picquet of the 29th Foot opened up on a mob of anti-British agitators: the first shots of the American Revolution.

Recruiting

Worcestershire, Derbyshire and Nottinghamshire. RHQ: Norton Barracks, Worcester.

Simkin's view of the East Lancashires on manoeuvres, 1893.

The Queen's Lancashire Regiment (30th, 40th, 47th, 59th, 81st, 82nd Foot)

Insignia

The Red Rose of Lancaster: the emblem of the county of Lancashire has pride of place in the centre of the Regimental Colour.

The Red Rose ensigned with the Sphinx: the crest of the East Lancashire Regiment was inspired by the device awarded to the 30th for its part in the Egyptian campaign of 1801.

A Sphinx ensigned with the Prince of Wales' Plume: the badge of the South Lancashire Regiment was composed of the Sphinx awarded to the 40th Regiment in 1802 and by the Prince of Wales' plume granted to the 82nd, by way of its founder Colonel, who was on the Prince's staff.

The Red Rose ensigned with the Royal Crest: the badge of the Loyal Regiment (North Lancashire).

Loyally I Serve: the Regimental motto is a conjunction of two mottoes: *Loyaute m'oblige* and *Ich dien* (I serve). The first was connected with the curiously titled Loyal Regiment and was the family motto of Albermarle Berti, 9th Earl of Lindsey, who formed the Loyal Lincoln Volunteers in 1793. When the Regiment became the 81st of Foot it was permitted the distinction of continuing with the unique title *Loyal* in recognition of the patriotic zeal displayed by the Loyal Lincoln Militia when they volunteered *en masse* for the fight against Revolutionary France. The motto was translated as

My loyalty compels me. *Ich dien* (I serve) comes from the Prince of Wales' badge of the South Lancashire Regiment.

Honours

Gibraltar 1704–05 (30th); Louisburg (40th/47th); Quebec 1759 (47th); Belleisle (30th); Havannah (40th); Cape of Good Hope 1806 (59th); Maida (81st); Monte Video (40th); Vimiera (40th/82nd); Java (59th); Tarifa (47th); Badajoz (30th/40th); Vittoria (40th/59th); St Sebastian (47th/59th); Pyrenees (40th/82nd); Nivelle (40th/82nd); Nive (47th/59th); Niagara (82nd); Orthes (40th/82nd); Toulouse (40th); Waterloo (30th/40th); Ava (47th); Bhurtpore (59th); Candahar, Maharajpore (40th); Alma, Inkerman (30th); Sevastopol (30th/47th/82nd); Lucknow (82nd); Canton (59th); New Zealand (40th); Ali Masjid (81st); Ahmed Khel (59th); Chitral (ELR); Defence of Kimberley (LNL); Relief of Ladysmith (SLR).

Mons (SLR/LNL); Retreat from Mons, Marne 1914, 1915, 1918 (ELR); Aisne 1914, 1918 (ELR/SLR/ LNL); Messines 1914, 1917, 1918 (SLR); Ypres 1914, 1917, 1918 (ELR/SLR/LNL); Neuve Chapelle (ELR); Somme 1916, 1918 (ELR/SLR/ LNL); Arras 1917, 1918 (ELR); Lys (LNL); Hindenburg Line (LNL); Doiran 1917, 1918 (ELR/ SLR); Helles (ELR); Suvla (LNL); Sari Bair (SLR); Gaza (LNL); Kut al Amara 1917 (ELR); Baghdad (SLR/LNL); Kilimanjaro (LNL); Baluchistan 1918 (SLR).

Afghanistan 1919 (SLR).

Dunkirk 1940 (ELR/SLR/LNL); Normandy Landing, Bourgebus Ridge (SLR); Falais (ELR/ SLR); Lower Maas, Ourthes (ELR); Rhineland (SLR); Reichswald, Weeze, Aller (ELR); Djebel

Escort to the Keys, HM Tower of London, 1983.

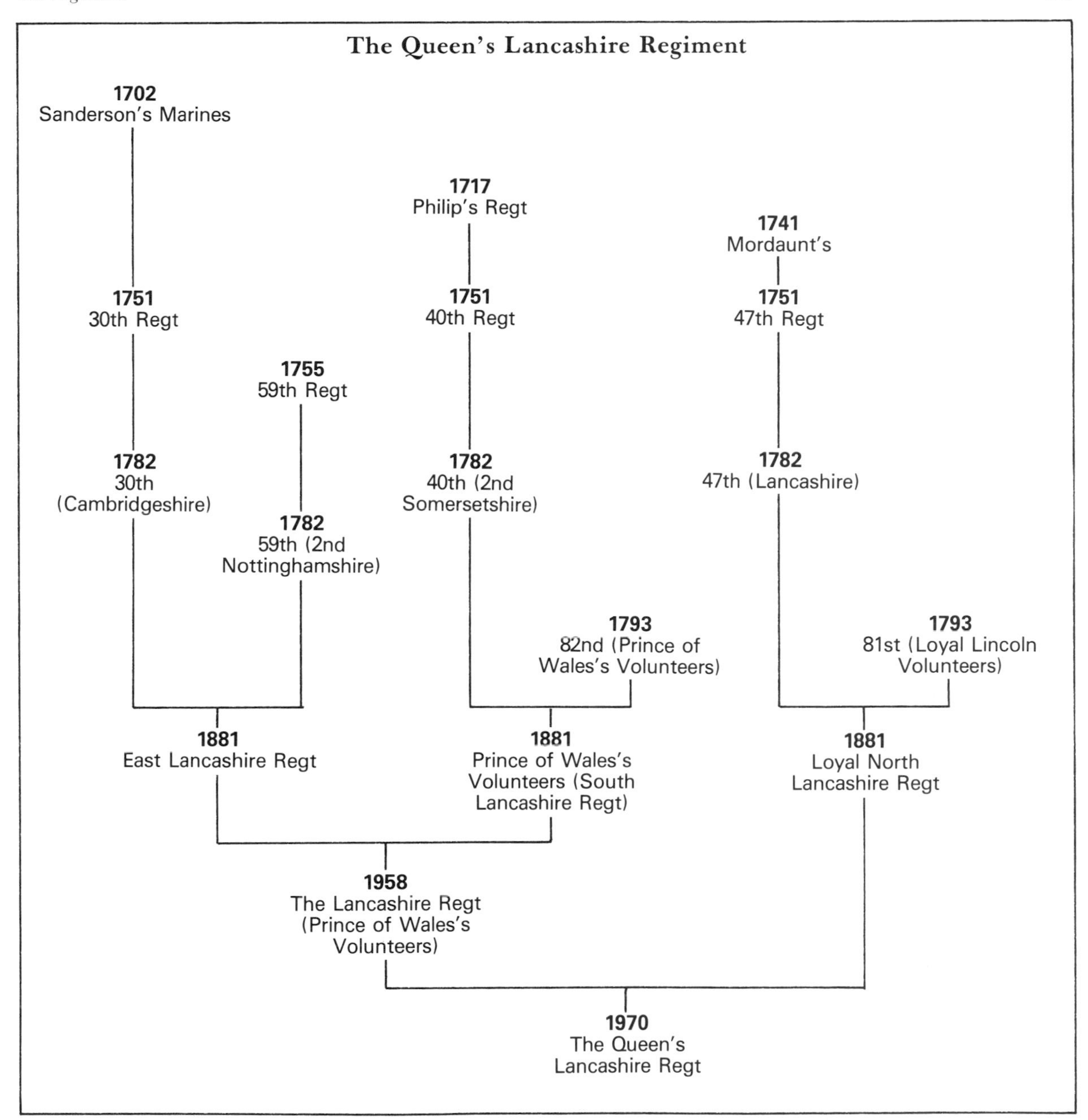

Above left *The blue Regimental Colour leads off the 'Old Guard' from Buckingham Palace in 1983.*

Left *The South Lancashire Regiment carries the last enemy position before the Relief of Ladysmith: Pieter's Hill, February 27 1900. General Buller afterwards gave a mention to the 'magnificent charge' in despatches, and the battalion was personally congratulated on its achievement in camp on the following day.*

Kesskiss, Gueriat el Atach Ridge, Anzio, Fiesole, Monte Grande (LNL); Madagascar (ELR/ SLR); Johore, Singapore Island (LNL); North Arakan, Kohima (SLR); Pinwe (ELR); Nyaungu Bridgehead (SLR).

'Egypt' was borne on the Colours of the 30th and 40th Regiments. The South Lancashires honoured March 8 as Aboukir Day in celebration of the successful landing of the 40th on the shores of Aboukir Bay in 1801.

'Louisburg' was granted to the 40th and 47th Regiments, as a result of which both units passed into the Wolfe Society, a privilege that has been inherited by the QLR.

'Maida' was granted to seven regiments and the 2nd Battalion Loyal Regiment used to keep Maida Day (July 4) for its Colour trooping ceremony.

'Tarifa' was awarded to three regiments in all. The Sergeants Mess of the Loyal Regiment customarily held a ball on Tarifa Night (December 31).

'Somme' was commemorated by the South Lancashire Regiment on July 1, in solemn memory of the 463 lives lost by the Regiment in one attack alone.

Anniversaries

Quebec Day (September 13): the prominent part taken by the 47th Foot at the Battle of Quebec led the QLR to observe September 13 as Quebec Day, even though the Loyals did not.

Waterloo Day (June 18): the anniversary of the Battle of Waterloo was important to the East Lancashires, who suffered great losses in the battle. It was customary for members of the South Lancashire Regiment to wear a laurel leaf in the cap on Waterloo Day.

Customs

In the Loyal Regiment the Loyal Toast was often proposed 'The Queen, Duke of Lancaster, Our Colonel-in-Chief.'

In the 1st Loyals a *Subalterns' Cup* was used before the Second World War to celebrate subalterns' promotions.

After the Battle of Maida Lieutenant Colonel Kempt made his supper off a tortoise and saved the shell as a memento; this was later mounted in silver as a snuff box for the mess.

Mascot

None.

Dress distinctions

A blue dress cap with a scarlet band and piping, mounted with the Regimental cap badge: the crowned Rose within an oval with the motto scroll beneath. The badge is worn on a diamond-shaped primrose patch on the beret. A maroon side hat with a black tip. Collar badges: the crowned Rose. Buttons are stamped with the Rose of Lancaster. The stable-belt is maroon.

Marches

L'Attaque, the Regimental March Past is a combination of *Attack* from the East Lancashires and *Red Red Rose* from the Loyals. *Long Live Elizabeth*, Queen Elizabeth II, Colonel-in-Chief of the Loyal Regiment from 1953, is the titular head of the QLR. *Quebec/The 47th* (Loyal Regiment). *The Lincolnshire Poacher*, the 2nd Battalion Loyal Regiment, the old 81st, was formed in Lincoln. *God Bless The Prince of Wales*: a former march of the South Lancashire Regiment. *Lancashire Witches* (South Lancashire Regiment). *The Lancashire Lad* (East Lancashire Regiment).

Scarlet-coated band and drums lead a contingent of QLR through Haslingden, Lancs, in the Freedom of the Town.

Nicknames

'The Blessed Images': an allusion to the smart appearance of the 47th Regiment.

'The Cauliflowers': the 47th Regiment, from its white facings, which were quite rare in the 18th century.

'The Excellers': the 40th Regiment, from its rank insignia (XL).

'The Fighting Fortieth': the 40th's reputation relates to the 1st Battalion's impressive range of service throughout the Peninsula War, when it was often left to operate in an independent capacity.

'The Lancashire Lads': the predecessors of the Loyal Regiment, the 47th, were the only regular corps to bear the name 'Lancashire' prior to 1881.

'The Triple X's': the 30th Regiment, from its rank in Roman numerals (XXX).

'Wolfe's Own': the 47th Regiment. Colonel Hale of the 47th was chosen to deliver the victory news of Quebec to London, and the Regiment honoured Wolfe's memory by wearing a black mourning line in the officers' lace.

Recruiting

Central Lancashire. RHQ: Fulwood Barracks, Preston.

The Duke of Wellington's Regiment (33rd, 76th Foot)

Insignia

A demi-lion issuing from a ducal coronet above the motto *Virtutis fortuna comes:* Arthur Wellesley served with the 76th as a subaltern, and with the 33rd as Lieutenant Colonel, during his early military career in India. He accepted the Colonelcy of the 33rd in 1806, and his crest and title were bestowed upon that Regiment in 1853, a year after his death. It has been a tradition since the 19th century for the Regiment to have a Duke of Wellington as Colonel-in-Chief. The DWR maintains the unique distinction of being the only Regiment to be named after a person not of Royal blood.

An elephant with howdah and mahout, circumscribed 'Hindoostan', and ensigned with the Crown: awarded to the 76th Regiment in 1808 for services to the Honourable East India Company from 1787 to 1807. The device was modelled on the emblem conferred on the Regiments at Assaye, but is peculiar to the DWR by virtue of design.

Honours

Dettingen (33rd); Mysore (76th); Seringapatam (33rd/76th); Ally Ghur, Delhi 1803, Leswaree, Deig, Corunna, Nive, Peninsula (76th); Waterloo, Alma, Inkerman, Sevastopol, Abyssinia (33rd); Relief of Kimberley, Paardeberg, South Africa 1900–1902.

Mons, Marne 1914, 1918, Ypres 1914, 1918, Hill 60, Somme 1916, 1918, Arras 1917, 1918,

'The Havercake Lads'.

Lovell

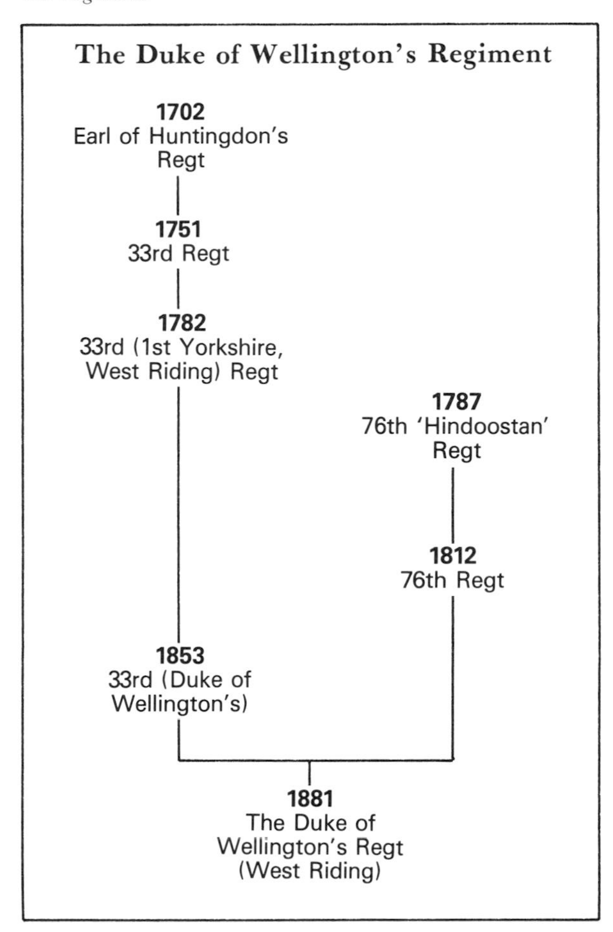

Cambrai 1917, 1918, Lys, Piave 1918, Landing at Suvla.

Afghanistan 1919.

Dunkirk, St Valery-en-Caux, Fontenoy-le-Pesnil, North-West Europe 1940, 1944–45, Djebel Bou Aoukaz 1943, Anzio, Monte Ceco, Sittang 1942, Chindits 1944, Burma 1942–44.

Anniversaries

St George's Day (April 23): white roses are worn on the left side of the cap.

Customs

The Honorary Colours: the DWR is the only regiment to have the privilege of carrying four Colours on parade; two regulation and two honorary. The Honorary Colours are descended from a pair presented to the 76th Regiment by the Honourable East India Company in 1808, and bear the achievements of that Regiment: the elephant with howdah and mahout in the centre, circumscribed *Hindoostan,* with the battle honours 'Ally Ghur, 4th September 1803', 'Delhi, 11th September 1803', 'Agra, 10th October 1803', 'Leswaree, 1st November 1803', 'Deig, 23rd December 1804', 'Mysore', 'Nive', 'Corunna', and 'Peninsula'. The 1803 honours, with the exception of 'Leswaree' which is shared with the Queen's Royal Irish Hussars, are borne by no other British regiment.

Mascot

None.

Dress distinctions

A blue dress cap mounted with the Duke of Wellington's crest on a red backing. A blue side hat, the body piped in gold. Collar badges: the elephant with howdah. Buttons are embossed with the elephant within a peripheral inscription: *Duke of Wellington's West Riding Regiment.* Scarlet lanyards and facings. Scarlet facings, worn by both the 33rd and 76th Regiments, were restored to the DWR in 1905.

Marches

The Wellesley. Ilkley Moor. I'm Ninety-five. Scotland The Brave (76th). On Guest Nights in the Officers Mess *Rule Britannia* is played along with a selection of rugby tunes. The DWR prides itself on its rugby.

Nicknames

'The Dukes'.

'The Havercake Lads': an old nickname of the 33rd which referred to a recruiting ploy used during the Napoleonic Wars, when able-bodied men were lured to the Colours by the promise of an oatcake, or haver, skewered to the point of the recruiting Sergeant's sword.

'The Old Immortals': a reputation held by the 76th, whose forebears astounded Lord Lake with their remarkable ability to get back to fighting strength after each devastating battle of the Mahratta Wars.

'The Pigs': the 76th Regiment, from its elephant badge.

'The Old Seven and Sixpennies': the 76th, from their Regimental numerals.

Recruiting

West Yorkshire. RHQ: Halifax.

Above left *Simkin's Grenadiers of the 76th, under the personal command of Arthur Wellesley, in the attack on Seringapatam, May 4 1799.*

Left *Freedom March in Huddersfield. The spearheads on the larger (Honorary) Colours are the originals, engraved and presented by the Honourable East India Company.*

The Royal Hampshire Regiment (37th, 67th Foot)

Insignia

A double red rose: the 'Hampshire Rose', together with the Crown and Garter, was bestowed upon the trained Bands of Hampshire by Henry V to commemorate their service with him at Agincourt in 1415.

The Royal Tiger superscribed 'India': awarded to the 67th Regiment by King George IV in recognition of its continuous active service in India between the years 1805 and 1826

Honours

Blenheim, Ramillies, Oudenarde, Malplaquet, Dettingen, Minden, Tournay (37th); Barrossa, Peninsula, Taku Forts, Pekin 1860, Charasiah, Kabul 1879, Afghanistan 1878–80 (67th); Burma 1885–87, Paardeberg, South Africa 1900–02.

Retreat from Mons, Ypres 1915, 1917, 1918, Somme 1916, 1918, Arras 1917, 1918, Cambrai 1917, Doiran 1917, 1918, Landing at Helles, Suvla, Gaza, Kut al Amara.

Dunkirk 1940, Normandy Landing, Caen, Rhine, Tebourba Gap, Hunt's Gap, Salerno, Cassino II, Gothic Line, Malta 1941–42.

Cuneo's painting of Major Le Patourel winning his VC at Tebourba Gap. King George VI said of the campaign, 'I recommend you to read the story of the 2nd Battalion The Hampshire Regiment in Tunisia in 1942. That was a triumph of individual leadership and corporate discipline.'

Laying up of the Colours, all battalions, at Winchester in 1964. The Hampshires were reduced to 'Minden Company' in 1970, with the prospect of amalgamation with the Gloucesters, but a reprieve in 1972 brought the Regiment back up to strength for a tour of Northern Ireland.

Anniversaries

Minden Day (August 1): the anniversary of the Battle of Minden is observed with meticulous ceremony to mark the part played by the 37th Foot in the magnificent defeat of the French army on August 1 1759. The 'Minden Rose' is worn by all ranks behind the cap badge on this day.

Gallipoli Day (April 25): the landings at Suvla Bay and Helles from the HMT *River Clyde* are remembered on April 25 for the heavy losses sustained by the 2nd Battalion at Gallipoli.

Customs

The Wolfe Society: the Regiment's connection with the Wolfe Society goes back to 1758, when the 67th received General Wolfe as its first Colonel. Wolfe spent most of the year campaigning in Canada, but found time to visit his Regiment twice at its camp near Salisbury before returning to Canada for the last time.

Trooping the Swede: in 1920 a ceremony called 'Trooping the Swede' was initiated in the 4th Battalion to honour 'The Swedebashers' who flocked to the Colours in 1914 and never came back. At the Annual Reunion of the Battalion the procedure is for swedes to be tied with ribbons of yellow and black and trouped around the dining table to *The Farmer's Boy*.

Mascot

None.

Dress distinctions

A blue dress cap with scarlet band and piping, mounted with (for soldiers) the Rose surmounted by the Royal Tiger within a crowned laurel wreath or

A Quartermaster of the 37th and a Private of the 67th in 1877, when the two battalions came together in readiness for the merger of 1881.

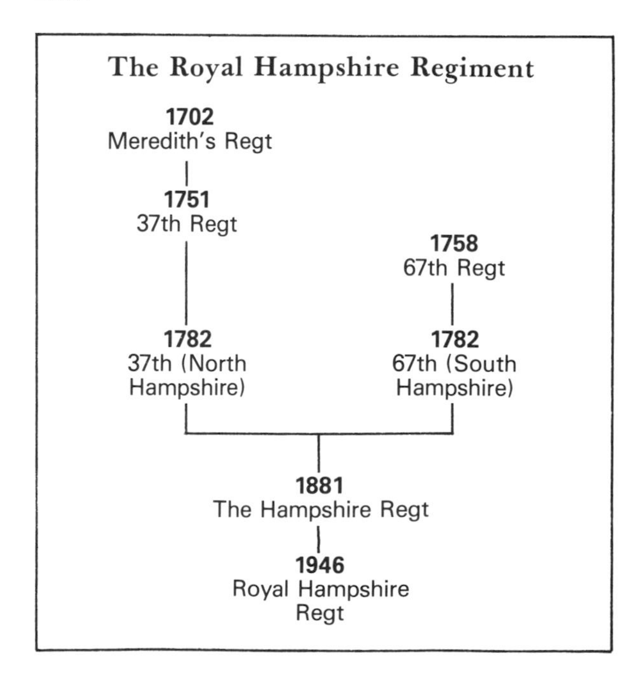

(for officers and warrant officers) an eight-pointed star with the Garter and Crown with the Rose within. The Royal Tiger was worn as the Regimental cap badge from 1881 until 1897, when officers assumed the badge of the Hampshire Militia and soldiers were issued with Tiger and Rose within the laurel wreath badge. The Crown was added in 1946. A blue side hat with a yellow tip and piping. Collar badges: the Rose within a laurel wreath. Buttons are embossed with the Tiger and Rose within a laurel wreath. The stable-belt is black with yellow/red/green/mauve stripes. Yellow facings were restored to the Regiment in 1904. Officers' Sam Browne belts are fitted with a whistle on the shoulder strap.

Marches

The Hampshire, the Regimental Quickstep is based on the March of the 37th Regiment, *The Highland Piper. We'll Gang Nae Mair To Yon Toon* (67th). *Cork Hill*, the March of the 3rd (Militia) Battalion. *The Farmer's Boy:*, the March common to all Wessex regiments is often played before the Regimental Marches on parade.

Nicknames

'The Stonewallers': the 1st Battalion gained this reputation during the First World War for never having lost a trench to the Germans. Tenacity in defence is still regarded as a characteristic of the Regiment.

Recruiting

Hampshire. RHQ: Winchester.

The Staffordshire Regiment (Prince of Wales's) (38th, 64th, 80th, 98th Foot)

Insignia

The Prince of Wales' Plume within the Stafford

Knot: the emblem of the Prince of Wales was conferred upon the 98th Regiment in 1876, when the Prince made a tour of Malta. On a visit of inspection to the Regiment, the Prince was told how a previous 98th had carried his title, and in October of that year the same honour was granted to the Regiment. The Knot of the de Stafford family was adopted by the 38th and 64th Regiments around 1782, when they were both affiliated to the county of Stafford for recruiting purposes.

The Sphinx superscribed 'Egypt': granted to the 80th Regiment in 1802 for service in the Egyptian campaign of 1801.

The Dragon superscribed 'China': awarded to the 98th Regiment for service in the 'Opium War' of 1840.

Honours

Guadaloupe 1759 (38th/64th); Martinique 1762 (38th); Martinique 1794, St Lucia 1803, Surinam (64th); Montevideo, Rolica, Vimiera, Corunna, Busaco, Badajoz, Salamanca, Vittoria, St Sebastian, Nive, Peninsula, Ava (38th); Moodkee, Ferozeshah, Sobraon (80th); Punjaub (98th); Pegu (80th); Alma, Inkerman, Sevastopol (38th); Reshire, Bushire, Koosh-ab, Persia (64th); Lucknow (38th/64th); Central India (80th); South Africa 1878–79, (80th); Egypt 1882, Kirbekan, Nile 1884–85 (S Staff); Hafir (N Staff); South Africa 1900–02 (S/N Staff).

Mons, Marne 1914, Aisne 1914 (S Staff); Armentières 1924 (N Staff); Ypres 1914, 1917, 1918 (S/N Staff); Loos (S Staff); Somme 1916, 1918 (S/N

A pen and ink sketch of the light company, 98th Regiment, during the 1840s. Flank companies such as this were abolished in 1860.

The 64th take the redoubt at Reshire for the loss of Colonel Stopford. The Persian campaign in the winter of 1856-7 was easily won, and few casualties were incurred overall.

Staff); Arras 1917, 1918, Messines 1917, 1918 (N Staff); Cambrai 1917, 1918, (S Staff); St Quentin Canal, (S/N Staff); Selle (N Staff); Vittorio Veneto (S Staff); Suvla, Sari Bair, Kut al Amara, North-West Frontier India 1915, (N Staff).

Afghanistan 1919 (N Staff).

Dyle, Ypres–Comines Canal (N Staff); Caen (S/N Staff); Noyers (S Staff); Brieux Bridgehead (N Staff); Falaise, Arnhem 1944, North-West Europe 1940, 1944–45 (S Staff); Medjez Plain (N Staff); North Africa 1940, 1943, (S/N Staff); Landing in Sicily, Sicily 1943 (S Staff); Anzio, Rome, Marradi (N Staff); Chindits 1944 (S Staff); Burma 1943, 1944 (S/N Staff).

Anniversaries

Ypres Day (July 31): the former Regimental Day of the North Staffords is the anniversary of the successful attack carried out by the 1st Battalion on the first day of Third Ypres.

Ferozeshah Day (December 21): the ritual of handing over the Colours to the Sergeants, which formerly characterised this Regimental Day of the South Staffords, is now normal procedure for all Regimental days. The ceremony was originally performed in honour of Sergeant Kirkland of the 80th, who was given a battlefield commission at Ferozeshah for his gallant capture of a black Sikh Standard. Wellington paid tribute to the Regiment in a Parliamentary address: 'Who but old soldiers could have done what the 80th did at Ferozeshah?'.

Anzio Day (January 22): a secondary day now, the original purpose of which was to commemorate the landing and engagement of the 2nd North Staffords at Anzio in 1944.

Arnhem Day (September 17): the old Regimental Day of the South Staffords is dedicated to the memory of the men who volunteered to wear the red beret and join the airborne assault on Arnhem in 1944.

Customs

The Regiment maintains an alliance with the Jamaica Defence Regiment and the Antigua Defence Force, in connection with its early history in the West Indies.

Mascot

None.

Dress distinctions

A blue dress cap mounted with the Stafford Knot badge surmounted by the Prince of Wales' Plume. The badge is worn with a buff Holland backing authorised to the South Staffords in 1935 to commemorate the 57 years of continuous service seen by the 38th Foot in the West Indies, from 1707 to 1764. This symbolises the sacking used in the sugar trade of the Leeward Islands, with which the men patched and finally replaced their neglected uniforms. A blue side hat piped in gold. Collar badges: the Stafford Knot with the Plume of the Prince of Wales within. Buttons are stamped with the Regimental

Above right *Ferozeshan Day. The Colours in the care of the Sergeants.*

Above far right *The Corps of Drums taken at the Governor's Residence at Gibraltar in 1983. The tunic facings are yellow after the South Staffords, while the wings are black (North Staffords).*

Right *Observation post. The cap badge, with the plume* above *the knot, is clearly shown.*

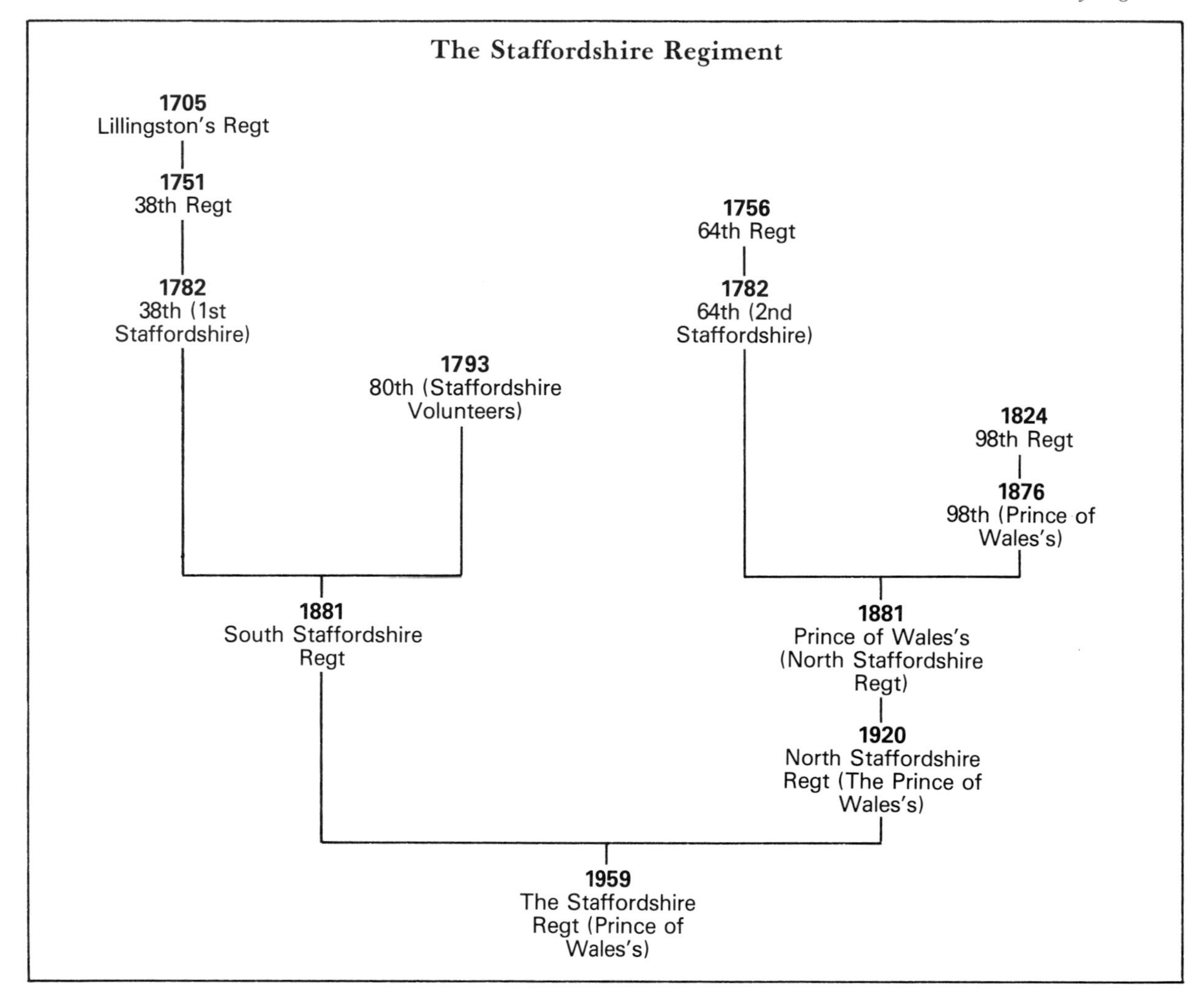

badge. A gold glider badge is worn on the upper right sleeve by all ranks as a tribute to the South Staffords' part in the airborne landings on Sicily, July 9 1943. The badge was originally awarded to the 2nd Battalion by George VI. The stable-belt and lanyards are black, the facing colour of the 64th Regiment restored to the North Staffords in 1937. Facings of yellow, formerly sported by the 38th and 80th Regiments, were restored to the South Staffords in 1936.

Marches

Come Lasses And Lads/The Days We Went A Gypsying, the Regimental March is a fusion of the marches played in the South and North Staffords respectively. *God Bless The Prince Of Wales* (North Staffords). *Gemel Jager*, the Approach March was adopted by the South Staffords during the Second World War as a salute to their Norwegian allies. It has an importance in Norway equivalent to *The British Grenadier* in Britain. *Zakmi Dil* or *The Afghan March* was adopted by the 2nd North Staffords on a tour of duty on the North West Frontier in 1912. *The 80th*, an Inspection tune introduced to the South Staffords' repertoire around 1930. *We'll Gang Nae More To Glasgae Toun*, a fife and drum march from the South Staffords; used now as the Colour Escort March.

Nicknames

'The Black Knots': the 64th Regiment, from its black facings and Stafford Knot badge.

'The Brown Regiment': a term used in the 18th century to describe the neglected detachments of the

38th Foot in the West Indies, where they spent 57 years, based on Antigua, repairing and constructing ships for the Fleet and providing men for the numerous expeditions against the French and Spanish in the Leeward Islands. The name comes from the local sacking which the Regiment used to replace worn-out red coats.

'The Pump and Tortoise': the 38th Foot, origin obscure.

Recruiting

Staffordshire and part of the West Midlands. RHQ: Whittington Barracks, Lichfield.

The Black Watch (Royal Highland Regiment) (42nd, 73rd Foot)

Insignia

The Royal Cipher within the Garter.

The badge and motto of the Order of the Garter.

The Royal Cipher ensigned with the Crown.

The Sphinx superscribed 'Egypt': granted to the 42nd Regiment in 1802.

Honours

Guadaloupe 1759, Martinique 1762, Havannah, North America 1763–64 (42nd); Mangalore, Mysore, Seringapatam (73rd); Corunna, Busaco, Fuentes d'Onor, Pyrenees, Nivelle, Nive, Orthes, Toulouse, Peninsula (42nd); Waterloo (42nd/73rd); South Africa 1846–47, 1851–53 (73rd); Alma, Sevastopol, Lucknow, Ashantee 1873–74 (42nd); Tel-el-kebir, Egypt 1882, 1884, Kirbekan, Nile 1884–85, Paardeberg, South Africa 1899–1902.

Marne 1914, 1918, Ypres 1914, 1917, 1918, Loos, Somme 1916, 1918, Arras 1917, 1918, Lys, Hindenburg Line, Doiran 1917, Meggido, Kut al Amara 1917.

Falaise Road, Rhine, Tobruk 1941, El Alamein, Akarit, Tunis, Sicily 1943, Cassino II, Crete, Burma 1944.

The Hook, Korea 1952–53.

'North America 1763–64' is shared only with the Royal Green Jackets, and records the little wars against the American Indians out of Fort Pitt. It was there that the 42nd learned the art of forest warfare, although their desperate assault on the breastworks of Fort Ticonderoga in 1758 is also highly regarded in military circles.

'Toulouse' represents another example of the 42nd's famous fighting qualities, even though the Battalion suffered the sad distinction in this battle of having the highest casualty rate in a conflict fought after peace had been declared.

'Waterloo' has always been remembered with due ceremony in both founder Regiments.

Anniversaries

Red Hackle Day (June 4): the Regimental Day takes its name from the Regiment's unique red feather worn on certain types of headgear in place of a badge. Red feathers were presented to the 42nd Highlanders at Royston on June 4 1795, to be worn 'as a mark of gallantry'. The exact reason for the award is open to speculation, but theorists are mainly divided between the Battle of Guildermalsen (1795), where the Highlanders were reputed to have saved the guns, and the American War of Independence, in which the 42nd distinguished itself at

The Black Watch at Tel-el-kebir, September 12 1882

Above *Colour Sergeant Murray, hackle visible, standing between the Bagdad Bell, captured at Samarra Station in 1917, and the Mutiny Gong.*

Below *The 42nd square attacked by French lancers at Quatre Bras during the Waterloo campaign.*

the battles in and around New York. The original feathers were obviously treated without regard for their true meaning because the normal order of company feathers were again worn in the Napoleonic Wars. It was not until 1825, when the new Colonel, Sir George Murray, asserted the General Order of 1822 which confirmed red vulture feathers to the 42nd, that the distinction was resumed on a permanent basis.

Customs

Two trophies of war have long been used to sound time in barracks. During the Indian Mutiny the 1st Battalion 'liberated' a brass gong from the mutineers of the Gwalior contingent at Seraghai, while the 2nd Battalion was the first unit of the Mesopotamian Expeditionary Force to enter Baghdad (on March 11 1917), capturing a bell at Samarra railway station on April 23.

Mascot

The Regiment had a stag called 'Donald' in Dublin

James Campbell, 'the valiant Highlander who kill'd nine men with his broadsword at . . . Fontenoy . . . & was making a stroke at a tenth but was prevented by a cannon ball's shooting off his left arm . . .'.

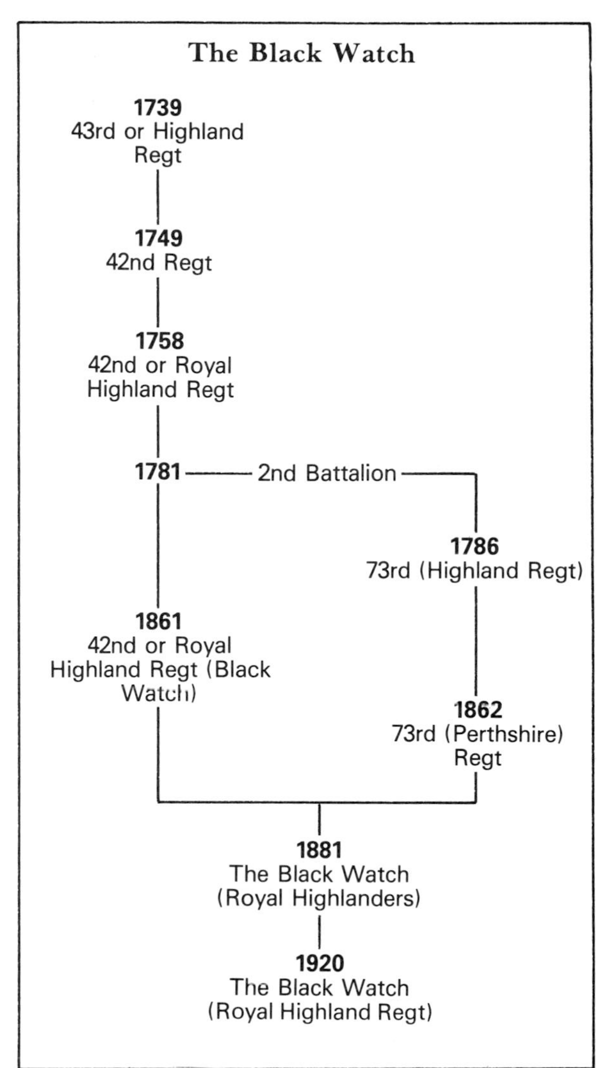

during 1836, which was walked on Guard mountings and parades in Phoenix Park.

Dress distinctions

A blue glengarry mounted with the Regimental badge. A red hackle is worn on the tam o'shanter and the full dress feather bonnet. Collar badges: St Andrew and Cross. Buttons bear a circular form of the cap badge, the Star of the Order of the Thistle with St Andrew and cross within. On the lower point of the Star, the Sphinx. A kilt of Black Watch tartan and a white hair sporran with five short black tassels. The Government, or Military, tartan was designed for the Regiment in 1739, and by the time it came to be worn by the newly-raised Highland regiments of the latter part of the century, it had acquired the name *Black Watch*. The stable-belt is of Black Watch tartan. Spats are distinguished by a 'V' indentation. It was popularly believed that the Black Watch had to wear spats cut in this manner to remind them of the disgrace of the broken square at Tamii in 1884. Pipers wear the Royal Stewart tartan and, alone of Scottish infantry regiments, the feathered bonnet.

Marches
Highland Laddie. Lead On The Forty-Second (1970). *Garb Of Old Gaul* (Slow).

Nicknames
'The Black Watch': until 1861, when it officially became part of the Regiment's title, the term 'Black Watch' existed as a nickname for the 42nd. The name originated as *Am Freiceadan Dubh* with the birth of the Regiment, and was inspired by the sombre sett of the soldiers' kilts and their duties in policing the restive Highlands.

'The Cape Greyhounds': the 73rd Regiment under Colonel Eyre in South Africa during the 1846–47 War were dressed in grey cotton jackets and fought in rapid skirmish formation.

'The Forty Twa': the 42nd Regiment.

'Les Sauvages d'Ecosse': a French soldier's description of 'The Savages of Scotland'.

Recruiting
Tayside (Perthshire and Angus) and Fife. RHQ: Balhousic Castle, Perth.

The Duke of Edinburgh's Royal Regiment (49th, 62nd, 66th, 99th Foot)

Insignia
A dragon within two coils of rope surmounted by a ducal coronet, superimposed upon a cross pattée: the China Dragon and rope come from the Regimental insignia of the Royal Berkshire Regiment; the ship's rope was part of the badge worn by officers and commemorates the marine service of the old 49th Regiment. The coronet was granted to the 99th Regiment in 1874 as part of its distinction in becoming 'The Duke of Edinburgh's', and was later carried with the Duke's cipher on the badge of the Wiltshire Regiment. The cross pattée was adopted by the 62nd on Malta in 1806.

A dragon superscribed 'China': awarded to the 49th Regiment in 1843 for its part in the 'Opium War' of 1840–42.

A Naval Crown superscribed '2nd April, 1801': conferred on the Royal Berkshire Regiment in 1951 as a testament to the services of the 49th Regimentt, which fought with Sir Hyde Parker's fleet at Copenhagen in 1801. The date denotes the day on which Nelson, ignoring the Admiral's order, forced his way through the Danish fleet with devastating effect.

Honours
Louisburg (62nd); St Lucia 1778, Egmont-op-Zee, Copenhagen (49th); Douro, Talavera, Albuhera (66th); Queenstown (49th); Vittoria, Pyrenees, Nivelle (66th); Nive (62nd/66th); Orthes (66th); Peninsula (62nd/66th); Ferozeshah, Sobraon (62nd); Alma, Inkerman (49th); Sevastopol (49th/62nd); New Zealand, Pekin 1860, South

A glengarry badge of the 62nd Regiment.

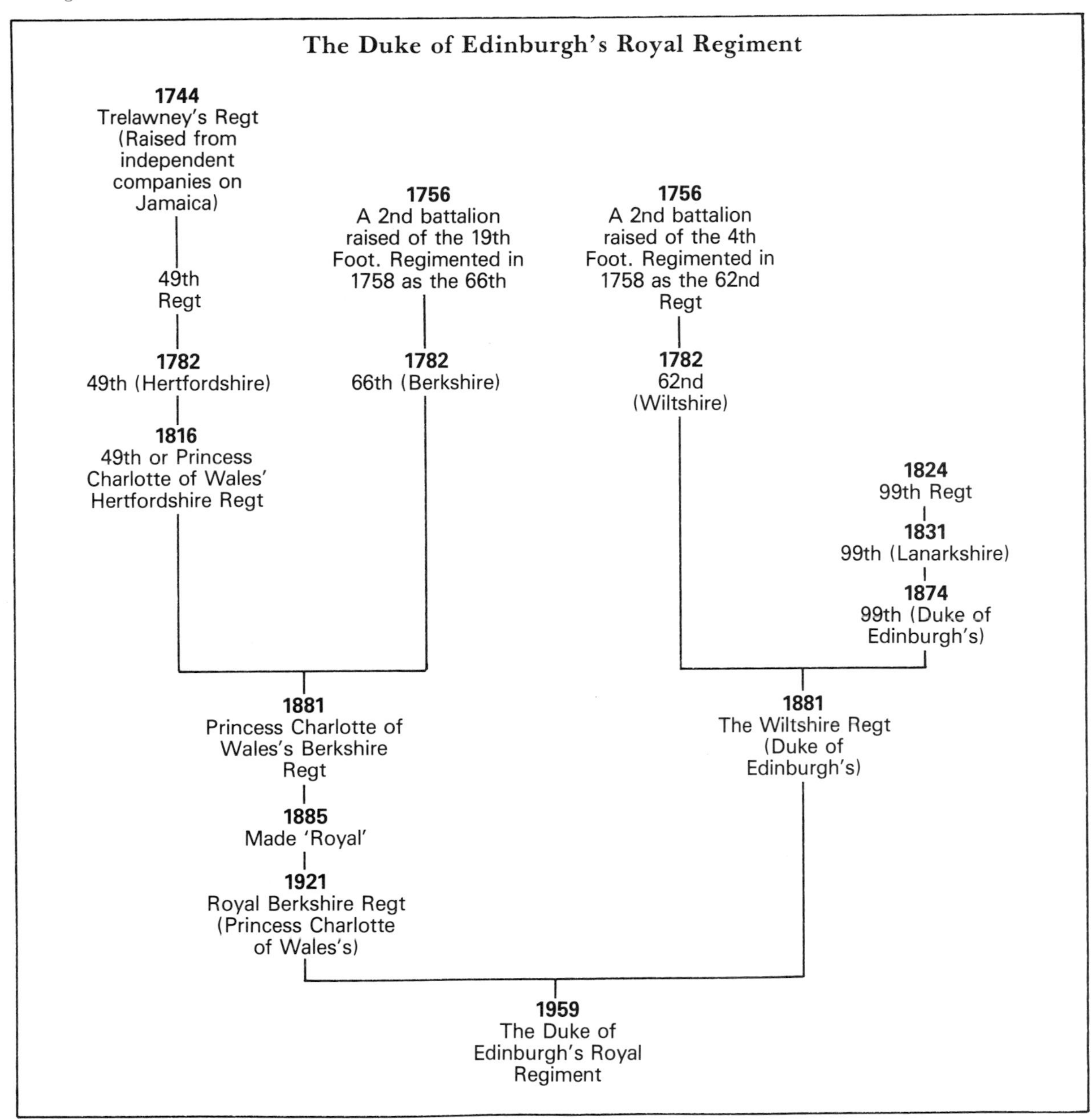

Africa 1879 (99th); Kandahar 1880, Afghanistan 1879–80 (66th); Egypt 1882, Tofrek, Suakin 1885 (Berks); South Africa 1899–1902 (Berks/Wilts).

Mons, Messines 1914, 1917, 1918 (Berks/Wilts); Ypres 1914, 1917 (Wilts); Neuve Chapelle, Loos (Berks); Somme 1916, 1918, Arras 1917, 1918 (Berks/Wilts); Cambrai 1917, 1918 (Berks); Bapaume 1918 (Wilts); Selle, Vittorio Veneto, Doiran 1917, 1918 (Berks); Macedonia 1915–18, Gallipoli 1915–16, Palestine 1917–18, Baghdad (Wilts).

Defence of Arras (Wilts); Dunkirk 1940, Normandy Landing (Berks); Hill 112, Maltot, Mont Pincon, Seine 1944, Cleve (Wilts); Rhine, Sicily 1943 (Berks); Garigliano Crossing (Wilts); Damiano (Berks); Anzio (Berks/Wilts); Rome, North Arakan (Wilts); Kohima, Mandalay, Burma 1942–45 (Berks).

Princess Charlotte bestowed her title on the 49th Regiment in 1816, when it returned from Canada and stood guard duty for her at Weymouth.

Prince Alfred, the Duke of Edinburgh after whom the DERR was named. The 99th adopted the Prince's title in 1874, some years after he had reviewed the Regiment in Cape Town.

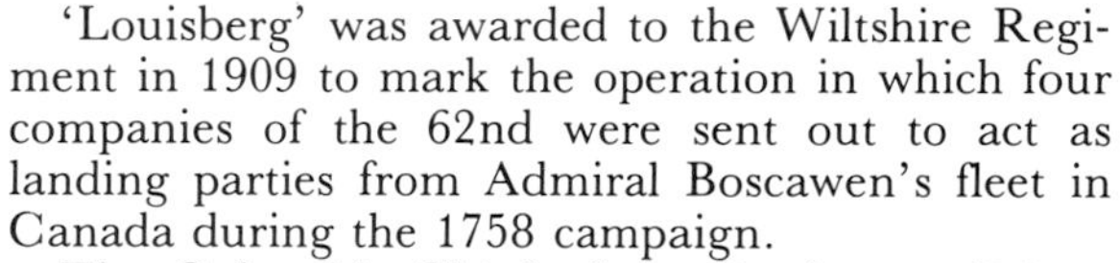

'Louisberg' was awarded to the Wiltshire Regiment in 1909 to mark the operation in which four companies of the 62nd were sent out to act as landing parties from Admiral Boscawen's fleet in Canada during the 1758 campaign.

The Colonel-in-Chief of the Regiment, Prince Philip, Duke of Edinburgh, is keen on the DERR preserving its inherited links with the Royal Navy and the Wiltshires' custom of sounding time on a ship's bell is perpetuated on a bell from HMS *Vernon*.

'Tofrek' is important in DERR history as being the battle in which the Berkshire Regiment won its Royal title.

Anniversaries

Ferozeshah Day (December 21): the victory at Ferozeshah in 1845 is celebrated in the way of the Wiltshire Regiment, with a ceremonial parade at which the Colours are entrusted to the Sergeants for the day. A Sergeants' Ball is held in the evening, and the Colours are handed back to the officers at midnight.

Maiwand Day (July 27): the Regimental Day of the Royal Berkshire Regiment is observed to honour the men of the last stand at Maiwand in 1880, when a small field force was overwhelmed by a massive army of fanatical Ghazis and irregulars under Ayub Khan. The only survivor of the last stand of the 66th Regiment was 'Bobby', a Sergeant's mongrel dog, whose loyalty was rewarded by Queen Victoria with the Afghan medal. Maiwand was technically a defeat and as such received no battle honour recognition, but in 1886 a great lion monument was erected in Forbury Gardens, Reading, as a lasting tribute to the men who perished in the battle.

Customs

Officers of the Royal Berkshire Regiment brought to the DERR some quaint mess customs which have survived to this day. The tune *Kiss Me Lady* was introduced into the Regiment's mess procedure by an amorous Colonel in the past and is played, as was the tradition, after the Loyal Toast. The

The stand of the Last Eleven at Maiwand. Sergeant Kelly's white mongrel escaped to Kandahar, and returned home to a hero's welcome.

On exercise with the BAOR. The triangular Brandywine Flash is just discernible behind the beret badge.

'Rolling In Ceremony' takes place on Guest Nights, and is characterised by the sight of two drummers in full dress 'rolling in' the diners on drums captured in the Crimean and First World Wars, to the tune *Roast Beef Of Old England.*

Mascot

None.

Dress distinctions

A blue dress cap with scarlet band and piping, mounted with the Regimental badge, the cross pattée superimposed by the China Dragon. The badge is worn on a red 'Brandywine Flash', which takes the form of a long triangle on the beret. This is worn by courtesy of the light company of the 49th, which reeked havoc on the sleeping American camp at Brandywine in 1777 and afterwards wore conspicuous red cap feathers in answer to the Americans' threat of revenge. A blue side hat piped scarlet. Collar badges: as the cap badge. Buttons are stamped with the Prince of Wales' plume to indicate the Regiment's place in the Prince of Wales's Division. The stable-belt is blue with two narrow scarlet bands.

Marches

The Farmer's Boy, the Regimental Quick March was chosen for its general appeal among the Wessex regiments. *Auld Robin Grey*, the Slow March of the

The Berkshires at Tofrek, March 22 1885. The DERR is the only British regiment to have inherited this battle honour.

Wiltshire Regiment comes from the 99th which was Scottish in origin. *The Royal Berkshire Regiment*, based on the Berkshires' *Dashing White Sergeant. Rule Britannia*, the DERR has permission to play the march after its Regimental March in commemoration of the marine service provided by detachments of the 49th at Copenhagen, and the 62nd at Louisburg. *The Wiltshires*, the former march of the Wiltshire Regiment is based on the 'Moonraker' legend with its rustic lyrics 'The Vly be on the turmat, but there bain't no vlies on we'.

Nicknames

'The Wonders': from the Battalion initials 1 DERR.

'The Biscuit Boys': the former nickname of the Royal Berkshire comes from the biscuit factories in the depot town of Reading.

'The China Dragons': the Royal Berkshires, from their dragon cap badge.

'The Emerald Greens': a self-imposed sobriquet of the 66th Regiment taken from a recruiting poster of 1825. The name referred to the green facings of the Regiment.

'The Jamaica Volunteers': a name given to the independent companies of the Jamaica Militia, which went to make up Trelawney's Regiment (the 49th Foot) in 1744.

'The Moonrakers': the nickname of the Wiltshire Regiment, from the county folk song which tells of how two yokels managed to trick excise men by 'raking' the moon's reflection from a puddle, thereby pretending to be too simple to be guilty of smuggling.

'The Queen's Pets': a name given to the 99th Regiment by other regiments resentful of their impeccable turn-out, which led them to be chosen to stand guard over the Queen's Pavilion at Aldershot in 1858. The 99th wore a diced glengarry, and its legendary smartness resulted in the saying 'to dress to the nines'.

'The Splashers': the 62nd Foot, from its reputed 'splash', or dent, in its buttons, said to have been a peculiarity of the Regiment's uniform to commemorate its lone defence of Carrickfergus Castle on February 21 1758. According to legend the men ran out of ball ammunition and resorted to firing buttons torn from their coats.

'The Springers': a term used to describe the light skirmishing tactics adopted by the 10th and 62nd Regiments during the American War of Independence; from the light infantry command 'Spring Up!'

Recruiting

Berkshire and Wiltshire. RHQ: Salisbury.

The Queen's Own Highlanders (Seaforth and Cameron) (72nd, 78th, 79th Foot)

Insignia

A stag's head caboshed, between the attires the

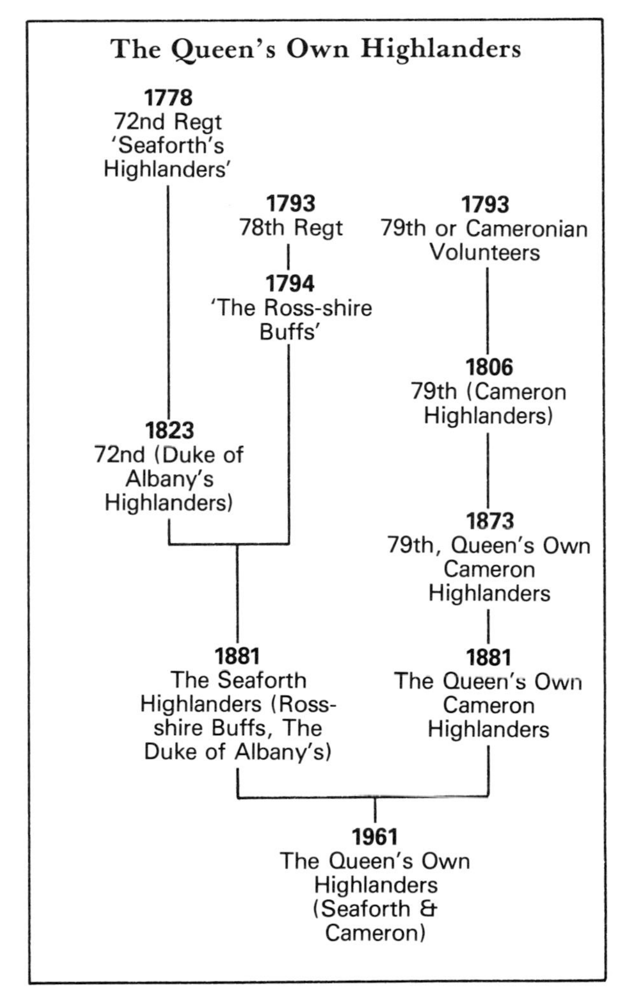

Simkin's Seaforth Highlanders' officer, 1900. The doublet facings were buff in this Regiment.

Thistle ensigned with a Crown: the stag's head emblem of the Mackenzie clan was worn by both the 72nd and 78th Highlanders before amalgamation, and then by the Seaforth Highlanders. The 72nd wore the badge in conjunction with the motto *Caber feidh* (The deer's antlers). The Thistle and Crown badge was granted to the 79th by Queen Victoria in 1873, when she presented new Colours to the Regiment and commanded that they should in future be styled 'The 79th Queen's Own Cameron Highlanders'.

The cipher of the Duke of York: granted to the 72nd Regiment in 1823 on becoming 'The Duke of Albany's Own Highlanders', after Prince Frederick, Duke of York and Albany.

The Sphinx superscribed 'Egypt': awarded to the 79th Regiment in 1802 for its part in the Egyptian campaign of the previous year.

The Elephant superscribed 'Assaye': awarded to the 78th Regiment on an Honorary Colour for service at the Battle of Assaye in 1803. The Regiment lost the original Colour, and thus the right to it, but an extra buff colour was purchased by the 2nd Battalion Seaforth Highlanders for the Officers' Mess in 1899.

The cipher of the Duke of Edinburgh: HRH Prince Philip, Duke of Edinburgh, is Colonel-in-Chief of the Regiment.

Cuidich'n Righ: the Regiment's Gaelic motto was inherited from the Seaforth Highlanders, who wore it, like the 78th before them, as part of the Mackenzie badge. Its translation depends on two theories of origin. The first invokes the story of King Alexander III of Scotland, who was unhorsed by an angry stag whilst out hunting and was saved

Seaforths and Camerons burying their dead after the Battle of Atbara, April 8 1898.

only by the prompt action of Colin Fitzgerald, an ancestor of the Mackenzies of Seaforth, who killed the stag with a cry of 'Cuidich 'n Righ!' (Help the King!).

The more formal explanation has the Arms and motto coming from the annual feudal tribute of a stag, which the Mackenzies of Seaforth were required to deliver to the Crown in payment for their lands at Kintail. The motto, in this case, would be translated as 'Tribute to the King'.

Honours

Carnatic (72nd); Hindoostan (78th); Mysore (72nd); Egmont-op-Zee (79th); Cape of Good Hope 1806 (72nd); Maida (78th); Corunna, Busaco, Fuentes d'Onor (79th); Java (78th); Salamanca, Pyrenees, Nivelle, Nive, Toulouse, Peninsula, Waterloo (79th); South Africa 1835 (72nd); Alma (79th); Sevastopol (72nd/79th); Koosh-ab, Persia (78th); Lucknow (78th/79th); Central India, Peiwar Kotal, Charasiah, Kabul 1879, Kandahar 1880 (72nd); Afghanistan 1878–80 (72nd/78th); Egypt 1882, Tel-el-kebir (S'forth/Cameron); Nile 1884–85 (Cameron); Chitral (S'forth); Atbara, Khartoum (S'forth/Cameron); Paardeberg (S'forth); South Africa 1899–1902 (S'forth/Cameron).

Marne 1914, 1918 (S'forth/Cameron); Aisne 1914 (Cameron); Ypres 1914, 1915, 1917, 1918 (S'forth/Cameron); Neuve Chapelle (Cameron); Loos, Somme 1916, 1918 (S'forth/Cameron); Delville Wood (Cameron); Arras 1917, 1918 (S'forth/Cameron); Vimy 1917, Cambrai 1917, 1918, Valenciennes, (S'forth); Sambre, Macedonia 1915–18 (Cameron); Palestine 1918, Baghdad (S'forth).

St Omer–La Bassée (Cameron); St Valery-en-Caux, Caen, Rhineland (S'forth); Reichswald, Rhine, Keren, Sidi Barrani (Cameron); El Alamein, Akarit (S'forth/Cameron); Sicily 1943, Anzio, (S'forth); Gothic Line (Cameron); Madagascar, Imphal (S'forth); Kohima, Mandalay, (Cameron); Burma 1942–45, (S'forth).

'Carnatic' is shared only with the Royal Highland Fusiliers and records the services of the newly-raised Scottish regiments of the 1780s in dealing with the invasion of the Carnatic region by Hyder Ali of Mysore.

'Waterloo' is remembered in the Regiment for the daring exploit of Piper McKay of the 79th, who left the comparative safety of his Battalion square and marched around the perimeter playing on his pipes the tune *Cogadh no Sith* (Peace or War).

'El Alamein' commemorates the action of both founding Regiments at the Battle of El Alamein in 1942. The 2nd and 5th battalions of the Seaforth Highlanders fought side-by-side with 5th Battalion, The Cameron Highlanders, in the 51st Highland Division.

Anniversaries

Amalgamation Day (February 7). Assaye Day (Sept 23). St Andrew's Day (November 30), officers and sergeants visit each other's mess.

Customs

At Hogmanay the eldest soldier, dressed as Father

Time, is carried on a cart and ceremoniously kicked out of barracks. At midnight the youngest soldier is escorted by a procession of torch-bearers to the gate and beyond.

Mascot

None.

Dress distinctions

A plain blue glengarry mounted with the Regimental badge and a blue hackle. The glengarry is worn without dicing after the style of the Cameron Highlanders. Officers and Sergeants wear a silver cap badge in three parts: a stag's head, thistle and crown, and the motto scroll. The tradition for Sergeants to share officers' privileges comes from the earliest days of the 72nd Regiment when officers and Sergeants were often recruited from the same family. The short blue hackle was first worn by the Cameron Highlanders at Arras in 1940 as a result of a suggestion put to King George VI by Lieutenant Colonel Wimberley, a staunch campaigner for the retention of the kilt. The Camerons were the last regiment to wear the kilt in action (Dunkirk 1940) and the hackle was adopted in compensation for its loss. Collar badges: the Elephant superscribed 'Assaye'. Buttons are embossed with the Regimental badge less the motto.

No 1 dress jackets are distinguished by buff slashes. The Regiment boasts two facing colours: blue (Camerons) and buff (Seaforth); the officers' mess jacket has buff lapels and blue collar and cuffs.

Pipe Major of the 1st Battalion in 1964. The Elephant collar badge is worn without the 'Assaye' inscription in the tradition of Seaforth Pipe Majors.

All for one. A Queen's Own Highlander, in barrack dress, with members of (from the left) the Gurkhas, Coldstream Guards, Welsh Guards and Royal Irish Rangers.

Kilts of Mackenzie of Seaforth tartan, and trews of Cameron of Erracht. The Mackenzie tartan was worn by both the 72nd and 78th Regiments, although trews of 'Prince Charles Edward Stewart' were being worn by the 72nd from 1823. The Erracht tartan of the Cameron Highlanders is unique in the Army for being based on no military or clan design, it is said to have been devised by the mother of Alan Cameron of Erracht, the founder of the 79th Regiment. The Royal Stewart was authorised to be worn by pipers of the Cameron Highlanders in 1943 on the occasion of the Regiment's 150th anniversary, but was discontinued on amalgamation with the Seaforths in 1961. Black hair sporran with two long white tassels (Camerons).

Pipers' uniform: a glengarry eagle feather; kilt and plaid of Cameron of Erracht tartan (trews of Mackenzie); a grey hair sporran with two long black tassels (2nd Seaforth); red and green hose (Camerons). The plaid brooch is designed to contain the cipher of the Duke of York and the Sphinx, separated by a bar bearing the honour 'El Alamein'. The bagpipes are covered in Mackenzie tartan, and the ceremonial banner is buff on one side and blue the other. Drummers' uniform: the feather Highland bonnet; scarlet doublet faced in blue; kilt of Cameron of Erracht tartan. Mackenzie trews are worn in barrack dress.

Marches

Scotland The Brave/March Of The Cameron Men, the Regimental March consists of the former marches of the founding Regiments. *The Pibroch o' Donuil Dhu*, the Pipes March Past was common to both the Seaforth and Cameron Highlanders. *Garb Of Old Gaul*, the March Past in slow time.

Nicknames

'The King's Men': the 78th Regiment, from its motto *Cuidich 'n Righ* (Help to the King).

'The Wild Macraes': the 72nd Highlanders were originally men of uncertain temperament, from the Macrae clan's moors of northern Scotland.

Recruiting

Highland (Sutherland, Caithness, Ross and Cromarty, Inverness-shire, Nairn), Morayshire, the Western Isles and the Orkney Islands. RHQ: Inverness.

The Gordon Highlanders (75th, 92nd)

Insignia

The crest of the Marquess of Huntly within a wreath of ivy, with the motto *Bydand*: the stag's head and motto of the ducal family of Gordon was confirmed to the 92nd Regiment in 1872. The motto *Bydand* has been variously translated as 'Watchful' and 'Steadfast'.

The Royal Tiger superscribed 'India': awarded to the 75th Regiment for service in India between the years 1787 and 1806.

The Sphinx with 'Egypt': the 92nd served in Egypt during 1801 and there gained the Sphinx badge and battle honours 'Egypt' and 'Mandora' for the colours. 'Mandora' was awarded to only two regiments, the 90th and 92nd, and with the demise of the former, the Gordons are able to claim the honour as their own. The Sphinx was worn as the Regimental Badge of the 92nd until 1872.

Honours

Mysore, Seringapatam (75th); Egmont-op-Zee, Mandora, Corunna, Fuentes d'Onor, Almaraz, Vittoria, Pyrenees, Nive, Orthes, Peninsula, Waterloo (92nd); South Africa 1835, Delhi 1857, Lucknow (75th); Charasiah, Kabul 1879, Kandahar 1880, Afghanistan 1878–80 (92nd); Tel-el-kebir, Egypt 1882, 1884, Nile 1884–85, Chitral, Tirah, Defence of Ladysmith, Paardeberg, South Africa 1899–1902.

Mons, Le Cateau, Marne 1914, Ypres 1914, 1915, 1917, Loos, Somme 1916, 1918, Ancre 1916, Arras 1917, 1918, Cambrai 1917, 1918, Vittorio Veneto.

Odon, Reichswald, Goch, Rhine, North-West Europe 1940, 1944–45, El Alamein, Mareth, North Africa 1942–43, Sferro, Anzio.

'Pyrenees' is the blanket battle honour for all the engagements that took place in the Pyrenean mountains between the armies of the Duke of Wellington and Marshal Soult during the year 1813. The campaign stands out in the Gordons'

Left *The Duchess Jean of Gordon recruiting for the Duke's regiment, with the offer of the King's shilling to any who would take it from her lips with a kiss.*

Right *Piper Findlater at Dargai.*

Right *The floodlit arrival for HRH Prince Michael of Kent, Belize 1981. No 6 (Warm weather parade) dress is worn.*

history for the daring charge in the Pass of Maya, in which a depleted half battalion of the 92nd held at bay a full French infantry division (on the crest of the Chemin des Anglais).

'Waterloo' is remembered in the Regiment for the death of Colonel Cameron at Quatre Bras, and the celebrated charge of the Scots Greys and 92nd Highlanders with their combined war cry 'Scotland for ever!'.

'Tirah' marks one of the Regiment's greatest achievements, the assault on the Heights of Dargai on the North-West Frontier of India in 1896. Lieutenant Colonel Mathias initiated the attack with the words, 'The General says this hill must be taken at all costs, the Gordon Highlanders will take it', and to the sound of the pipes the Battalion went forward, and within 40 minutes took the crest that had previously defeated a whole brigade. One of the VCs won that day went to Piper Findlater, who, although shot through both legs, continued to urge on his Battalion by playing lively Regimental pibrochs.

Anniversaries

Information not available.

Customs

Some items of uniform contain an element of black

to commemorate the death of Sir John Moore at Corunna. After his midnight burial on the battlefield, officers of the 92nd made a request for the blue line in their lace to be changed to black as a sign of mourning.

Mascot

None.

Dress distinctions

A blue glengarry with diced band, mounted with the Regimental cap badge, a stag's head within a wreath of ivy with the motto *Bydand*. Soldiers' collar badges: the Royal Tiger with 'India'. Officers' collar badges: the Sphinx with 'Egypt'. Buttons are embossed with the Sphinx over the Tiger embraced by a thistle wreath and superimposed upon St Andrew's Cross. Kilt and trews of No 3 (Gordon) tartan. A white hair sporran with two long black tassels. Spats are distinguished by black buttons for this Regiment, a mark of respect for Sir John Moore and his soldier's death at Corunna.

Marches

Cock o' The North replaced *Highland Laddie* as the Regimental March in 1935, as being more intrinsic

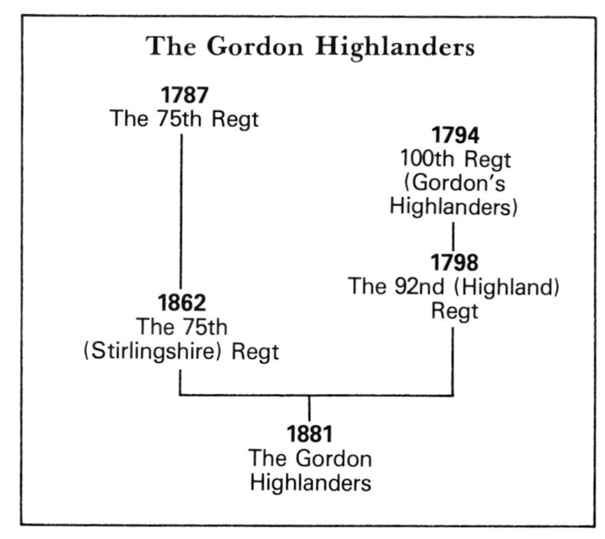

to the Regiment's tradition. The March was one of the tunes played by Piper Findlater at Dargai. *In The Garb Of Old Gaul/St Andrew's Cross* (the Slow).

RSM (left) and Colonel of the 1st Battalion with a visiting General. Colonels of Highland regiments are allowed to carry a cromag *(shepherd's crook), a symbol of their responsibility for their 'flock'.*

Nicknames

'The Cheesy Gordons' a nickname given to the 92nd Highlanders shortly after formation when the distinctive yellow line was added to their tartan by the 4th Duke of Gordon to 'liven up' the Black Watch sett.

'The Gay Gordons': from the song *Gay Go The Gordons To A Fight*.

Recruiting

Grampian (Aberdeenshire, Banffshire and Kincardineshire) and the Shetland Islands. RHQ: Aberdeen.

The Argyll and Sutherland Highlanders (91st, 93rd Foot)

Insignia

Princess Louise's cipher and Coronet. A boar's

Colour Party. Note the badger's head decoration above the sporran tassels (known in the Regiment as 'The Swinging Six').

head with motto *Ne Obliviscaris*, within a wreath of myrtle, and a wild cat with motto *Sans Peur* within a wreath of broom, surmounted with Her Royal Highness' crest: the cipher of Princess Louise and the boar's head with motto (Do not forget) from the Arms of the Dukes of Argyll were granted to the 91st (Argyllshire) Highlanders in 1871, in honour of the marriage of Princess Louise to the Marquess of Lorne. The 91st provided the Guard of Honour at the marriage ceremony. The wild cat and motto (fearless) of the Dukes of Sutherland was borne on the Colours of the 93rd (Sutherland) Highlanders Regiment, which was originally raised on the estate of the young Countess of Sutherland in 1799.

Honours

Cape of Good Hope 1806 (93rd); Rolica, Vimiera, Corunna, Pyrenees, Nivelle, Nive, Orthes, Toulouse, Peninsula, South Africa 1846–47, 1851–53 (91st); Alma, Balaklava, Sevastopol, Lucknow (93rd); South Africa 1879 (91st); Modder River, Paardeberg, South Africa 1899–1902.

Mons, Le Cateau, Marne 1914, 1918, Ypres 1915, 1917, 1918, Loos, Somme 1916, 1918, Arras 1917, 1918, Doiran 1917, 1918, Gaza.

Odon, Rhine, Sidi Barrani, El Alamein, Akarit, Longstop Hill 1943, Italy 1943–44, Crete, Grik Road, Malaya 1941–42.

Pakchon 1950–51, Korea.

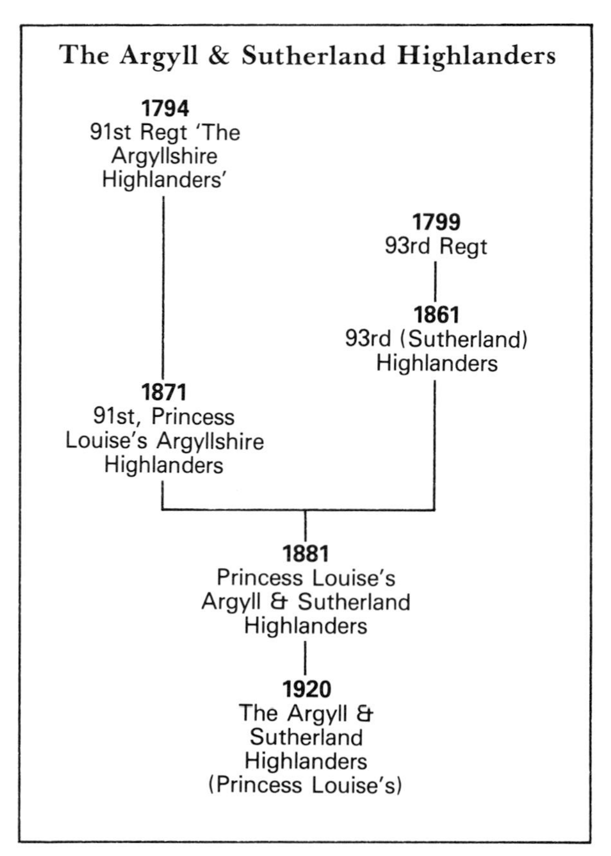

Anniversaries

Balaklava Day (October 25): the battle honour 'Balaklava' is unique to the A&SH among infantry regiments and no entrant is considered fully trained until he is completely *au fait* with the story of the 93rd at Balaklava. The tide of Russian cavalry, which swept through the Turks' redoubts and opened hostilities on October 25 1854, were poised to threaten the British base camp in the Port of Balaklava, and all that stood between them and the camp were 550 men of the 93rd Highlanders, a few guardsmen hurried up from the base camp and a group of invalids collected to swell the numbers. The Russian cavalry lumbered forward to eradicate the stubborn little group and Sir Colin Campbell

'The Thin Red Line' at Balaklava.

The 1st Battalion at Balmoral Castle — the Queen's Colour dipped in salute.

moved along the line exhorting his men, ' . . .remember there is no retreat from here. You must die where you stand'. But the horsemen wavered at each volley delivered by the Highlanders and Campbell had his work cut out to restrain the 93rd from advancing with the bayonet. At the third volley the Russians wheeled off and Balaklava was saved.

Customs

Information not available.

Mascot

A Shetland Pony by the name of 'Cruachan II' was presented to the Regiment on its return from the Korean War.

Dress distinctions

A blue glengarry with diced band, mounted with the Regimental cap badge, a circle inscribed with the Regiment's title within a thistle wreath; in the centre the *L* cipher of the late Princess Louise reversed and interlaced and surmounted by her Coronet. To one side of the cipher, the boar's head, and to the other, the wild cat. Collar badges: two circles of laurels, within one the boar's head, within the other the wild cat. Buttons are embossed with the cap badge design surmounted by a coronet. Kilt and trews of No 1 (Black Watch) tartan, known within the Regiment as 'Sutherland'. A black hair sporran with six short white tassels. Officers and Sergeants sport the badgers head decoration to the purse lid, a Regimental peculiarity of the 93rd. Yellow facings are worn in full dress.

Marches
The Thin Red Line/Garb Of Old Gaul (Quick) and *The Skye Boat Song* (Slow March on pipes).

Nicknames
'The Thin Red Line': the famous image of the 93rd at Balaklava has evolved as a common saying to indicate a brave, forlorn stand against great odds.

'The Rorys': origin unknown.

Recruiting
Central Scotland (Stirlingshire), and that part of Strathclyde which was Argyllshire, Bute, Renfrewshire and Dunbartonshire. RHQ: Stirling Castle.

The Parachute Regiment

Insignia
Upon a spread of wings, an open parachute; above, the Royal Crest.

Utrinque Paratus: the Regimental motto (Ready for anything).

Honours
Bruneval, Normandy Landing, Breville, Arnhem 1944, Rhine, Southern France, Oudna, Tamera, Primosole Bridge, Athens, Falkland Islands 1982, Goose Green, Mount Longdon, Wireless Ridge.

Anniversaries
Information not available.

Customs
Information not available.

Mascot
A pony called 'Pegasus' after the winged horse of mythology.

Dress distinctions
A maroon beret mounted with the Regimental badge. Collar badges and buttons carry the Regimental badge design. Lanyards are worn to battalion pattern. Brigade HQ, light blue and maroon; 1st Battalion, red; 2nd Battalion, blue; and 3rd Battalion, green. Trained soldiers who have made the required number of parachute jumps are issued with 'wings' to be worn at the top of each sleeve.

Marches
Ride Of The Valkyries, the Regimental Quickstep is based upon an arrangement by bandmasters Keeling and Rippon in 1950 from Wagner's *Die Walkurie*. *Pomp and Circumstance No 4*, the Regimental Slow March.

When in the RHQ town of Aldershot the band is normally led on parade by the Regimental Mascot.

Parachute Regiment training exercise in the 1950s.

The Parachute Regiment

1940
1st Parachute Battalion developed from No 2 Commando

1942
The Parachute Regiment. Volunteers serve on detachment from their own regiments

1953
The regiment is allowed to recruit in its own right

1958
Officers allowed to transfer from other corps on a permanent basis

Nicknames

'The Maroon Machine': from the Regiment's distinctions in dress and its reputed efficiency in battle training.

'The Paras': regular battalions are named thus — 1 Para, 2 Para, 3 Para.

'The Red Devils': a term bestowed upon the Regiment by German paratroopers in Tunisia during World War 2 (from the colour of their berets).

Recruiting

Nationwide. RHQ: Aldershot.

The 2nd King Edward VII's Own Gurkha Rifles (The Sirmoor Rifles)

Insignia

The Prince of Wales' Plume, the Royal and Imperial Cipher of King Edward VII.

Kaphar Hunnu Bhanda Marnu Ramro (It is better to die than be a coward): motto of the Gurkha regiments.

Honours

Bhurtpore, Aliwal, Sobraon, Delhi 1857, Kabul 1879, Afghanistan 1878–80, Kandahar, Punjab Frontier, Tirah.

La Bassee 1914, Festubert 1914, 1915, Givenchy 1914, Neuve Chapelle, Aubers, Loos.

El Alamein, Akarit, Tunis, Cassino I, Gothic Line, Jitra, Slim River, North Arakan, Irrawaddy, Tamandu.

Anniversaries

Delhi Day (September 14): the Regiment's outstanding service at Delhi in 1857 was initially rewarded with an Honorary Colour, which bore the battle honour in English, Hindu and Persian. The 2GR wear red facings in honour of a request made by the King's Royal Rifle Corps, that 'the Sirmoor

A 1914 watercolour of the Truncheon Jemadar and rifleman.

The 2nd King Edward VII's Own Gurkha Rifles

1815
Raised in Sirmoor

1823
8th (or Sirmoor) Local Battalion

1826
6th (or Sirmoor) Local Battalion

1850
The Sirmoor Battalion

1858
The Sirmoor Rifle Regt

1861
17th Regt of Bengal Native Infantry

1864
2nd Goorkha (The Sirmoor Rifles) Regt

1876
2nd (Prince of Wales' Own) Goorkha Regt (The Sirmoor Rifles)

1886
2nd (The Prince of Wales's Own) Gurkha Rifles Regt (The Sirmoor Rifles)

1901
2nd (The Prince of Wales's Own) Gurkha Rifles (The Sirmoor Rifles)

1906
2nd King Edward's Own Gurkha Rifles (The Sirmoor Rifles)

1948
Becomes part of the British Army

Rifles Regiment should be permitted to conform to the dress of the 60th Rifles in memory of the English riflemen with whom the Goorkhas served side by side in the stress of the Delhi siege'.

Customs

The Queen's Truncheon: Rifle regiments are known not to carry Colours, and when the Sirmoor Battalion was upgraded to a Rifle regiment in 1858 Queen Victoria ordered that a six-foot bronze truncheon be made to compensate for the loss of the Honorary Colour presented for Delhi the year before.

The truncheon commands a degree of respect not seen in any other regiment and is known to the men as *Nishani Mai* (The Great Mother). It is placed outside the Quarter Guard on Delhi Day, and also on the anniversary of the crossing of the Tigris at Shumran in February 1917, and every member of the Regiment will salute it during the course of the day. The truncheon was made to be dismantled and carried into action by five soldiers; it is surmounted by the Royal Crown supported by three figures of riflemen; on a ring of silver below is inscribed 'Main Picquet, Hindoo Rao's House, Delhi 1857'.

Mascot

None.

Dress distinctions

A black 'pill-box' kilmarnock with diced band and black toorie, mounted with the Regimental badge, the plume of the Prince of Wales on a red backing. A rifle green dress cap with diced band (officers). A khaki slouch hat with the Regimental badge mounted on a red and black patch. Black buttons embossed with an Edwardian Crown above an entwined *ERI*, over crossed kukris. The stable-belt has a green centre band flanked by scarlet bands and black outer edges. Officers wear a black patent-leather shoulder-belt with a silver ram's head mask, chain and whistle. The ram's head commemorates the assault on Fort Koonja in 1824.

Marches

Lutzow's Wild Hunt/Wha's The Steer Kimmer.

Nicknames

Information not available.

Recruiting

Nepal. British officers are transferred from other regiments, whilst native officers are promoted from within the 'Brigade. Based in Hong Kong.

The 6th Queen Elizabeth's Own Gurkha Rifles

Insignia

Two crossed kukris, thereunder the figure *6*, the whole ensigned with the Crown.

Honours

Helles, Krithia, Suvla, Sari Bair, Gallipoli 1915, Suez Canal, Khan Baghdadi, Mesopotamia 1916–18, Persia 1918, North-West Frontier India 1915.
Afghanistan 1919.
Monte Chicco, Medicina, Italy 1944–45, Kyaukmyaung Bridgehead, Mandalay, Fort Dafferin, Rangoon Road, Sittang 1945, Chindits 1944, Burma 1944–45.

Anniversaries

Information not available.

Customs

Information not available.

Mascot

None.

Pipers of 6 GR and drummers of 7 GR at the Aldershot Army Display 1965.

Dress distinctions

A black kilmarnock with a scarlet toorie, mounted with the Regimental badge. A rifle green dress cap with black piping (officers). Black buttons stamped with the Regimental badge. The Eagle badge of the

6th Queen Elizabeth's Own Gurkha Rifles

1817
Raised at Orissa as The Cuttack Legion

1823
The Rangpur Light Infantry Battalion

1826
8th (or Rangpur) Local Light Infantry Battalion

1828
8th (or Assam) Local Light Light Infantry Battalion

1844
1st Assam Light Infantry

1861
46th Regt of Bengal Light Infantry

1864
42nd (Assam) Regt of Bengal (Native) Light Infantry

1886
42nd Regt Goorkha Light Infantry

1891
42nd Gurkha (Rifle) Regt of Bengal Light Infantry

1901
42nd Gurkha Rifles

1903
6th Gurkha Rifles

1959
6th Queen Elizabeth's Own Gurkha Rifles

14th/20th King's Hussars is worn on the upper sleeve in commemoration of the bond forged between that Regiment and the 6GR in the Italian campaign of World War 2. Lanyards of green and black. Officers wear a black patent-leather shoulder-belt fashioned with a silver lion's head mask, chain and whistle.

Marches

Queen Elizabeth's Own.

Nicknames

Information not available.

Recruiting

Nepal. British officers are transferred from other regiments, whilst native officers come from within the Brigade. Based in Hong Kong.

The 7th Duke of Edinburgh's Own Gurkha Rifles

Insignia

Two kukris, points upwards, the handles crossed in saltire, blades upwards. Between the blades the numeral *7* and ensigned with the cipher of HRH The Duke of Edinburgh.

Honours

Egypt 1915, Megiddo, Sharon, Palestine 1918, Kut al Amara 1915, 1917, Ctesiphon, Defence of Kut al Amara, Baghdad, Sharquat, Mesopotamia 1915–18.

Afghanistan 1919.

Cassino I, Poggio del Grillo, Tavoleto, Sittang 1942, 1945, Kyaukse 1942, Imphal, Bishenpur, Meiktila, Rangoon Road, Falkland Islands 1982.

Anniversaries

Information not available.

Customs

Information not available.

7th Duke of Edinburgh's Own Gurkha Rifles

1902
Raised at Thayetmyo as the 8th Gurkha Rifles

1903
2nd Battalion, 10th Gurkha Rifles

1907
7th Gurkha Rifles

1959
7th Duke of Edinburgh's Own Gurkha Rifles

Mascot

None.

Dress distinctions

A kilmarnock with a black toorie, mounted with the Regimental badge. A rifle green dress cap and side hat (officers). Black buttons embossed with the Regimental badge. Officers wear a black patent-leather shoulder-belt mounted with a silver Maltese Cross within a laurel wreath, a lion's head mask, chain and whistle. Pipers and drummers wear trews, scarf and plaid of Douglas tartan in honour of the Regiment's association with the former Scottish Rifles.

Sharpening kukris for the Falklands conflict, 1982.

Marches
Old Monmouthshire.

Nicknames
Information not available.

Recruiting
Nepal. British officers are transferred from other regiments, whilst native officers come from within the Brigade. Based in Hong Kong.

The 10th Princess Mary's Own Gurkha Rifles

Insignia
A bugle horn stringed and interlaced with a kukri in fess. Above the kukri the cipher of HRH Princess Mary (The Princess Royal) and below it the numeral *10*.

Honours
Helles, Krithia, Suvla, Sari Bair, Gallipoli 1915, Suez Canal, Egypt 1915, Sharquat, Mesopotamia 1916–18.

Afghanistan 1919.

Coriano, Santarcangelo, Bologna, Imphal, Tuitam, Tnegnoupal, Mandalay, Myinmu, Bridgehead, Meiktila, Rangoon Road.

Anniversaries
Information not available.

Customs
Information not available.

Dress distinctions
A black kilmarnock mounted with the Regimental badge. A rifle green dress cap (officers). Black

10th Princess Mary's Own Gurkha Rifles

1890
1st Regt of Burma Infantry

1891
10th Regt (1st Burma Bn) of Madras Infantry

1892
10th Regt (1st Burma Rifles) Madras Infantry

1895
10th Regt (1st Burma Gurkha Rifles) Madras Infantry

1901
10th Gurkha Rifles

1949
10th Princess Mary's Own Gurkha Rifles

Right *2nd Battalion drummers in ceremonial whites.*

buttons embossed with the Regimental badge. Officers wear a black patent-leather shoulder-belt mounted with a silver badge, lion's head mask, chain and whistle. Pipers and drummers wear Hunting Stewart tartan.

Marches

A Hundred Pipers.

Nicknames

Information not available.

Recruiting

Nepal. British officers are transferred from other regiments, whilst native officers come from within the Brigade. Based in Hong Kong.

The Royal Green Jackets (43rd, 52nd, 60th, RB)

Insignia

A Maltese Cross inscribed with selected battle honours, thereon a bugle horn stringed and encircled with the title of the Regiment, all within a wreath of laurel ensigned with the Crown resting upon a plinth inscribed 'Peninsula'. Across the tie a Naval Crown superscribed 'Copenhagen 2 April, 1801': the device is basically the same as that worn by the Rifle Brigade, although the KRRC wore a similar Maltese Cross, and the bugle horn, shared with the Light Infantry and now the symbol of the Light Division, was common to all the founding regiments. The Naval Crown was ordered to the Rifle Brigade (and the Royal Berkshire Regt) in 1951 to commemorate their service with the Fleet at the Battle of Copenhagen in 1801.

Celer et Audax: the Regimental motto (Swift and bold) comes from the KRRC, and originated as a term of praise for the 2nd and 3rd Royal Americans at the Battle of Quebec in 1759.

Honours

Louisburg (60th); Quebec 1759, Martinique 1762, Havannah (43rd/60th); North America 1763–64, (60th); Mysore, Hindoostan (52nd); Martinique 1794 (43rd); Copenhagen, Monte Video (95th); Rolica (60th/95th); Vimiera (43rd/52nd/60th/95th); Corunna (43rd/52nd/95th); Martinique 1809, Talavera (60th); Busaco (43rd/52nd/60th/95th); Barrosa (95th); Fuentes d'Onor (43rd/52nd/60th/95th); Albuhera (60th); Ciudad Rodrigo, Badajoz, Salamanca, Vittoria, Pyrenees, Nivelle, Nive (43rd/52nd/60th/95th); Orthes, Toulouse (52nd/60th/95th); Peninsula (43rd/ 52nd/60th/95th); Waterloo (52nd/95th); South Africa 1846–47, (RB); Mooltan, Goojerat, Punjaub (60th); South Africa 1851–53 (43rd/ 60th/RB); Alma, Inkerman, Sevastopol (RB); Delhi 1857 (52nd/ 60th); Lucknow (RB); Taku Forts, Pekin 1860 (60th); New Zealand (43rd); Ashantee 1873–74, Ali Masjid (RB); South Africa 1879, Ahmed Khel, Kandahar 1880 (60th); Afghanistan 1878–80 (60th/RB); Tel-el-kebir, Egypt 1882–84

1955. A Royal Green Jackets rifleman displaying one of his regiment's singular drill positions. The custom of carrying the rifle 'at the trail', or 'reversed' from the shoulder, began in the forests of North America, where the 60th used to move in like manner to avoid having their muskets fouled in the undergrowth.

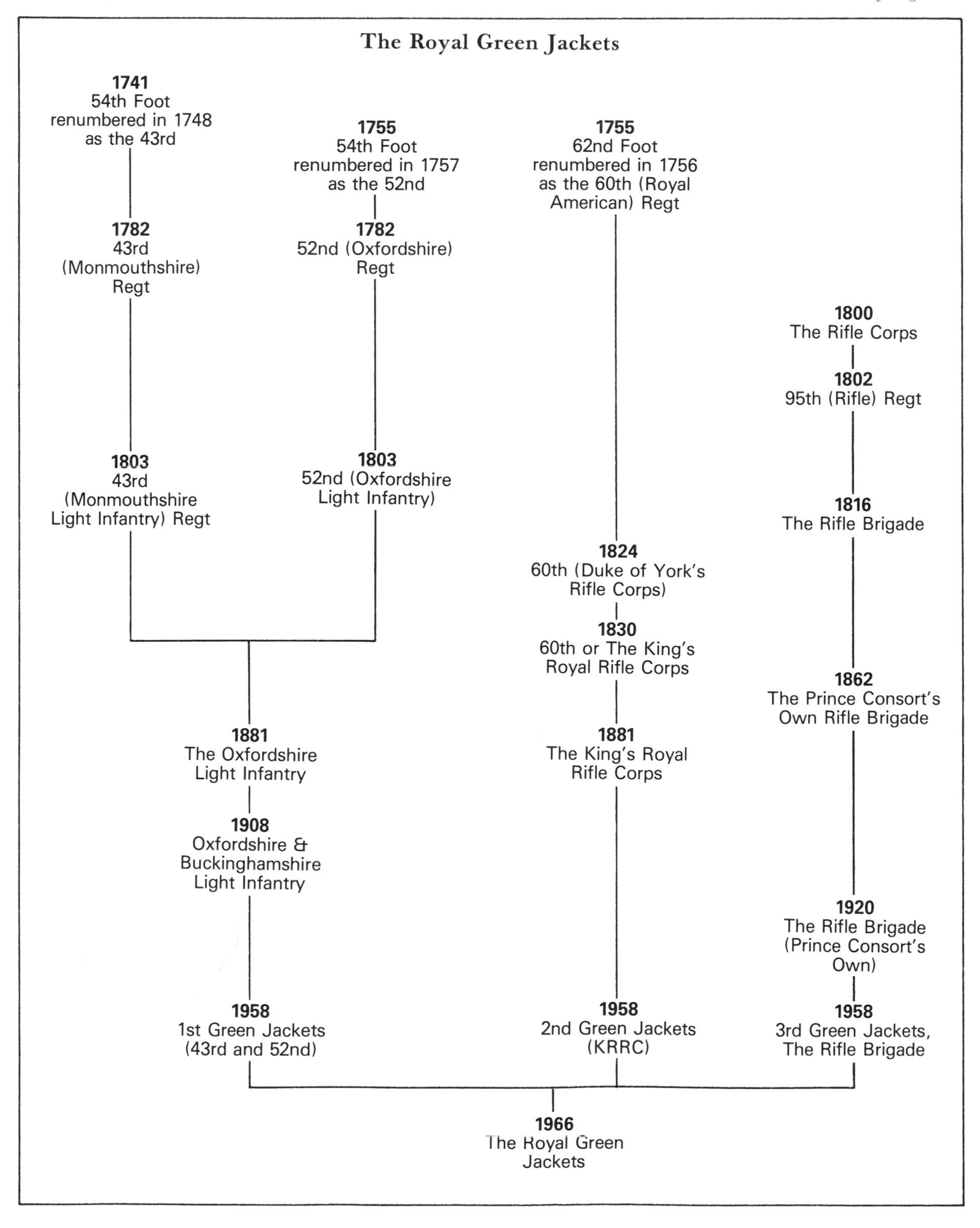
The Royal Green Jackets
1741
54th Foot
renumbered in 1748
as the 43rd
1755
54th Foot
renumbered in 1757
as the 52nd
1755
62nd Foot
renumbered in 1756
as the 60th (Royal
American) Regt
1782
43rd
(Monmouthshire)
Regt
1782
52nd (Oxfordshire)
Regt
1800
The Rifle Corps
1802
95th (Rifle) Regt
1803
43rd
(Monmouthshire
Light Infantry) Regt
1803
52nd (Oxfordshire
Light Infantry)
1816
The Rifle Brigade
1824
60th (Duke of York's
Rifle Corps)
1830
60th or The King's
Royal Rifle Corps
1862
The Prince Consort's
Own Rifle Brigade
1881
The Oxfordshire
Light Infantry
1881
The King's Royal
Rifle Corps
1908
Oxfordshire &
Buckinghamshire
Light Infantry
1920
The Rifle Brigade
(Prince Consort's
Own)
1958
1st Green Jackets
(43rd and 52nd)
1958
2nd Green Jackets
(KRRC)
1958
3rd Green Jackets,
The Rifle Brigade
1966
The Royal Green
Jackets

Elements of the Peninsular Light Division: a rifleman (95th), light dragoon (23rd), and light infantryman (43rd). Although different in name, the RGJ embodies all the qualities and traditions of that famous formation.

Painting of the King's Royal Rifle Corps in 1885, before the re-introduction of the busby.

(KRRC); Burma 1885–87 (RB); Chitral (KRRC); Khartoum (RB); Defence of Ladysmith (KRRC/RB); Relief of Kimberley, Paardeberg (OLI); Relief of Ladysmith (KRRC/RB); South Africa 1899–1902 (OLI/KRRC/RB).

Principal battle honours of World Wars 1 and 2 number only six (*) and appear on the Regimental badge. Below are listed the principal honours of the founder regiments:

Mons (OLI/KRRC); Le Cateau (RB); Marne 1914 (KRRC); Ypres* 1914, 1915, 1917, 1918 (OLI/KRRC/RB); Langemarck 1914, 1917, Nonne Bosschen* (OLI); Neuve Chapelle (RB); Somme* 1916, 1918 (OLI/KRRC/RB); Arras 1917, 1918, Messines 1917, 1918 (KRRC/RB); Cambrai 1917, 1918 (OLI/RB); Hindenburg Line (RB); Epehy, Canal du Nord, Selle, Sambre (KRRC); France & Flanders 1914–18 (RB); Piave, Doiran 1917, 1918 (OLI); Macedonia 1915–18 (RB); Ctesiphon, Defence of Kut al Amara (OLI).

Calais 1940* (KRRC/RB); Cassel, Ypres–Comines Canal, Normandy Landing, Pegasus Bridge* (OLI); Rhineland (KRRC); Reichswald, Rhine (OLI); North-West Europe 1940, 1944–45 (KRRC/RB); Egyptian Frontier 1940 (KRRC); Beda Fomm (RB); Sidi Rezegh 1941 (KRRC/RB); Alem al Halfa, El Alamein* (KRRC/RB); Enfidaville (OLI); North Africa 1940–43 (KRRC/RB); Salerno, Anzio (OLI); Cassino II, Capture of Perugia (RB); Gemmano Ridge (OLI); Italy 1943–45 (KRRC/RB); Greece 1941, 1944–45 (KRRC).

'Louisburg' and 'Quebec' permit the RGJ membership of the Wolfe Society. These honours, and the rare 'North America 1763–64' testify to the unequalled service of the 60th (Royal American) Regiment in their homeland during the French and Indian Wars.

'Peninsula' embodies the record number of Peninsula War battle honours gained by the regiments of the Light Division, which came together again 160 years later as The Royal Green Jackets. The Light Division, formed by Sir John Moore in 1803, was a *Corps d'Elite* whose achievements in Spain may be summed up in the words of Napier: 'Six years warfare could not detect a flaw in their system nor were they matched in courage and skill'.

'Waterloo' was the principal battle honour of the Oxfordshire & Buckinghamshire Light Infantry and Waterloo Day was observed in the Regiment to celebrate the brilliant flanking manouevre carried

Colonel Commandment's Inspection, 3 RGJ, 1971.

out by the 52nd, which decided the fate of Napoleon's Old Guard.

'Pegasus Bridge' is unique to the RGJ and marks the glider-borne mission of the Oxfordshire and Buckinghamshire Light Infantry to secure the bridges of Ranville and Benouville on the canal and River Orne before the Normandy Landings. Benouville proved particularly hard to take, but the 'Ox and Bucks' were reinforced by the 7th Parachute Regiment and Operation *Benouville Bridge* was renamed *Pegasus Bridge* to commemorate this.

Anniversaries

July 25 is celebrated as the day on which HM Queen Elizabeth II first visited the Royal Green Jackets as Colonel-in-Chief of the Regiment. With the exception of Waterloo Day, dates for celebration among the founding corps were confined to Regimental birthdays. December 25 was observed in the KRRC to celebrate General Lord Loudon's appointment as Colonel-in-Chief of the Royal Americans on Christmas Day 1755, from which date they were officially regarded as a regiment. The Rifle Brigade's day was August 25, being the day in 1800 when the Sharpshooters, barely four months in existence, first came under fire (at Ferrol).

Customs

The Loyal Toast is drunk only when there is a member of the Royal family present, a tradition inherited from the Oxfordshire & Buckinghamshire Light Infantry.

In order to preserve the trend towards a more tolerant kind of discipline, which was inherent to the methods of the Light Division, ranks are not recognised in the mess and badges of rank not worn. The only exception to this understanding is the Colonel, who is addressed by his rank.

In keeping with the tradition of the Rifle

Green Jackets in Calais on the 25th anniversary of their heroic rearguard action in 1940. A single Brigade of Rifles sacrificed itself to hold off two German armoured divisions for four days — only 30 unwounded men were brought out by the Royal Navy.

regiments the Royal Green Jackets do not carry Colours. This custom derived from the dispersed formations often used by the Rifles in the Peninsula War, where a centre of regiment would have been impractical.

The Regiment's position at the end of the infantry list was inherited from the Rifle Brigade, who chose to occupy this traditional place of honour for rifle regiments when it was taken out of the line in 1816. Marching is done at the Rifles' traditional tempo of 140 paces to the minute, and all marches are accordingly played in double time.

The 'Rifle Walk' refers to the Bugle Major's short parade cane, which is walked in the way that one walks an umbrella.

Mascot

None.

Dress distinctions

A rifle green dress cap (and beret) mounted with the Regimental badge. Collar badges: the bugle horn, bronzed. As the premier regiment of light infantry, the Oxfordshires saw no reason to advertise their tribal emblem on the collar as well as the cap and proudly chose to wear no collar badges at all. Officers of the Regiment could be distinguished by a gorget button in the collar, reminiscent of the type worn by officers in the 18th century. Black buttons embossed with a crowned bugle horn. Lanyards of black and green. The stable-belt is rifle green. Officers wear a black patent-leather shoulder-belt, a relic of the cavalry style of dress favoured by Rifles' officers since 1800.

The band and Corps of Bugles are dressed in rifle green regimentals with black appointments and a

Officers of the 60th or Duke of York's Own Rifle Corps, 1824.

busby of the pattern adopted by the Rifle regiments in 1890.

Marches

The Royal Green Jackets, the Regimental March. *Lower Castle Yard/Nach Flager von Granada* (OLI). *Lutzow's Wild Chase* (KRRC). *I'm Ninety-five*, adopted by the Rifle Brigade in Malta in 1842 to reflect its old position in the line prior to 1816, when the Regiment was taken out of the line because its four battalions committed it to brigade status. The March *I'm Ninety-five* became so popular with other regiments that a directive had to be issued forbidding its play by any other band in the presence of the Rifle Brigade.

Nicknames

'The Black Buttons': from a distinctive feature of the Regiment's dress.

'The Black Mafia': a modern name for factions within the RGJ.

'The Green Jackets': a name first used for the 95th (Rifle) Regiment, whose revolutionary green coatees caused a feeling of elitism as against the more common red coat regiments.

'The *Jägers*': the 5th (Rifle) Battalion of the 60th Regiment, which served as skirmishers for Wellington's divisions in the Peninsula, contained a high proportion of Germans, most of them proficient in the skills of the hunter (*Jäger*).

'The Light Bobs': 18th century slang for soldiers of the light companies of infantry, but applied regimentally to the 43rd and 52nd in the Peninsula. The nickname was taken on again by the Oxfordshire & Buckinghamshire Light Infantry.

'The Ox and Bucks': an understandable abbreviation for the Oxfordshire and Buckinghamshire

Light Infantry, who, themselves, forbade any form of abbreviation for Regimental use.

'The Sixtieth': after 1881, when Regimental numbers were abolished in the infantry, officers of the KRRC continued to refer to their Regiment as 'The Sixtieth'. KRRC was sometimes transcribed as 'The King's Rich Rude Rifles'.

'The Kaiser's Own': a jibe of the First World War inspired by a resemblance between the Maltese Cross badge of the KRRC and the German Iron Cross.

Recruiting

Greater London, Buckinghamshire and Oxfordshire. RHQ: Peninsula Barracks, Winchester.

The Special Air Service Regiment

Insignia

A winged dagger striking downwards, with the motto *Who dares wins.*

Honours

North-West Europe 1944–45, Tobruk 1941, Benghazi Raid, North Africa 1940–43, Landing in Sicily, Termoli, Valli di Comacchio, Italy 1943–45, Adriatic, Middle East 1943-44, Falkland Islands 1982.

Anniversaries

Information not available.

Customs

The customs of the Regiment emanate from the secret and dangerous nature of its work. Soldiers and officers work together, often as equals and without the trappings of rank, in an atmosphere of highly specialised efficiency. Awards of merit, which must be many, are made to members as a team, and rarely to individuals.

Mascot

None.

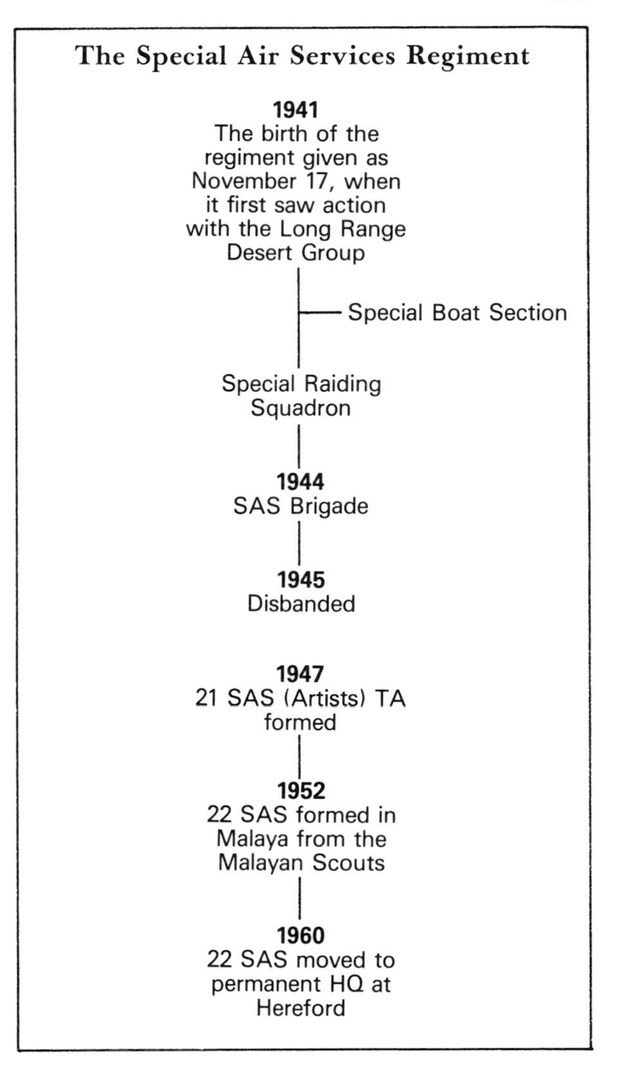

Dress distinctions

A beige beret with an embroidered badge: a silver dagger with light blue wings and motto scroll outlined in red, on a blue patch. Collar badges and button design after the Regimental badge. Cambridge blue facings (after the Army Air Corps).

Marches

Marche des Parachutistes Belge (Quick).

Nicknames

'The SAS': the famous initials' nickname evokes the anonymity and daring that is intrinsic to the Regiment.

Recruiting

General, from other regiments. RHQ: Hereford.

Appendices

Appendix I: Disbanded Regiments

The Royal Irish Regiment

The Regiment was summoned from Ireland by King James II in 1688 and kept on by William III, to be placed as the 18th of Foot in 1751. Its service at the Siege of Namur, in 1695, was rewarded with the title *Royal Regiment of Ireland*, the Lion of Nassau from the Arms of William III, and the motto *Virtutis Namurcensis Proemium*. Later battle honours, apart from four gained for service with the Duke of Marlborough, were limited to Queen Victoria's 'Little Wars' and included the Dragon with 'China'. Its proudest nicknames were 'The Namurs' and 'Paddy's Blackguards'. Like others regiments which relied on southern Irish recruits the Royal Irish was disbanded in 1922.

The Cameronians (Scottish Rifles)

In 1968, at a meeting of the Council of Scottish Colonels, it was decided that no more Scottish regiments were to be amalgamated, and on May 14 the Cameronians paraded for the last time near to their ancestral stronghold at Castle Dangerous, where they had first mustered as a regiment 279 years before.

'The Cameronians' were formed in Lanarkshire 'all in one day and without tuck of drum, nor expense of public money' from a band of Covenanters named after their martyred leader Richard Cameron. The Regiment was constructed on the Covenanters' religious principles: officers were appointed for their religious integrity and each man carried a Bible in his kit. The Regiment was placed as the 26th in line in 1751, and was linked with the 90th (Perthshire Light Infantry) in 1881.

The 90th was raised as 'The Perthshire Volunteers' in 1794 by Thomas Graham of Balgowen to avenge an act of dishonour made on the body of his deceased wife by French Revolutionaries. The Volunteers were known as 'The Perthshire Greybreeks' from the grey breeches worn at this time by the inmates of Perth Prison.

The two Regiments came together in 1881 as The Cameronians (The Scottish Rifles), and were uniformed in a unique manner of dress which is kept alive by The Cameronians TA: a rifle-green doublet, green chaco with a black plume and trews of Douglas sett (the tartan of the Regiment's founder, the Earl of Angus). The whole appearance cost the Regiment the nickname of 'Glasgow Sweeps'. The Regimental badge showed the bugle horn of the 90th surmounted by a five-starred mullet (a spur-rowel from the Arms of the 1st Earl of Angus) enclosed by two sprays of thistle. Battle honours of the Regiment went back to Blenheim, and included two devices: the Sphinx (with the 90th's additional battle honour 'Mandora') and the China Dragon (26th).

The Cameronians' unique customs originated from their religious background. Rifles were carried on Church Parade when there was a rack provided, a hangover from the troubled days of the Stuarts, when the Covenanters were forced to live by their wits in order to practise their own brand of religion. Their ancient services, or *Conventicles*, were observed to the last. The mess could not partake of the Loyal Toast because of the old beliefs and a procedure was devised whereby a glass was passed from officer to officer with no spoken word of fealty.

The York and Lancaster Regiment

The 'Yorks and Lancs' were disbanded in 1968 as the junior regiment of the Yorkshire Brigade. The Regiment was constituted in 1881 with the combination of the 65th (2nd Yorkshire North Riding) and the 84th (York and Lancaster) Regiments; its curious title dates from the year 1808, when the 84th formed a second battalion which was raised at Preston and completed at York. Recruiting was made in an area of South Yorkshire called 'Hallamshire', from a depot, first at Pontefract and then Sheffield.

The uniform was unexceptional but for the badge, which twinned the Royal Tiger (65th) with the Union Rose, a design variously known as 'The Cat and Cabbage' or 'Rabbit and Geranium'. The Regiment's title was open to similar misinterpretation and frequently came out as 'The Young and Lovelies' or 'The Cork and Doncaster'. The campaigning 65th were known to the Maoris of New Zealand as 'Hickety Pip'. The Royal Tiger was approved for the 65th in 1823 with the honours 'India' and 'Arabia'. The latter was awarded to no other regiment, and marked two small expeditions to quell pirates operating in the Persian Gulf.

Lucknow Day was held to commemorate the tragic massacre at Cawnpore, which involved men of the 84th Regiment. St George's Day was observed in memory of the 1st Battalion's attack at Ypres in 1915; and Warren Hastings Day (January 14) honoured the perfect discipline exercised by the regiment on board the Indian Marine Transport *Warren Hastings*, wrecked on rocks off the coast of the Island of Reunion in 1897.

The Connaught Rangers

This Regiment was the product of the 1881 Order which combined infantry battalions, in this case the 88th and 94th. It was disbanded in 1922 following a 'mutiny' in India brought on by the Irish troubles of that year.

The 88th Regiment was raised in Connaught by the Hon John Thomas de Burgh in 1793, and the 94th was reconstituted from elements of the old Scots Brigade disbanded in 1818, at Scotland and Cork in 1823. The 94th nickname 'Garvies' came from the old Scottish term for men of small stature. As an Irish regiment the Rangers wore green facings and an elephant collar badge awarded to the old 94th in 1808.

Battle honours of the Regiment were notable for a Sphinx and an impressive range of Peninsula War honours won by the 88th in Picton's famous 3rd 'Fighting' Division. The Regiment's intrepid nickname 'The Devil's Own' was probably inspired in these campaigns.

The Prince of Wales's Leinster Regiment

The Regiment was formed in 1881 by the combination of the 100th (Prince of Wales's Royal Canadian) and the 109th (Bombay Infantry) Regiments. It was disbanded on the formation of the Irish Free State in 1922. Battle honours prior to 1914 numbered only 'Niagara', 'Central India' and 'South Africa'. Nicknames reflected the Regiment's Canadian origin ('The Beavers'), the old 100th ('The Centipedes') and a long history of service in India by the 109th ('The Poona Pets').

The Royal Munster Fusiliers

This Regiment came into being in 1881 with the merger of the 101st (Royal Bengal Fusiliers) and the 104th (Bengal Fusiliers), and was disbanded in 1922. Full dress of the Regiment was recognised by a white/green side plume and the grenade badge embossed with the Royal Tiger. The latter was granted to the Bengal Fusiliers for their long service in India, where 22 battle honours were gained. The nicknames 'Dirty shirts' and 'Delhi rebels' were conferred by the enemy at the siege of Delhi in 1857, where coats were discarded in the bitter heat of fighting.

The Royal Dublin Fusiliers

The Regiment was formed by the linking of the 102nd (Royal Madras Fusiliers) and the 103rd (Royal Bombay Fusiliers) in 1881, and was disbanded at the inception of the Irish Free State in 1922. The fusilier cap was personalised by a blue and green side plume and the grenade badge superimposed by the Tiger and Elephant.

Appendix II: The Brigade System

Listed hereunder are the brigades of 1948 as they had evolved by 1962.

The Brigade of Guards
The Grenadier Guards
The Coldstream Guards
The Scots Guards
The Irish Guards
The Welsh Guards

The Lowland Brigade
(A thistle within a circle bearing the motto of the Order of the Thistle, all upon the Cross of St Andrew.)
The Royal Scots (The Royal Regiment)
The Royal Highland Fusiliers (Princess Margaret's Own Glasgow and Ayrshire Regiment)
The King's Own Scottish Borderers

The Home Counties Brigade
(A Saxon crown embracing a sword point upwards.)
The Queen's Royal Surrey Regiment
The Queen's Own Buffs
The Royal Sussex Regiment
The Middlesex Regiment (Duke of Cambridge's Own)

The Lancastrian Brigade
(The Rose of Lancaster within a laurel wreath, ensigned with the Royal Crest.)
The King's Own Royal Border Regiment
The King's Regiment (Manchester and Liverpool)
The Lancashire Regiment (Prince of Wales's Volunteers)
The Loyal Regiment (North Lancashire)

The Fusilier Brigade (Formed 1957)
(A grenade, with St George and the Dragon and a Crown superimposed.)
The Royal Northumberland Fusiliers
The Royal Warwickshire Fusiliers (from the Forester Brigade in 1963)
The Royal Fusiliers (City of London Regiment)
The Lancashire Fusiliers

The Forester Brigade (dispersed in 1963)
(An antelope with the Garter upon a Maltese Cross, all within an oak wreath. Above, the Royal Tiger.)
The Royal Warwickshire Regiment (transferred to the Fusilier Brigade in 1963)
The Royal Leicestershire Regiment (transferred to the East Anglians in 1963)
The Sherwood Foresters (transferred to the Mercian Brigade in 1962)

The East Anglian Brigade
(The Castle and Key of Gibraltar upon an eight-pointed star.)
1st East Anglian Regiment (Royal Norfolk and Suffolk)
2nd East Anglian Regiment (Duchess of Gloucester's Own Royal Lincolnshire & Northamptonshire)
3rd East Anglian Regiment (16th/44th Foot)

The Wessex Brigade
(A wyvern.)
The Devonshire & Dorset Regiment
The Gloucestershire Regiment
The Royal Hampshire Regiment
The Duke of Edinburgh's Royal Regiment (Berkshire and Wiltshire)

The Light Infantry Brigade
(A stringed bugle horn.)
The Somerset & Cornwall Light Infantry
The King's Own Yorkshire Light Infantry
The King's Shropshire Light Infantry
The Durham Light Infantry

The Yorkshire Brigade
(The Rose of York ensigned with the Crown.)
The Prince of Wales's Own Regiment of Yorkshire
The Green Howards (Alexandra, Princess of Wales's Own Yorkshire Regiment)
The Duke of Wellington's Regiment (West Riding)
The York and Lancaster Regiment

The Mercian Brigade
(A double-headed eagle with a Saxon Crown above.)
The Cheshire Regiment
The Worcestershire Regiment
The Sherwood Foresters
The Staffordshire Regiment (The Prince of Wales's)

The Welsh Brigade
(The Prince of Wales's Plume, Coronet and motto.)
The Royal Welch Fusiliers
The South Wales Borderers
The Welch Regiment

The North Irish Brigade
(An angel harp ensigned with the Crown)
The Royal Inniskilling Fusiliers
The Royal Ulster Rifles
The Royal Irish Fusiliers (Princess Victoria's)

The Highland Brigade
(A stag's head upon a cross with the motto *Cuidich 'n Righ.*)
The Black Watch (Royal Highland Regiment)
The Queen's Own Highlanders (Seaforth and Cameron)
The Gordon Highlanders
The Argyll & Sutherland Highlanders (Princess Louise's)

The Brigade of Gurkhas (Crossed kukris)
The 2nd King Edward's Own Gurkha Rifles (The Sirmoor Rifles)
The 6th Queen Elizabeth's Own Gurkha Rifles
The 7th Duke of Edinburgh's Own Gurkha Rifles
The 10th Princess Mary's Own Gurkha Rifles

The Green Jackets Brigade
(A Maltese Cross superimposed by a stringed bugle horn, all within a laurel wreath and ensigned with the Crown upon a tablet inscribed 'Peninsula'.)
The Oxfordshire and Buckinghamshire Light Infantry
The King's Royal Rifle Corps
The Rifle Brigade (Prince Consort's Own)

Appendix III: The Division System 1968

The brigade groups that had been in existence since 1948 were dissolved in 1968 and superseded by larger groups called divisions. The hated brigade badges had long been dispensed with, but recruits were still fed to the regiments through a central depot.

The Household Division
The Life Guards
The Royal Horse Guards (Blues)
The 1st or Grenadier Regiment of Foot Guards
The Coldstream Guards
The Scots Guards
The Irish Guards
The Welsh Guards

The Royal Armoured Corps (established in 1939)
1st The Queen's Dragoon Guards
The 3rd Carabiniers (Prince of Wales's Dragoon Guards)
The 4th/7th Royal Dragoon Guards
The 5th Royal Inniskilling Dragoon Guards
The 1st (Royal) Dragoons
The Royal Scots Greys (2nd Dragoons)
The Queen's Own Hussars
The Queen's Royal Irish Hussars
The 9th/12th Royal Lancers (Prince of Wales's)
The 10th Royal Hussars (Prince of Wales's Own)
The 11th Hussars (Prince Albert's Own)
The 13th/18th Royal Hussars (Queen Mary's Own)
The 14th/20th King's Hussars
15th/19th The King's Royal Hussars
16th/5th The Queen's Royal Lancers
The 17th/21st Lancers
The Royal Tank Regiment

The Scottish Division
The Royal Scots (The Royal Regiment)
The Royal Highland Fusiliers (Princess Margaret's Own Glasgow & Ayrshire Regiment)
The King's Own Scottish Borderers
The Cameronians (Scottish Rifles)
The Black Watch (Royal Highland Regiment)
The Queen's Own Highlanders (Seaforth and Cameron)
The Gordon Highlanders
The Argyll & Sutherland Highlanders (Princess Louise's)

The Queen's Division
The Queen's Regiment
The Royal Regiment of Fusiliers
The Royal Anglian Regiment

The King's Division
The King's Own Royal Border Regiment
The King's Regiment (Manchester and Liverpool)
The Prince of Wales's Own Regiment of Yorkshire
The Green Howards (Alexandra, Princess of Wales's Own Yorkshire Regiment)
The Royal Irish Rangers
The Lancashire Regiment (Prince of Wales's Volunteers)
The Duke of Wellington's Regiment (West Riding)
The Loyal Regiment (North Lancashire)

The Prince of Wales's Division
The Devonshire and Dorset Regiment
The Cheshire Regiment
The Royal Welch Fusiliers
The South Wales Borderers
The Gloucestershire Regiment
The Worcestershire Regiment
The Royal Hampshire Regiment
The Staffordshire Regiment (The Prince of Wales's)
The Welch Regiment
The Sherwood Foresters (Nottinghamshire and Derbyshire Regiment)

The Light Division
The Light Infantry
The Royal Green Jackets

Picture credits

National Army Museum 14, 17, 18, 19, 22 (bottom), 24 (bottom), 26 (top right), 27, 30 (bottom), 32, 35 (top), 37, 39 (left), 40, 45 (top), 46, 47 (bottom), 50, 55, 57, 59, 60, 62 (top), 66 (top), 67, 71 (top), 73 (left), 76 (top), 77 (bottom), 79 (right), 80, 83, 93, 94, 95, 105 (right), 107, 108 (top), 112 (top), 115 (top), 117, 120 (right), 121 (top), 124 (left), 128, 129, 132, 136 (bottom), 139, 140 (top right), 142, 148 (top), 152, 157, 158, 159, 160, 165, 166, 168, 169 (top), 172 (top), 174, 181. *Soldier Magazine* 9, 10, 11, 12, 13, 26 (top left), 30 (top), 31, 34 (top left), 39 (right), 48 (right), 54 (bottom), 61, 62 (bottom), 63, 64, 70, 71 (bottom), 74, 87, 99, 100, 106 (top), 118 (bottom), 120 (left), 121 (bottom), 122, 131, 136 (top), 138, 151, 155, 167, 171, 172 (bottom), 173, 176, 177, 178, 179, 182, 183, 186. *Tank Museum* 28, 53 (bottom). *English Life Publications* 66 (bottom). *Leicester Mercury* 88 (bottom). *Bristol City Museum* 134. *PR BAOR* 127. *HQ UKLF* 91 (left).

Index